FATHER BRUNO DE JESUS-MARIE, O.C.D.,
was born in Bourbourg, France, in 1892,
and attended the Institut Catholique of
Lille and the Collegio Angelico in Rome.
He is an authority on the psychology of
religious experience and is the founder
and director of an international organization devoted to its study, as well as the
director of Etudes Carmélitaines of Paris.

LOVE AND VIOLENCE

LOVE AND VIOLENCE

SHEED AND WARD

NEW YORK · 1954

NIHIL OBSTAT: DANIEL DUIVESTEIJN, S.T.D.
CENSOR DEPUTATUS
IMPRIMATUR: E. MORROGH BERNARD
VIC. GEN.
WESTMONASTERII, DIE 30A MARTII, 1954

This book is based upon the 1946 volume of the series "Études Carmélitaines", *Amour et Violence*, published by Desclée de Brouwer under the editorship of Père Bruno de Jésus-Marie, O.C.D.

ACKNOWLEDGMENTS

THE PUBLISHERS' thanks are due to Mlle Jeanne-Adèle Bergson for permission to quote from *The Two Sources of Morality and Religion*: to Messrs. William Heinemann, Ltd., for the quotation from Constance Garnett's translation of *A Raw Youth* and *The Brothers Karamazov*: to the Harvill Press, Ltd., for the quotation from Roy Campbell's translation of the poems of St. John of the Cross: to Geoffrey Bles, Ltd., for the quotation from Jacques Maritain's *True Humanism*: to Messrs. Routledge and Kegan Paul, Ltd., for the quotation from Simone Weil's *Gravity and Grace*: to the S.P.C.K. and the Westminster Press for the quotation from Bishop Nygren's *Agape and Eros*: to the Princeton University Press for the quotation from Kierkegaard's *Attack Upon Christendom*: to Adam and Charles Black, Ltd., and Harper and Brothers for the quotations from *Love* (Manuals from Kittel's *Theologisches Wörterbuch*): to Messrs. Burns, Oates and Washbourne for the quotations from Professor Allison Peers' translation of the works of St. John of the Cross and François Mauriac's *Margaret of Cortona*: to Messrs. Burns, Oates and Washbourne and Benziger Brothers, Inc., for the quotations from the translation of the *Summa Theologica* made by the Dominican Fathers of the English Province: and to the Hogarth Press, and W. W. Norton, Inc., for the quotation from *Civilization and its Discontents*.

*The translations in this volume were
made by George Lamb*

CONTENTS

CONTENTS

ILLUSTRATIONS

The plates are here reproduced by courtesy of
the Mansell Collection

WAR AND LOVE

GUSTAVE THIBON

THE MOST hellish war in history has come to an end,[1] but mankind is still pulverised and infected in its inmost being. The end of hostilities has not removed the inner causes of the war, and though we may have laid down our arms we have not all got rid of the hatred in our hearts. A brood of future wars is stirring in the womb of the war that has ended.

Not only the Christian conscience but even the simple human conscience is gripped with anguish when it surveys the spectacle of the depth to which this spiritual and material disaster reaches. Is there a single corner left in the world or in the souls of men which has not been devastated and ruined by the war? The retreat and defeat of love are so evident that one needs to ascend into heaven itself to be reassured of the possibility of peace. And yet one has to go on living on the earth. . . . It is no use defeating the enemy if the war goes on existing in the minds and habits of men. How is war itself to be defeated? That is the great question that beats with devilish insistence in the mind of every person of goodwill today.

FALSE PEACE

War goes deep. Heraclitus, Nietzsche and Marx, each from his different point of view, looked upon it as the mother of all things, the queen of the world. And undoubtedly war has its virtues, its own positive ends. It is by fighting against himself and against nature and against his own kind that man tests and strengthens his spirit: most civilizations have grown out of struggle and conquest, as grain only grows if the soil is properly worked. It is not permissible to speak of peace until one has measured the depth and the extent of this conflict. In other words, to reach to true peace it is necessary to enter into the very thick of the battle and get beyond war only by transcending it.

Unfortunately, instead of transcending it, men generally escape from war by dodging round it. Let us take a look round and probe a little into the hearts of some of the so-called peace-lovers. Is this man really a lover of peace, for instance, this queer, evasive creature

---

[1] This essay was written in 1946.

who never contradicts anybody in company but who, when he finds he can lose his temper without any danger to himself (amongst his family, especially) becomes the most unbearable man alive? Or this public figure who is so afraid of responsibility or of creating any enemies against himself that he allows all manner of error and evil to exist around him, his motto being " Let sleeping dogs lie "? Or this spineless creature who can flop like a jelly into the mould of any and every character and event? No doubt these different kinds of behaviour can flatter themselves with fine names like good-naturedness, benevolence, tolerance, but in reality they are simply the result of cowardice, a longing for peace and quiet, scepticism, indifference to good and evil. If the teachings of pacifists, the appeals to human concord and love, generally lack magnetism and authority, this is because they emanate from minds which exist on this side of war and not the other. When the man of peace seems less alive to us than the man of war it can only be assumed that real peace is not in him. The coward is even further from the saint than the warmonger.

This kind of peace, which means being satisfied with mediocrity or sin and temporising with evil, was condemned by Christ when He said: " I did not come to bring peace but a sword ".

THE JUSTIFICATION OF VIOLENCE

Truth, like justice, has different levels. Something that is true and good at one level of thought or the inner life can be untrue and evil at a lower level. At the level on which Nietzsche and Lenin, for example, lived (it is only on this particular point that I dare to link these two names), moral health obviously meant rejecting the Christian precepts concerning resignation, forgiving one's neighbour, the love of one's enemies, and so on, for at the level of Heraclitus's conception of the world, the level of fallen human nature and the will to power, these Christian virtues can only be masks, stratagems of war, weakness and cowardice. At this level hatred and violence are virtues (in the etymological if not the moral sense of the word) because they need more courage and involve greater risks and therefore demand more strength. Love of one's enemies and universal benevolence only become genuine virtues in the context of Christian sanctity—in the super-natural order in which the ego and its will to power no longer exist. St. Paul said that the weakness of God is stronger than men. For our weakness to be stronger and purer than strength it needs to come from the love of God within us. Christian non-violence no more resembles cowardice than chastity resembles impotence. Nietzsche and Lenin, who looked upon war as the motive force of progress and the great progenitor of human society, were right, on their own level and within their own limits, to defend human nature against diseases wearing the mask of virtue.

Gandhi, the apostle of non-violence, echoed the apostles of war when he said: " If the only choice was between violence and cowardice, I should not hesitate to choose violence."[1] Nietzsche and Lenin had no other choice. Love alone gives us the wings to rise above this dilemma.

THE SWORD AND THE CROSS

Ultimately there are no contradictions in life: they are all rooted in one single seat, the individual, self-enclosed ego. Between violence[2] and cowardice there is a difference of degree, but not of nature. The man of violence is a coward turned " tough ". The expression about being " puffed up " is highly significant: a tyre that has been pumped up has no other virtue except that of being full of wind. The connection between violence and cowardice is the same as that between a bow stretched taut and a bow that has been relaxed: in essence they are both the same. And so these passions follow each other quite naturally in the same soul: it was the very Disciple who drew his sword to wound the servant of the high priest who, a few moments later, so feebly denied his Master. Allowing for differences of circumstance and inner condition, it is the same exclusiveness of the ego, the same longing to preserve ourselves or to extend our sphere of influence that makes us either fight our fellow-men or run away from them. He whose soul was all love refused to draw the sword, but He was not afraid of the cross.

Only the folly of the cross can enable us to overcome the tension between violence and cowardice. Let us endeavour for a moment to summarise (without, however, identifying ourselves with it) the non-violent way of thinking.

The wisdom of India asks: If evil is answered by evil, when will evil end? The moment I take out my sword I have already been defeated by the evil that I imagine myself to be fighting, for my enemy has already injected his soul into my own, and even though I come out on top physically I can do no more than substitute for the evil I hate another evil at least equivalent to it, with the additional horror

---

[1] Quoted by Lanza del Vasto in *Pèlerinage aux sources*.

[2] Here I am simply speaking of the kind of blind ungoverned violence which arises from anger, hatred, pride, or ambition, and which has been exalted in some doctrines into an absolute good, an end in itself. The kind of aggressiveness that is directed against evil and oppression and is put at the service of peace, on the other hand, is perfectly sound and legitimate: it has a purely instrumental and temporary task to perform.

of the warfare that has taken place between us. Proper resistance to evil means saying to the transgressor: I am not sufficiently like you to be able to consent to fighting against you. What point is there in my getting the better of you and killing your body, if in return I have to contract the evil that is destroying your soul? I intend to preserve the purity of my own soul though it cost me the death of my body—first, out of love for myself, and secondly from love of you, for I hope that my example will affect you. If I resisted you, I should partake of the evil that is in you; by laying myself open to you and not offering any resistance, I hope to enable you to partake of the good that is in me. I reject the sword, I accept the Cross.

" Whoever takes up the sword will perish by the sword." The evil projected by the aggressor into the souls of those he aims to destroy or oppress comes back upon him and kills him. The more contagious it is the more it reacts upon his own head and the more punishment it brings. War does not therefore get rid of evil, it simply moves it into a different place and diffuses it (modern wars and revolutions are very instructive on this point). The only thing that gets rid of evil is pure goodness, the supernatural love that loves its enemies, turns the other cheek and dies upon the Cross. The Cross alone can expunge the evil caused by the sword.

Absolute resistance to evil therefore implies non-resistance to the evil person, whilst resistance to the evil person involves a certain participation in evil. The old rule about loving the sinner and hating the sin thus appears in a new light: hatred has to choose between the sinner and the sin, since they cannot both be hated at the same time.[1]

Make no mistake about it: absolute non-resistance to evil can only be sound and fruitful in the climate of Christian sanctity—in other words, the only possible justification for refusing to take up the sword is to be prepared to be stretched out on the Cross. The balance of forces in this world of guilt and punishment depends partly on evil and war (de Maistre, Nietzsche and many others have shown this again and again), and anyone who refuses to play the world's game must be prepared to accept all the evil that he refuses to commit. A mystical pacifism, which does not demand at least as much courage and as many risks as the religion of war, is simply a mask for weakness and fear. It must not be forgotten what the fate of the God of peace was on this earth—the torture endured on

---

[1] This principle, despite its element of concrete truth, could not be made into an absolute law. It is possible to fight against an evil person without sharing in the evil. The only thing that this needs is a considerable amount of purity. St. Louis and Joan of Arc were fighters.

Calvary is the logical consequence, the strict application, of the Sermon on the Mount.

Simone Weil gets to the heart of this matter of supernatural non-violence when she says: " He who takes the sword will perish by the sword. And he who does not take the sword—or relinquishes it—will perish on the Cross." To transform the violence of others into suffering for oneself is to participate in Christ's redemption. " The sin which we have in us emerges from us and spreads outside ourselves setting up a contagion of sin. Thus, when we are in a temper those around us grow angry. But at the contact of a perfectly pure being there is a transmutation and the sin becomes suffering. Such is the function of the just servant of Isaiah, of the Lamb of God. Such is redemptive suffering. All the criminal violence of the Roman Empire ran up against Christ and in Him it became pure suffering. Evil beings, on the other hand, transform simple suffering (sickness for example) into sin . . . The false God changes suffering into violence. The true God changes violence into suffering."

THE PURIFICATION OF WAR

Today hatred has such means of material destruction at its disposal (already there is talk of the possible annihilation of our planet) and such a capacity for influencing morals (is there a single soul left who has not been affected by the poison of propaganda?), that it is worth while asking whether Gandhi's kind of non-resistance to evil may not be the least harmful solution of the problem.

It is necessary to say at the outset that despite the growing horror of modern warfare mankind as a whole is not yet ready for absolute, universal non-violence. The Christian vocation is an entirely personal thing; as Richelieu said, in no uncertain terms, the salvation of society is not always achieved by the same means as that of the individual; and even the saint has no right to allow his fellow-men to be sacrificed to the oppressor if his country is attacked. The kind of pacifism, for instance, that leads to conscientious objection, arises from an individualistic attitude which must be condemned: the conscientious objector is a "transcendent" egoist who is prepared to sacrifice to his ideal of *personal* perfection the most sacred interests—and even the very existence—of the community of which he is a part.

Thus, out of obedience to the laws of his country, the man of peace may be obliged to take up the sword. The question then becomes: How is violence to be purified? In such an extreme case every effort must be made to resist the contagion of hatred and *transmute action into passion*. The sword is to the man of peace condemned to wage

war what the Cross is to the martyr. It is not right to kill unless the
state of one's soul is such that one would wish to die in it.

On the human level it is impossible to put violence at the service
of peace and perform all the actions of hatred whilst maintaining love
in one's heart; grace alone can enable us to overcome such a contradiction. For war is exacting: the absolute risk (i.e. of death) which it
involves summons up in the soul a counterpoise no less absolute, and
if this is not the true God it is bound to be an idol. Thus it is that
very few of those engaged in war manage to kill and die without making
an idol of the cause they are defending, and another idol, of the opposite
kind, of their enemies. " I know that you are brave and that the
blood of the true warrior flows in your veins ", one must say to the
young man marching to war; " I am not afraid of your not being heroic,
but rather that you will be satisfied with merely being heroic. Sanctity
is to human heroism what the heavens are to the highest points on
earth. Fight to the death, but do not idolize war: in the very thick
of the battle never forget the love and the ultimate weakness into which
war will melt and be resolved."

Another way of purifying violence is to use it in the service of
those who are weak and oppressed. For St. Paul's " animal man "
moved by " the pride of life " is naturally sensitive to the attractions
of power, and his instinctive inclination is to side with the powerful
and victorious. It is more difficult and ultimately superhuman to side
with the weak, especially if they are pure and their defeat seems unavoidable. Napoleon and Hitler found millions of men ready to die
for them, but Christ on the cross had only one Disciple at His side.
This does not mean, of course, that we must attempt to justify or
worship weakness and defeat as such: that would be a kind of idolatry
no better than the idolatry of power and success. It simply means that
we must attempt to realise the principle of justice, whose symbol is a
pair of scales, and devote all our courage to the task of keeping the
scales balanced. Now if the vanquished—whether this means an
individual, or a class, or a nation—are, a priori, no better than the
victors, it is only too clear that in general the scale will incline towards
the benefit of the latter and the balance be broken. It is not an accident
that justice has been called " that fugitive from the camp of conquerors."[1]

[1] This does not mean that one must rush to help the vanquished, no matter
who they may be; nor above all does it mean that if the vanquished are also
guilty one must fight against the rigours of the justice dealt out to them. The
punishment of the guilty is precisely the way the balance is restored! The
vanquished are only to be helped to the extent that they have been unjustly
oppressed. And if they are guilty they must be punished for their guilt, not
for having been defeated. The absolute vae victis, the motto of all predatory
men and nations, is at the opposite pole from the spirit of the Gospels.

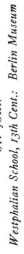

ST. JOHN
Westphalian School, 13th Cent.: Berlin Museum

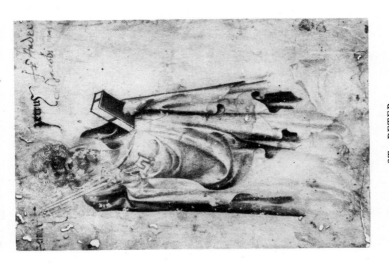

ST. PETER
French School, 14th Cent.: Louvre

THE PURIFICATION OF WEAKNESS

Plato says somewhere that love has nothing in common with force. But this love which has nothing in common with the force that is based on pride and domination has no connection either with the masked weakness of envy and resentment. It is weakness, pure weakness—not the kind that tries to get the better of violence by underhand means (denigration, appeals to pity, etc.) and then step into its shoes. Only in this perfectly pure sense is it permissible to say that " the weakness of God is stronger than men ".

We have seen that the strong and violent must purify war in their own souls by means of love. But what way is there for those whose " gentleness " arises chiefly from weakness, those who are psychologically incapable of waging war because of the feeble stamp of their character? I believe that a similar purification is incumbent upon them too, involving not the rejection but the denudation of their weakness.

The first thing is to be able to see oneself clearly. This needs a good deal of integrity and a good deal of humility. If I believe myself to be a peace-lover, the first thing I have to do is to find out the inner causes of my " gentleness ", and separate the part that arises from love from that which is simply camouflaged egoism. I do not avenge wrongs done to me: is this because I prefer an easy time and fear reprisals, or is it because I really love the person who has offended me? Does my " virtue " operate according to a scale laid down by the separated fleshly ego, or at the level of a soul in communion with the universe and God? There is a quite simple standard to judge by: if I were sure that the consequences of forgiveness would involve me in greater efforts and more suffering than revenge, would I still go on forgiving? If the answer to this question is yes, I am right to forgive; if not, it would be more truthful, on the human level, for me to take my revenge.

Does this mean to say that, on the pretext of fighting against their own nature, the weak and cowardly are to declare on their neighbours a war which, subjectively, they are quite incapable of waging and which, objectively, may be a sin? Not at all; it simply means being naked before one's own eyes. There is a vast gulf between the man who is so weak that he is incapable of taking his revenge and who therefore puffs himself up with pride, assiduously fostering his deficiency in a sort of travesty of religious virtue, and the man who knows with all the bitterness of self-knowledge that he avoids taking his revenge because he is weak, and who thereupon has enough supernatural love to acquiesce in such a humiliation of his nature.

And then again there is no creature so weak that he will not find around him creatures weaker still, on whom he may inflict suffering.

It is here that he must redeem and purify his weakness. " The warlike virtues are outside your range," one may say to the man who can only be weakly irritable. " You are not tough enough to be able to cope with those who are stronger than yourself; then at least learn to be gentle with those who are weaker than yourself. This is your golden rule: every day, whenever you can behave badly without danger to yourself (particularly with those who love you), do out of goodness of heart what you so often do out of cowardice, when there would be a certain amount of courage and danger involved in getting angry or taking your revenge."

THE DEFEAT OF WAR

When Christ said, " The violent will take the kingdom of heaven " and " I came not to bring peace but a sword ", it was false peace which He condemned. But when He said, " Blessed are the peacemakers " and " I leave you my peace, I give unto you my peace ", it was true peace that He meant. He was careful to say on another occasion, " I do not give as the world gives ", for the world is separated from God and hence does not bear within itself any principle of genuine peace; what it calls peace is simply a stratagem of war, a sort of armistice or a balance of power between forces that neutralize each other. True peace is the fruit of supernatural love.

It is this true peace, the peace that includes and overcomes war, that we must endeavour to foster. This is a hard task, for which the forces of nature do not in themselves suffice. From the human point of view we are bound to fail. And when this failure occurs we are very ready to attribute it to our Christian faith, because it forbids us to use impure means. Let us decide, then, to use means which are *fundamentally* pure. The deepest cause of our failures is that we have a superficial polish of Christian virtue but not its essence; we are too good to succeed in the world, but not good enough to overcome it. We are unable to follow great realists of nihilism like Machiavelli or Nietzsche, and so we get defeated. But let us follow Christ to the very end—to the Cross—and we shall be conquerors. This is the meaning of the mysterious promise given in the Gospels: " Blessed are the meek, for they shall inherit the earth." But we shall only be conquerors of the world when we have conquered ourselves sufficiently by means of the Person who Himself conquered the world.

It is nothing to defeat the enemy. We know only too well that there are new wars sprouting from our last victory, like the tenacious shoots thrown out by a felled tree. The only victory worthy of a disciple of Christ is victory over war. All the violence we bear within ourselves must be subordinated to love for the sake of this supreme struggle.

LOVE AND AGGRESSIVENESS IN ART

René Huyghe

We find it difficult to appreciate the importance of revolutions in which we actually take part: instead, we tend to go on living in the past, ignoring all that is new in the world around us. So it may be worth reminding ourselves once again that for a century now our knowledge of man has been undergoing a more profound transformation than any that has taken place since Christianity first appeared on earth, perhaps indeed since the great days of classical Greece.

In the old days, a simple dualism sufficed: body and soul, matter and spirit, physiology and psychology. Life was regarded as a kind of lighthouse, with its brute masonry below, and a lighted cabin at the top—the one thing visible in the surrounding darkness. Then, one day, it was suddenly realized that the light at the top that caught one's eye was connected with some sort of obscure machinery down below that helped to produce it and make it what it was, something that went on ceaselessly shaking and throbbing down in the depths: the inner life found itself no longer limited to that single room with its lighted windows, where everything could be seen and understood; it was something much deeper, going down out of sight into the dark hidden parts of the body in which it had its source. From then on, the inner life was not simply the life of the mind: it had become something much bigger, much weightier, for it included the vast new field of the unconscious.

The extent of this transformation has still not been properly estimated. Previously, the clear life of thought and reflection had seemed to be the cause of all our ideas and actions, all that we did; with brutal suddenness it became instead simply the end-product of a whole process, a reaction, a mere effect. And not only the individual emerged transformed from this revolution: the study of history was likewise affected. History had been looked upon as a process determined by " famous men ", by thought acting on event; suddenly it was discovered that history too had an unconscious—the anonymous masses, and the hidden forces by which they are so blindly led. Thus Taine asserted that art was determined by the conditions in which it appeared; Marx explained society as a function of dialectical materialism.

The nineteenth century ended on a wave of determinism, and conscience became for many no more than an automatic record, an epiphenomenon.

Since then there has been an attempt to restore the balance. Faced with the boundless world of the unconscious, which by its very nature is utterly foreign to it and yet on which it depends so closely, reason has reasserted itself. Since, by definition, there is nothing which it cannot reduce to its own terms, not even the things furthest removed from its own nature, it attempted in the time of Bergson and Proust to reorganize its methods so that instead of denying whatever contradicted it, it should be able to analyse it instead. With Valéry it went a stage further: it aimed to recover all its responsibilities, its complete autonomy. More lucid, more acrobatic than ever, developing such skill that it could follow the unconscious in all its ramifications and understand it to its very depths, it went so far in asserting its independence that it even denied the fact of inspiration as something too vague to be valuable, so that it could the better assert its own perpetual self-mastery. This is perhaps Valéry's real place in the history of thought: perhaps in this way he continued Bergson's work even while reacting against it.

However that may be, for the past fifty years man has been engaged in a double " reading " of himself, one straightforward, the other, so to speak, in code; the first based on his consciously avowed ideas, on his thought-processes and intentional aims—the traditional method of the old moralists—the second studying the clues, the involuntary signs of his spontaneous, unconscious life, and trying to discover " what they correspond to " in the depths of the individual life—the method which in its systematic form has come to be known as psychoanalysis. The history of art cannot afford to ignore this development; from now on it must take it into account. It will thus have a threefold method of investigation at its disposal: first, the " straightforward reading ", which means studying the artist's conscious aims, his aesthetic intentions, and deciding to what extent he realizes them in his work; but then, following Taine's principles—which remain true within their proper limits—the historian must go beyond this field of conscious activity: he must consider the surrounding conditions, both social and historical, which inevitably affect the work of art, almost to the extent of determining its form. But even this is not enough: he must then proceed to a sort of decoding of the work, in the widest sense of the word a kind of psycho-analysis, entering the work from the back, so to speak, by the hidden door of the unconscious: he will then see every line, every form, every stroke of the brush, as a movement no less instinctive than it is voluntary, through which the artist

expresses not only his conscious intention but also his own fundamental nature, unconsciously stamping upon the work of art the
characteristics of his most intimate being, characteristics which he is
himself unaware of in the moment of creation, just as he is unaware
of the expressions on his face, his gait, his mannerisms—the whole
of his spontaneous behaviour. His whole being is there, hidden in these
undeniable manifestations of his personality. Thus the work of art
is like a piece of writing which reveals the character of its author both
by its content, which only needs to be understood, and by its handwriting, which has to be interpreted. Like writing, too, it can be studied
by both the reader and the graphologist.

There is no art, and perhaps no medium of expression, that lends
itself to this kind of investigation better than painting; in all other
cases the created work appears at the end of a long process—the
writer, the musician, the architect, offer us simply the final fruit,
detached from the stalk that gave it life. In a picture, on the other
hand, practically the whole process is present along with the final
result: the two things are inseparable. The painter aims to give us a
picture; but in his picture, the touches, the strokes, even the very
movements of his hand that enabled him to create it, are there, not
to be denied—in fact the picture is nothing less than a permanent
record of every creative act that went into it, presented with a clarity
and a suggestive power not to be found in any other of the arts.

We may seem to have wandered far from our theme of love and
aggressiveness, but we can now come back to it better equipped, for it
should be clear that every mental attitude has its corresponding method
of transcribing the real: tenderness has its own personal language which
it expresses spontaneously in its varieties of brush stroke, its handling
of light, its colour harmonies; cruelty has its own special kind of calligraphy, its contrasts, its particular way of applying the brush. Love
and aggressiveness can be discerned just as clearly in the different ways
a picture is created as in a person's facial features.

Calligraphy is the first and most obvious element to be interpreted, so it will be convenient to begin our enquiry with that. It is
immediately apparent—and I hope no one will suspect me of any
national prejudice, any bowing to circumstance when I say this, but
realize that it is the statement of a well-nigh proven fact—that
the graphic line of love is found at its highest in the art of France,
whilst that of aggression is, if anything, too violent in the art of
Germany.

It is remarkable that the graphic line of love, with its ample contours,
appears in France at the height of the Middle Ages, at a time when

the dominant style is the Gothic, whose drawing tended to be rather crude and angular. Not until the Renaissance were the harmony and refinement of classical antiquity to reappear in European art in general —this can be seen by comparing any sample of pre-sixteenth-century handwriting with a later hand—and so it is not surprising to find that in northern, Germanic Europe, which the Renaissance spirit affected much later and far less profoundly than the south, angularity of line was very slow to die out; whilst a more flowing line developed wherever the classical influence spread abroad. It is instructive to compare a Flemish drawing of about 1500, with its stiff, broken lines, with a contemporary Italian drawing, so supple and round; and to see how the same angularity persists in Dutch drawings even at the height of the seventeenth century, when it was gloriously transformed under the influence of Rembrandt's dramatic lighting; whilst in Flanders the Italian influence can be seen in the graceful contours that with Rubens become almost too opulent. (And yet often in a sketch the natural tendency will suddenly intrude like a local accent; and in a pen-and-ink drawing by Rubens or Van Dyck all Rembrandt's broken lines will reappear.)

The Middle Ages, then, in themselves hardly favoured fluent, flexible, graceful draughtsmanship; and yet it was in such unpropitious circumstances that France, even as far back as the twelfth century, developed this kind of drawing, which was to become her own special property. It appeared in its first perfection in the work of Jean Pucelle, and blossomed forth fully in the School of Paris, radiating through Europe until it was rudely shattered in 1415 by the disaster of Agincourt. In this kind of drawing, as in the later decorative Gothic, curve answers curve in an easy, consistent rhythm that is as simple as in real life, and the eye moves freely, without encountering a single harshness or stiffness, occasionally coming across a gentle fold or volute, like the skater's arabesque on the ice (Plate I, p. 6). The style spread over Europe, and was found wherever our spiritual influence was dominant —in England, where it became a little sharper; along the Rhine, grown slightly sentimental; even in Bohemia and beyond the valley of the Po; rarely, however, keeping in all its purity the airy, limpid grace conferred upon it by the School of Paris.

One has only to let one's eye follow the meandering line, so pure and simple, and yet so subtle, of our thirteenth- and fourteenth-century miniaturists and fifteenth-century primitives, to realize how eloquently this style suggests a loving flexibility, the longing to create harmony out of discord, to soften contours, to join with curves instead of emphasising contrasts by the use of broken lines, to win the heart with its grace and elegance, portraying all things in sweetness and light: no musical phrase could speak more impressively or more eloquently to the sensitive ear than this speaks to the eye. Only one other school of painting can bear comparison for delicacy of style, and that is the Sienese—and what was the motto of that gentle city but love: " Siena tibi cor pandit.".

At the opposite pole stands the German school, with its harsh drawing that seems full of a kind of negative electricity. The Flemish school is crude, uncivilized, unpolished, brutal; the lines change direction sharply, in jerks; the style is neutral, insensitive to the subtleties of the physical object. The German style of draughtsmanship goes one better (historically it derived from it, in fact); it becomes aggressive; instinctively it inclines towards the visual equivalents of cruelty—the line no longer adheres lovingly to the form; it is abrupt, haughty, hostile, suggesting all the things that cut and scratch and sting and rend to pieces. It will suddenly twist into those little hooks which it cannot resist using to clutter up its lines, whether the subject calls for them or not; pushes out sharp points, setting them up in frenzied juxtaposition one against the other so that they look like the hectic scribbles of delirium, like the toothmarks of a saw; it summons up images of knife-edges, beaks, talons, swordblades—all the obscure symbols through which the diseased imagination expresses its obsessions and which in our own day have been—too systematically—explored by psycho-analysis.

The choice of subject-matter, the unconscious impulse by which the artist's eye is moved towards this thing or that, is very revealing. The fifteenth-century draughtsmen of the School of Paris loved the flowing lines of aristocratic draperies, phylacteries blown out in the wind, clouds like the curly heads of angels; the German draughtsman of the fifteen hundreds, transforming the Flemish style of the previous century, which was merely arid, goes in for torn clothing that is all rents and scallopings, barbed feathers, and highly aggressive-looking plants. People generally imagine that the artist has his choice of subject-matter determined for him by local conditions—forgetting all the obscure impulses which lead men to seek their satisfactions further afield. Why should Grünewald, for instance, introduce a foreign plant like a palm-tree into his compositions, except that its leaves are like a panoply of serried bayonets? Even Dürer, though, like Goethe, he was won over to the Latin serenity—a kind of Faust, turning tenderly towards Helen—scanned in vain the golden numbers of Paccioli and da Vinci for the key to visual harmony: his evil genius takes a step, and there beneath the hem of his cloak appears its cloven hoof. How significant in this respect is his self-portrait in the Louvre! Painted for his fiancée, it must have been an act of love; and it is quite clear that he has attempted to take the emaciation out of his face and substitute an expression of romantic reverie instead. But if you look closely you will see that the flower he is holding in his hand as a symbol of his faithful heart is not a shy, modest forget-me-not, but—and this German equivalent of the forget-me-not is highly revealing—a thistle, bristling with prickles. And just look at the bony hand with its bent fingers all shrivelled up—try as it will, it cannot conceal its family-likeness to those hands of Grünewald's that contract like claws (Plate II, p. 38).

Crows, eagles, the birds of night, with their stiff feathers suggesting the bristling crest of a helmet or the cluster of pikestaffs in a martial trophy—such are the creatures we find flying in these green, glaucous landscapes, or perched in the artificial segments of heraldic design.

Besides portraying things for us, or evoking them in our memory or imagination, a picture is a cryptogram from which we must learn to decipher the soul of its creator. If we do this, we shall find some light shed on all the great problems of psychology—including the problem of love, both divine and human.

I will go further and say that representational arts like painting themselves raise the problem of love—or rather their own problem is analogous to the problem of love: for it concerns the relationship between the ego and the external world, the self and the " other ": " Ego et alter ". Can there be a better description of the artist than as a strongly defined ego who, so to speak, asserts himself by focussing his attention on the external world and opposing it?

Love, too, is simply one of the solutions of the self-other equation; it develops out of the ego's desperate efforts to escape from its own subjection, to transcend itself, to go beyond its own limits and shatter its egoism by subordinating itself to that which is other than itself. It annihilates itself and is absorbed into God, or into created nature, or into the creature, into another being. The great artist fosters all the powers of his own ego so that he can love or admire better, and communicate the fire that burns within him and consumes him. Love (human or divine) sheds its transfiguring light on Rembrandt's Christ in " The Pilgrims at Emmaus " and on the humble figure with its meek countenance in Hendrickje's " Bethsheba ", just as it transfigures those landscapes by Corot that seem to tremble with the intensity of the artist's feeling.

One stage lower and this fire grows cooler; from love we come down to knowledge; from the divine to the human; from art to science. Between the ego and the other there is now merely communication;

the painter becomes a kind of scientist, facing an object; now he thinks only of taking possession of it, mastering it, rifling the secrets of its appearance as the scientist seeks the secrets of its structure. This process is characteristic of possession in real life, of understanding in the sphere of the mind and of realism in art. Love, which means giving, gives way to avidity, which means taking.

In art, too, love is made up of " sacrifices "—as Delacroix so often insisted; whereas realism is insatiable, it wants everything, is determined to have everything. Set beside Delacroix, who is full of passion, if not of love, an artist like Ingres, whose enthusiasm is only aroused by sensuality, and the difference is plain: Ingres has an eye that loves every detail and can record it; Delacroix is attracted only to what moves him and inspires him with fervour; Delacroix's colour (which for this very reason often deceives beginners, who have developed quite different ideas as to what constitutes " a great colourist ") brings out the secret correspondences, the affinities, which it perceives between different tones, and reduces them all to a harmony. Ingres gets the most out of every separate tone, often at the cost of sacrificing the colour harmony: his strongest emotion is an avid sensuality, Delacroix's is compassion. Thus in these two masters we see the difference, not so much between two different schools, as between two different levels in the scale of values which we are endeavouring to establish.

The relentless scientific precision of the realists takes hold of things, but it does not give itself to them. Line and colour are perfect; but they state more than they evoke. How remote they seem from the mute or trembling tones of the artists roused by love, from the magically warm chiaroscuro in which artists like Rembrandt bathe their world, or the feeling that gives such a shy delicacy to Corot's colour, making his hand tremble with devotion! Here the picture is no more than a cage in which the painter displays his prey, conquered and tamed. Nature has been subjugated; she only presents her external appearance; her soul is absent; for she belongs to those who love her, not to those who subdue her. Realism is like science; their nets have the same kind of mesh; they catch the same things—and they let the same things escape, things of a kind less easily grasped.

There exists on this level, however, a colossal artist who by the sheer force of his genius overcame this bondage of the heart—I mean Leonardo da Vinci. For Leonardo certainly remained a stranger to love: he was the man of knowledge *par excellence*, and as such, indeed, as passionately interested in science as he was in art, for he sought both knowledge and power. Not only love was foreign to him, but even human tenderness. No doubt he is infinitely more subtle than the simple realist avid for every little detail of appearance. He scorns inventories, for he is interested in analysis; he refuses to collect facts, he aims to penetrate secrets. The sublimity of his search, the arid passion with which it is animated, confer upon him a poetical quality as intense as that of the artists who have created out of love. But how different he is from them! His chiaroscuro does not arise, like Rembrandt's, from any love of dreams; it springs from his insatiable urge to investigate his subject-matter. The human soul is not for him an unfathomable mystery affecting the heart, but an annoying puzzle which must be taken to pieces. Curiosity takes the place of inspiration. He does not penetrate things by identifying himself with them but by subjecting them to a close scrutiny. Rembrandt, like all the artists moved by love, suggests the mystic; da Vinci, like all those consumed with avidity, the scientist.

Beyond this neutral frontier, the middle way of objective knowledge, there exists, as a sort of negative answer to the positive force of love, a third thing—aggressiveness. And with this we reach the third stage of our investigation: with this we descend as low into the earth as we rose high into the air in the celestial light of love—the two things existing above and below the level ground of realism. At this stage the connection between the self and the other reappears: the ego feels a need to assert itself by cruelly or destructively possessing the other—in the case of intellectual work by means of knowledge, and in the case of artistic work by reproduction; it must subjugate, exploit, degrade, annihilate. The ego's only interest in the external world is to feed on it and use it to justify its own hypertrophy; proud of itself, it is cruel towards everything else.

With this we come to the last of the three great stages—the divine, the human, the demoniac; to which correspond, in the sphere of relationship, love, possession and sadism. The last of these three states has found its most triumphant incarnation in our time in the madness of Nazism. Now it is a really remarkable fact that in the sphere of art the characteristics of this third stage are found to a greater or less degree throughout German art. (If it was properly utilized, the history of art could be highly instructive because of the kind of ethnological psycho-analysis it makes possible.)

Do not mistake me: it would be puerile to say that German art expresses the " demoniac " state which we are now about to discuss. But it is nevertheless quite clear that German art does bear all the signs of aggressiveness and cruelty, which thus seem as though latent in the race, ready to waken into activity whenever the necessary stimulus is applied. One school, however, is certainly not to be included in this category—that which existed along the Rhine at the beginning of the fifteenth century, at the time of the great mystical outburst of Eckhart, Tauler, Suso and the rest. This great river artery seems at this stage to have been far more of a German frontier than actual German territory, and its painting, in full conformity with the principles we are endeavouring to establish, reflects all the characteristics of the mystical outpouring of the time—above all in its delicacy of line, which approaches that of the School of Paris. But then the Reformation breaks out: there is a complete break with the Catholic South: Germanism immediately aggravates all its own particular characteristics: its painting is transformed into something hysterical, sensational, cruel. The colour becomes violent, strident, developing a harshness unknown in the other schools. The line, as we have seen, is constantly suggesting the forms of aggressiveness, the things that sting and tear, cut and rend to pieces. This is not simply a matter of chance: spontaneous gestures are rare—and when they are involuntary, unintentional, unconscious even, they only serve to bring out more clearly the deepest tendencies and impulses behind this painting. If there was any need for more direct proof, this could be found in the choice of subject-matter: the caricatured bestiality of the types represented, particularly of Christ's executioners, has long been recognized; the painters enjoy portraying the ferocity of these people with a realism unknown in any other school, just as they love using Christ's supreme sacrifice or the martyrdom of the saints for their images of atrocities, blood, suffering. Manuel Deutsch is not satisfied with portraying less than ten thousand martyrs, all with bodies impaled or dismembered or broken. Could there be more frightful nightmares than those that obsess Grünewald? Round St. Anthony he sets monstrosities covered over with sores and gangrene; his Christ crucified revels in the ghastliness of death, the horror of the body blackened with blows, pierced with thorns, sweating with blood, contracted in the extremest agony of suffering, the face swollen, the mouth gaping. The clenched and contorted hands, set like talons against the background of the dark night, are a theme that obsesses him (Plate III, p. 70).

But it is by comparing different treatments of the same theme that one can best appreciate the expressive language of form. One has only to put this picture by the side of a crucifixion by a French miniaturist to feel at once the contrast between the spirit of love and the spirit of cruelty. Perhaps in Grünewald's case this spirit of cruelty is simply a painful way round to the reality of love through the shock of outraged compassion; but this does not alter the fact that the actual picture exists as a record of cruelty and is expressed in the language of cruelty.

Between these two extremes we may place a Crucifixion by Antonello da Messina, which is invested with an objectivity that seems, perhaps, by contrast, more absolute than it really is: the strong, almost geometrical lines, the ample volumes, simplified, boldly defined, the solidly-placed forms set in a space whose lighting is uniform and, so to speak, impartial—all this means that " pathos " and inspiration are both equally absent: intelligence, observation and knowledge play a bigger part in a picture like this than emotion or the divine or subterranean movements of the soul (Plate IV, p. 102).

To bring the discussion up to our own times, there is a fourth Crucifixion, by one of the most eminent representatives of the younger school, André Marchand, which throws a great deal of light on ourselves. Before the war Marchand showed a preference for forms that were calm and venerable with age, for large volumes and muted, contemplative colours: he clearly derived, by way of Cézanne, from Roman art and Le Nain. And then the war came. Marchand's painting underwent a profound change in every respect: his colour suddenly became strident and violently unrestrained; his brushwork was broken up into fragments, the paint slashed on, the whole thing done in jerks; what had been hieratic, somewhat lacking in feeling, became passionately emotional.

Now this remarkable development is not the only one of its kind: it is that of many of our younger painters. Their art has been described as cruel. And it cannot be denied that there is an aggressive spirit at work in it. Does this mean that there is cruelty in their souls? I should say not; I should say that cruelty has passed over them. Inescapably present to them throughout the war, the defeat, the German oppression, it exists in them now as a kind of obsession. Like a piercing blast from a whistle, against which the ear can find no protection, the cruelty of that indescribable time penetrated to the inmost centre of their inner life, hammering away relentlessly at their eyes and minds until the line of their stylistic development suddenly snapped. The spirit of love struggles within them but it is wounded, a prey to that spirit of aggressiveness whose characteristics have now appeared in the art of France for the first time.

Here we reach the very heart of the spiritual crisis of our age. Has Nazism been defeated? The answer is no: Nazism is everywhere. The beast has been brought to the ground, but its body still poisons the air, and now with a stench more noisome than when it was actively ferocious, because it is now more pervasive. We live in a changed world, a world that still bears the mark of the claw that fastened upon it— and not only the mark, but the raw wound.

Is there to be found in any other sphere such a clear and precise presentation of the drama latent in the years ahead as exists in this transformation in the style of painting? Art is one of the most convincing pieces of evidence that man can bring forward either for or against himself. Perhaps one day the historian and the psychologist will show a greater desire to question it about man's most intimate secrets.

THE RESOLUTION OF
LOVE AND VIOLENCE IN MICHELANGELO

Anthony Bertram

THERE is a late poem of Michelangelo's which describes his wavering and weary search for salvation, lost in the dark wood. He does not mention the wood, but the opening of *The Divine Comedy* was clearly in his mind, for he was a perpetual student of Dante. The poem begins:

> " Ora in sul destro, ora in sul manco piede
> Variando, cerco della mia salute.
> Fra 'l vizio e la virtute
> Il cor confuso mi traviglia e stanca,
> Come chi 'l ciel non vede,
> Che per ogni sentier si perde, a manca." [1]

My purpose in this essay is to ask what psychological circumstance or what flaw in his character made his life an agony and his work fragments. All other circumstances were so combined that life and work might have been as integrated and serene as Raphael's. He had ardour and facility in his youth: he had quick success, rich and powerful patrons and immense opportunities. He lived in the age and place that, above all others, could and did appreciate his genius. Why, then, his tragedy? What prevented him from ever enjoying what life offered him so generously? What plunged him into unremitted suffering, into squalor and loneliness?

On a sheet of miscellaneous drawings[2] he wrote these four terrible lines:

> " Sol io, ardendo, all 'ombra mi rimango,
> Quand'il sol de' suo' raggi il mondo spoglia;

---

[1] *Rime*, CLXXXXIX. I give the numbers in Piccoli's edition of the poems in the *Collezione di Classici Italiani*, 1944; but as they differ from other standard editions, I add the opening words of the poem when the quotation does not include them.

[2] Plate 19 in *Michelangelo Drawings* by Ludwig Goldscheider (Phaidon Press, 1951). For the reader's convenience I shall only refer to works reproduced in this publication or the *Sculptures* (revised ed., 1950) or the *Paintings* (n.d., about 1939) by the same author and publishers. The two latter are now available in one volume (1953). I shall give no further references as it will always be obvious to which volume I should refer.

Ogni altro per piacere, e io per doglia,
Prostrato in terra, mi lamento e piango." [1]

Not out of the depths, but from the height of his tremendous fame,
in the clear blaze of a recognized supremacy among the artists of Italy,
why should he see himself burning in the shadows, prostrate on the
earth, mourning and weeping?

In a letter to his brother, Buonarotto (17 October 1509), he wrote:
" Non ho amici di nessuna sorte, e non ne voglio." Why should he
say he had no friends? It was not true. Why should he say he wished
for none? It was a thousand times not true. His poems are a sustained
cry of hunger for love. The tragedy and the pity of his desolation is
that he hungered in the midst of plenty; he could not accept what all
his world was only too anxious to offer him. The psychological circumstance, I shall suggest, was in the nature of his love, the violence he
did it and the violence it did him. His quarrel was not with the world,
because the world did not quarrel with him but only with his quarrel-
someness; and that was no more than the superficial eruption of his
quarrel with himself. Yeats said, as we all know, that out of that quarrel
poetry is made. In his public works, Michelangelo projected his private
quarrel into man's quarrel with God. The violence of sin fills the
Sistine Chapel with its thunders. God is terrible even in the loving
act of creation and the incarnate Love is only offered at the moment
when He rises in anger and majesty to launch His sentence of damnation. But however much Michelangelo was conscious of his own part
in sin and his own danger of damnation, he keeps himself, biographi-
cally considered, out of his public works. In his private works—his verse
and drawings—Michelangelo turns in on himself almost exclusively.
Since our business here is with a biographical matter, it is chiefly in
them and in his letters that we shall look for our material. But when at
last the inner discord is resolved, the public works also reflect that resol-
ution.There is no violence in the serene and assured majesty of the dome
of St. Peter's, his most public work. And in the last sculptured *Pietàs*,
in that theme of love and redemption which he had also contemplated
tenderly and calmly in youth, before the storm got up, his private
sorrows, the poetry of his verse and drawings pass into stone and are
made public . . .

I have not the space here to detail the symptoms of Michelangelo's
inner conflict as we find them in the events of his life. I must be content with pointers. The most conspicuous, of course, is the immense
scale of his failure. It is not that he ended his life on any St. Helena
but that during it he lost every battle. He who at Carrara had proposed

_____
[1] *Rime,* XXII.

to carve a mountain into a colossus finished none of his larger undertakings in sculpture and few even of his single statues. This was
partly because he planned on a scale far beyond the powers of one man
to execute and was temperamentally unable to work with assistants.
There is here a great indiscipline of the imagination—a fault in the
technique of planning his work so that it was bound to fall short of
his vision. It is a fault also in the order of beauty, the proportioning
of means to end, the integration of the work of art with the artifact.

Another symptom is implicit in his difficulties with assistants: he
was altogether a " difficult " man. This is the best-known mark of
him, this easily-dramatized turbulence, particularly in his squabbles
with patrons. He was not wholly responsible for them, of course:
some of his patrons were difficult too. The most patient and submissive
of men would have found Pope Julius II a handful to work for, but
Michelangelo contributed more than his share to the tumultuous
situations. He recognized this affliction—for we must call it that—
and he spoke of it as " some trick of temper, or some madness, which
they say is in my nature, which hurts nobody except myself".[1] This
difficulty was most acute with his family. He was proud of its nobility
but inconsistent as usual. He was petulant with a man who addressed
him as " Sculptor " as if he kept a shop, but he often signed documents
with that description of himself. He was much concerned that his
family should not die out, but in one letter, he shrugged his shoulders
—" not that the world would be disturbed if it did, but every animal
tries to preserve its kind". He poured abuse and money on his family
in equal proportions. A letter of abuse would often end with a loving
and gentle postscript.

This quarrel with his family was, of course, an extension of his
quarrel with himself. They were his own, and what was his own he
was never at ease with. Likewise, though he loved Florence, he continually abused it. He mostly lived away and suffered home-sickness.
He was a patriot republican and a follower of Savonarola, but even
while engaged in republican military service, he continued to work
for the Medici as artist.

Michelangelo's attitude to money is again inconsistent. He made a
great deal but gave most of it to his family. He was lavish with drawings
to his friends and in the care of his servants. And yet he lived in the
squalid discomfort of a miser, though not from miserliness, for he
would refuse comfortable quarters even when they were offered free.

[1] J. A. Symonds's *Life of Michelangelo Buonarroti*, London, 1893. Any
future quotations for which I give no reference are from this source. It is so
easily available and so well indexed that the irritation of constant footnotes can
thus be avoided.

Perhaps he was punishing his body for its ugliness. That may well have been a particular cause of discord in him, since his ideal of beauty was the male body; but it seems to me, rather, that it may have been a mark of his religious temper—an ascetic, almost Franciscan attitude, an act of dedication.

" Be contented that bread does not fail you," he wrote to his father, " and live well with Christ, and poorly as I do here . . . It is now about fifteen years since I had a single hour of well-being, and all that I have done has been to keep you, and you have never recognized this or believed it. God pardon us all! I am ready to go on doing the same as long as I live, if only I am able."

This patience and resignation, this wide pity—" God pardon us all "—this distaste for the pomp and comfort of the world was accompanied—not always, far from it, but sometimes—by expressions of deep humility. " I am a poor man and of little merit, who plod along in the art which God gave me." He was not poor, but he made himself poor: he stripped himself. It is tempting to associate this with his view of sculpture as an act of stripping and with his passion for the nude in art. He was impatient of all " lendings " but what he sought to expose was not, like Lear, " a poor, bare, forked animal " but the image of God. And he struggled for this exposure *with violence*.

But this violence, this attack on the stone, was intermittent. In all artists there must be some alternation between the active and the contemplative life, between Leah and Rachel, but, as usual with Michelangelo, the alternations were to extremes. And yet, when he carved these symbolic figures for the tomb of Julius, his Leah is far from violent—a calm pensive creature who droops her head as if troubled that she has chosen the lesser part. There is no bombast of activity, no trace of the self-satisfied obtuseness of the exclusively active person. It is as if Michelangelo regretted the very medium of his greatness, the activity that is inevitable if contemplation is to bear fruit in art.

We are so impressed by the record of Michelangelo's feverish activity, of the huge scale of his undertakings, that we tend to overlook the long periods when he brooded alone, reading Dante and writing his poems. Symonds even surprises us by calling him " a meditative man, glad enough to be inert when not spurred forward " and often " sunk in a wise passiveness". While he wooed Rachel, Leah was neglected. The statue remained emergent from the stone, most often never to emerge completely. But perhaps Michelangelo is most fully expressive when, by this interpenetration in the image, we see in one form the fruit and the womb. In his last works the unfinished state seems not so much a failure as the image of the unutterableness which Dante discusses in the *Convivio*. It is as if Michelangelo had stayed his hand, fearing that if he did the stone more violence he might frighten away the ineffable vision he had half-exposed. For Michelangelo's violence was no consistent *attack*. It was itself another centre of contradiction in his behaviour, and as often took the form of *flight*. This man who defied the formidable Pope Julius in a way which, the Signory of Florence told him, " the King of France would not have dared ", was overwhelmed on other occasions by panic.

We are accustomed to think of his *terribilità*. We must also remember that his friend and first biographer Condivi wrote of him as " timorous . . . except when roused to righteous anger . . . but for the rest, most patient and enduring ". A great lady of Rome described him as " a nobleman of such delicate and fascinating manners that his equal hardly exists in Europe ".[1] But there was none of this when he was at work: then he attacked, and his violence became most significant —a battle with the stone to lay bare God's image. It was the loved image which he always wooed with violence; and that, I suggest, is because of the ambiguity of that image. It was also the image of the male physical beauty which troubled his whole life. I need not quote in full the description of him at work which is given in every biography.[2] Its contemporary author tells us that when over sixty he could knock off more chips in a quarter of an hour than three young stone-cutters in three or four hours, " hurling great fragments to the ground at one blow " and risking the whole work by the impetuosity with which he chiselled even in the most delicate places. He was fighting to expose the imprisoned statue and he worked like a rescuer who knows there is life under the wreckage. The greatest artist, he wrote, has nothing to say which is not already present in the marble, nothing to do but to release it:

> " Non ha l'ottimo artista alcun concetto,
>   C'un marmo solo in sé circoscriva
>   Col suo soverchio; a solo a quello arriva
>   La man che ubbidisce all'intelletto." [3]

It was not only the resisting marble that he attacked with this violence. In the earlier drawings he seemed, in Symonds's phrase, " to hew with the pen ". In fresco he painted with such fury that the Sistine ceiling reminded Stendhal of a sudden cannonade at night during the retreat from Moscow.

If we are to understand why this battle for the loved image was so terrible a process, we must examine the nature of love in Michelangelo's

---

[1] Quoted by Romain Rolland, *Vie de Michelange*, 1920, p. 151.
[2] Symonds, op. cit., vol. i, p. 101, for example.
[3] *Rime*, LXXXIII.

experience. It is here that we come at last to the crux of our problem. The paradox of Michelangelo was that he was naturally a gentle and loving creature. For him, as for the young and untravelled Dante,

" Amore e cor gentil sono una cosa."

The Gonfalonier of Florence assured the authorities in Rome, after the quarrel with Pope Julius, that only kindness and affection were necessary to ensure Michelangelo's ardent service. With servants, with the humble and the foolish, he was most gentle, most concerned and most tender. His pity ranged from the sufferings of Christ to the least sympathetic of human sins. He could write sadly of " the poor ungrateful man " and of his ingratitude as an affliction to be forgiven. He had great charity. He saw love as a splendour from the stars:

" Dalle piú alte stelle
    Discende uno splendore,
    Che 'l desir tira a quelle;
    E qui si chiama amore." [1]

But this love that could soften his heart to the suffering and the abased was engaged also by the triumphant power of physical beauty; and it was then that it became a tyranny to him. His susceptibility was narrowed to one form of physical beauty, the male body; and that concentration intensified it almost to mania. He described himself as having a heart like sulphur, a flesh like tow and bones like dry wood, so that he flamed at the least touch of fire.[2]

But indeed this particular susceptibility and the suffering it caused him fill his poems and letters and are manifest in all his works. He never introduced nature, except when his subject compelled him to, as in the *Fall* and *Deluge* of the Sistine ceiling. " He has traced no flowers . . . No forest scenery like Titian's fills his backgrounds, but only blank ranges of rock, and dim vegetable forms as blank as they, as in a world before the creation of the first five days."[3] He contemplated the whole universe in man alone, a stripped man suspended in the void. But it was also his image of the soul and of God, and nothing is allowed to come between us except the body that is its last veil, without which he could find no visual image. And his love for the beauty of that male body conflicted with his love for the soul and for God.

[1] *Rime*, CCI. " Gli occhi mie' vaghi . . . ",
[2] *Rime*, CLXXXXVI. " Al cor di zolfo . . . "
[3] Walter Pater in his essay on Michelangelo's poetry in *The Renaissance*.

As with nature, so with the female body—he never introduced it into his work except where the subject compelled him to; and when he did, it was masculine in character. Symonds is categoric: " Michelangelo neither loved nor admired nor yielded to the female form ". The fact must be faced that Michelangelo was homosexual. There is no evidence of any sexual love for any woman in all his long life. The poems which seem to be addressed to women are either formal exercises in the Petrarchan manner or possibly concerned with Vittoria Colonna. But this famous friendship of his late years was certainly not sexual, so far as we can be certain of any such thing. All this is clear enough; beneath it is only obscurity. But we cannot avoid looking into that depth if we are to treat our theme honestly. We must ask whether he was guilty of homosexual practices. The answer to our original question on the nature of the psychological circumstance or the flaw in his character most probably lies here. If he was guilty, then his profound horror of sin and the tragic penitential temper of his late years are explained. He would have felt his guilt not only as a betrayal of the crucified Christ, with whom in those years he was obsessed; but also of his Platonic ideal of beauty as a spiritual manifestation and the love of it as a spiritual activity.

Among those most familiar with the sources, Henry Thode,[1] Symonds and Charles De Tolnay do not accept this possibility. Symonds was outraged at the suggestion. He is again categoric: " There is nothing in his letters, in the correspondence addressed to him, in his poetry, or in any of the contemporary notices of his daily life, to raise any suspicion regarding his moral conduct." He goes on to suggest that the weight of evidence is in favour of his having been a man " of physically frigid temperament . . . who habitually philosophised his emotions " and he points out that only one of his four brothers married and that *he* had only one child. " The Buonarroti-Simone breed, in his generation, appears to have been partially sterilised."[2]

But that statement, that there is *nothing* to raise suspicion, is not strictly accurate. When Aretino was disappointed at Michelangelo's not giving him a drawing, he wrote his famous abusive letter on the nudes of *The Last Judgment*, in which he says that had he done so it would have silenced " the envious tongues that say that only certain Gherardos and Tommasos dispose of them ". This reference to Michelangelo's young friends Gherardo Perini and Tommaso dei Cavalieri is dismissed as sheer malice by most writers, especially because of its tainted source. De Tolnay asserts positively

[1] *Michelangelo und das Ende der Renaissance*, 6 vols., Berlin, 1902–13.
[2] See particularly the Appendix on this issue dealing with the contrary opinion, vol. ii, p. 384.

that " his friendship with Tommaso Cavalieri was to be in truth a love-passion without anything impure."[1] It may be so. But it may seem more difficult to get round another passage, also quoted by Symonds himself. Writing to a friend, Michelangelo relates how he has told a father that he does not want his son for his service, " e lui non la intese ma rispose, che se io lo vedessi, che non che in casa, io me lo caccere, nel letto. Io vi dico che rinunzio a questa consolazione, e non la voglio tòrre a lui ". It is, as Symonds rightly observes " a singular example of Italian sentiment and custom "; but it does not *prove* anything except that Michelangelo took such a suggestion rather lightly.

When Michelangelo the Younger published his great-uncle's poems in 1623, he changed the gender of all pronouns wherever " misinterpretation " could be possible. That again does not prove that he knew anything against his reputation, although it certainly suggests that he feared scandal. None of these slighṭ facts indeed proves anything, nor need we give much weight to Walter Pater's suggestion that " he who spoke so decisively of the supremacy in the imaginative world of the unveiled human form had not been always, we may think, a mere Platonic lover ". Indeed, it is inconceivable that Michelangelo found the nude in any way " suggestive ". It was for him, as I have said, the nearest possible approach to the spirit, the last " lending " and that which the visual artist cannot strip off. His drawings of our Lady are sometimes of the unclothed or transparently clothed body.[2] That is convincing evidence that his attitude to the nude in art was absolutely chaste. We cannot imagine this profoundly religious man using a vehicle that carried any salacious associations to express that high love of our Lady which he showed from his earliest works to his latest.

I have said that broadly speaking Michelangelo's personal conflict, whatever its exact nature, had no *direct* influence on his public work. The great exception may be the *Victory*. Various interpretations have been offered of this enigmatic work. At least one authority believes it to have been a political allegory of the destruction of liberty in Florence. Others have seen it as an allegory of Platonic love, but yet others have seen it as erotic and have even identified the defeated old man as a portrait of Michelangelo and the triumphant young man as one of Tommaso. Goldscheider is not inclined to accept this for various reasons[3] but the implicit admission of Michelangelo's guilt is not among them, it would seem, if we are to judge by his

[1] *The Youth of Michelangelo*, Princeton University Press, 1943, p. 19.
[2] See, for examples, Goldscheider's *Drawings*. Plates 82, 122 and 130.
[3] See his note in the Catalogue to the *Sculptures*.

attitude in his introduction to the *Drawings*. He writes there of Michelangelo: "Fear of sin gnawed at his breast like a vulture, yet he remained an addict of that vice which Savonarola described as the worst defect of the Florentines", and he seems, in the same place, to take Aretino's gibe seriously. His very interesting interpretation of certain drawings must, therefore, be considered in the light of this opinion. I have not the space to quote his arguments, which will be found in the notes to the drawings concerned. I can merely state that he interprets the so-called *Damned Soul* in the Uffizi as the fury of love in an old man; and the *Venus, Mars and Cupid*, also in the Uffizi, as an expression of "that terrible form of love which resorts to arms and destruction". If we accept this, then it is indeed an expression of the very heart of our theme. He sums up his interpretation of the religious symbolism of certain other relevant drawings as follows:

THE ARCHERS: The invulnerability of the protected soul.

TITYUS: The sin and punishment of illicit sexual indulgence, or the torments of a man who through sensuality has become godless (Plate V, p. 134).

PHAETON: The penalty of arrogance, or the fall resulting from desire for that which is not permitted.

THE DREAM: The five sins of passion, or the terrible awakening of the sinner to consciousness of himself.

THE BACCHANAL OF CHILDREN: The abasement of mankind through sin.

In the depth of Michelangelo's tortured soul, we discern the image of God as "a deep, but dazzling darkness". In the sonnet which begins "Colui che fece . . .",[1] Michelangelo declared how God had created light and darkness; and how the Fates had apportioned darkness to him:

> "Et a me consegnaro il tempo bruno,
> Come a simil nel parto e nella cuna."

As the darkness deepens, so deepens his consciousness of sin, but he has one comfort—that his darkness is a foil to the brightness of Another. It would be more than a mere figure of speech to interpret this as a proclamation that out of the abasement of Tityus, Christ may rise; for he held his drawing of Tityus up to the light and traced the recumbent figure on the back. Then he turned it upright and added a tomb and its open lid. The result, as Goldscheider has pointed

---

[1] *Rime*, CXXVII.

out, becomes an early sketch for the *Risen Christ* of the British Museum (Plate VI, p. 166).

If, from certain works, then, and on frail documentary evidence, we *may* conclude that Michelangelo had sinned homosexually, we *must*, on the other hand, conclude that his soul never accepted that sin as anything but a stain on his exalted conception of love. The majority of his relevant poems specifically declare his Platonic attitude, that love is a spiritual experience. Again and again, he praises the chastity of those he loves and his love as the image of eternal love. That is not love, he says, which belongs to a temporal beauty, but that which the *pure* heart knows as the image of paradise.

> " Fallace speme ha sol l'amor, che muore
> Con la beltà, c'ogni momento scema,
> Ond'è soggetta al variar d'un bel viso.
> Dolce è ben quella in un pudico core
> Che per cangiar di scorza o d'ora strema
> Non manca, e qui caparra il paradiso." [1]

As Michelangelo found beauty at the heart of the marble when he had stripped off its " lendings " with his chisel, so he found the divine Image at the heart of human beauty, and it was for that alone, when he was most himself, that he loved it.

> " Né Dio, sua grazia, mi si mostra altrove,
> Piú che'n alcun leggiadro e mortal velo;
> E quel sol amo, perch'in lui si specchia." [2]

Therefore, since this revelation of God was the mission of the artist, Michelangelo held that it was not enough for him to be an artist. " I maintain that he must also be a man of good conduct and morals, if possible a saint, in order that the Holy Ghost may rain down inspiration on his understanding." [3]

We understand then how, if Michelangelo was morally guilty, all the violence of his inner conflict is accounted for. But we have been led, rather, it seems to me, to the opposite probability—that he was chaste. Of course, if we accept Symonds's theory of his " physically frigid temperament ", which I find difficult, that may account for his chastity, but then we are left with nothing to account for the

---

[1] *Rime,* CCIII. " Ben può talor col mio . . . "
[2] *Rime,* CCVII. " Per ritornar là donde . . . " Cf. *Rime,* CI. " Se il mio rozzo martello . . . "
[3] Conversation reported by a contemporary. See Symonds, op. cit., vol. ii, p. 113.

violence. But if he was chaste because he was unable, for psychological reasons, to satisfy his sexuality in marriage and refused, for religious and moral reasons, to satisfy it in other ways, then indeed we see him as perpetually chained in the dark prison of his perversity. He had not accepted chastity like the priest, by an act of will, but been obliged to it by a vast misfortune. And it was the pressure of this, perhaps, which led him to the compensation of turning on that of which he was deprived and stigmatising even normal and legitimate sex acts as low and vile—" cose basse e vile "—a kind of tragic sour grapes.

There is one particular sonnet where he exalts Uranian love precisely because it does not, like the love of women, lead to such acts; and the fact that its argument derives from Plato is no reason for not accepting it as a genuine expression of Michelangelo's own belief.

" Non è sempre di colpa aspra e mortale
    D'una immensa bellezza un fero ardore,
    Si poi si lascia liquefatto il core,
    Che'n breve il penetri un divino strale.
Amore isveglia e desta e 'mpenna l'ale
    Né l'alto vol prescrive al van furore;
    Qual primo grado, c'al suo creatore,
    Di quel non sazia, l'alma ascende e sale.
L'amor di quel ch'i' parlo in alto aspira;
    Donna, è dissimil troppo; e mal conviensi
    Arder di quella al cor saggio e virile.
L'una tira al cielo, a l'altro in terra tira;
    Nell'alma l'un, l'altro abita ne' sensi,
    E l'arco tira a cose basse e vile." [1]

Such an enforced chastity could well account for all that is morbid and enigmatic in his personality. But perhaps we may also see it as having other fruit. The religious exaltation of his late years may well have grown from the transference of his barren sexual love to the mystic love of the crucified Christ. On this view we may interpret his whole ascetic life as a substitute, a Franciscan marriage with Poverty not of his free choice but psychologically forced on him at first, and only in maturity consciously accepted and welcomed as his Cross.

Goldscheider has said that " Michelangelo's deepest passion was religion ". It is to that passion, then, that we shall now look for some resolution of his quarrel with himself. The earliest indication of it is

[1] *Rime*, XCI.

that, although connected with the court of Lorenzo de' Medici, he was a follower of Savonarola. It is what we would expect. The prophetic and violent spirit of Savonarola's denunciations of sin was precisely what would be most apt to move Michelangelo. It is that spirit, not the sensuous and humanist paganism of Lorenzo, that inspired the Sistine frescoes. " The purity of the soul of the Dominican, the ardour with which he gave himself to his ideal, his disdain for the baseness of the world, his need of an interior renewal by asceticism, and finally his prophetic gift are traits that Michelangelo himself possessed to a certain degree."¹ But he had not Savonarola's single-mindedness, and could also entertain the prevalent love for classic form and mythology. He could work at the same time on the wholly sensuous and sensual *Bacchus* and the deeply Christian *Pietà* in St. Peter's. But this discord was eventually resolved by his concentration on religious themes, so that during his last thirty years all his work, without exception, can be interpreted as religious, even when the language of classic form and mythology may remain, as in the Tityus drawing.

We must partly attribute this to his friendship with Vittoria Colonna, his only recorded intimacy with a woman. It seems to have begun when he was over sixty and she a middle-aged widow, devoting her life to religion and philosophy. She was a member of that group of reforming Catholics which was gathered round Cardinal Pole, who were known as the *Spirituali*. Some of them, like Carnesecchi, were condemned for heresy: others, like Ochino, became Protestants. Vittoria herself was under some suspicion: but not Michelangelo. We must conclude that he kept an uncharacteristic balance in this dangerous circle. His relations with Vittoria were of respect and devotion, a love wholly free from passion; and the time of their greatest intimacy, from about 1540 to her death seven years later, was the most tranquil of his life. Under her influence Michelangelo's religious experience was deepened and simplified. He was able to give himself up to long hours of solitary prayer and is even credited in one con-temporary account with the gift of mystical vision.²

It is very difficult to date Michelangelo's poems, but it seems clear that the majority of those with purely religious themes, especially the Penitential Sonnets, must have been written in those last years. There is one madrigal which tells what he owed to Vittoria. "A man, even a God, speaks through the mouth of a woman " it begins. That is a strange statement, but we can understand it in the light of that habitual identification of the male form with the divine image which we have already noted. The poem goes on to say that he has listened to that

¹ De Tolnay, op. cit., p. 20.   ² Quoted by Rolland, op. cit. p. 169.

voice and been changed. The woman has led him to repentance and
her beauty has overshadowed all others. That beauty, we must remember, was purely spiritual; but even had she been physically beautiful,
we know that it would have meant nothing to Michelangelo.

> "Un uomo in una donna, anzi uno dio,
> Per la sua bocca parla,
> Ond'io per ascoltarla
> San fatto tal, che ma' piú sarò mio.
> I' credo ben, po' chi'io
> A me da lei fu' tolto,
> Fuor di me stesso aver di me pietate;
> Si sopra 'l van desio
> Mi sprona il suo bel volto,
> Ch'i' veggo morte in ogni altra beltate.
> O Donna, che passate
> Per acqua e foco l'alme a' lieti giorni,
> Deh, fate, c'a me stesso piú non torni!"[1]

She led him to joy through fire and water. I hope it is not too far
fetched to see them as symbols of our theme: violence in the fire of
repentance or frustration and serene love in the purity of water—a
love at last serene because it is freed from physical sex. But that fire,
also, was the ardour of his illicit loves. What penance must he do for
that, he asks her in another poem, now that she has chastened and
taught him?

> "Qual penitenza aspetta
> Mi' fero ardor, se mi castiga e 'nsegna?"[2]

In the poems on her death, he expressed his fear of what might
happen to him now that her help was withdrawn, unless Divine Love
came to his aid.[3]

I have no space to discuss the Penitential Sonnets. I can only draw
attention to the most famous and most significant, that beginning
" Giunto è già 'l corso della vita mia ",[4] in which he repudiates even
his own art, that had been his idol and king, stripping himself in the
end of the last earthly tie. Neither painting nor sculpture, he cries,
can give him rest. His soul turns to that Divine Love whose arms are
spread on the cross to receive us:

---

[1] *Rime*, CCXXXIII.
[2] *Rime*, CCXXXII. " Se ben concetto . . . "
[3] *Rime*, CII. " Qual maraviglia è . . . "
[4] *Rime*, CCXLV. Wordsworth translated this, from a very faulty text. See the
Clarendon Press edition, vol. iii, p. 408.

" Né pinger né scolpir fia piú che quieti
L'anima volta a quell'Amor divino
C'aperse, a prender noi, 'n croce le braccia."

In these years he worked on the completion of St. Peter's and refused all payment. " Many believed," he wrote, " and I believe, that I have been given this task by God. Old as I am, I do not wish to give it up: for I serve for the love of God."[1] It was then also that he carved the three infinitely pitiful and tender *Pietàs*, now in the cathedral and academy of Florence and in the Castello Sforzesco at Milan.[2] We have no reason to doubt Vasari's statement that the Nicodemus in the first of these was Michelangelo's self-portrait. The old man, whom perhaps we saw crushed and abased in the *Victory*, now stands in tranquil love over the dead Christ and His mother. His left hand supports her with a gesture of enormous pity. Out of his strength and violence has come forth sweetness.

Again and again he drew the Crucifixion, where, instead of the pen hewing out the clear form, we find the mystery of chalk adumbrating forms which say more than precise statement, " no longer communications but monologues . . . entries in a diary or book of confessions ".[3] Rachel has invaded and filled the world of Leah and we see her form as, when the decanter is filled with wine, we see a form of wine which, complete in itself, could none the less not survive the breaking of the container—the work of art. But in the act of contemplation, no effort of the will nor muscularity in the drawing is any longer necessary.

In the example which I reproduce (Plate VII, p. 198) we may identify Michelangelo with that mourning enigmatic figure at the foot of the cross, which lays its head against the dead body and caresses it as St. Anne caresses the cheek of St. Joachim in Giotto's fresco at Padua. Here at the Golden Gate Michelangelo's form flows into the form of the Crucified and loses its separating identity. He prays that he may be purged of self-love:

" Manca la speme, e pur cresce 'l desio,
Che da te sia dal proprio amor disciolto."[4]

There were times when Michelangelo was near despair, near to death and far from God—" si presso a morte e si lontan da Dio ".[5]

[1] Letter to his nephew, 7 July 1557.
[2] Until 1952 in the Palazzo Sansevarino Vimercati at Rome.
[3] Goldscheider, *Drawings*, p. 22.
[4] *Rime*, CCXLVIII: " Le favole del mondo . . . "
[5] *Rime*, XLVIII: " Forse perché d'altrui . . . "

This man of huge vitality had come to long for the shadow of death, which ends the sufferings of the heart, the last and best cure of the afflicted:

> " O ombra del morir, per cui si ferma
> Ogni miseri', a l'alma, al cor nemica,
> Ultimo degli afflitti e buon rimedio."[1]

But at last he finds his hope and assurance in the Crucifixion. Although we must believe in the promises of Christ, he says, yet he asks what man can dare to count on pity when repentance is long delayed? And he answers that the measure of God's gifts must be as infinite as His sufferings.

> " Che, benché alle promesse tue s'attenda,
> Sperar forse, Signore, è troppo ardire,
> C'ogni soverchio indugio amor perdoni.
> Ma pur par, nel tuo sangue si comprenda,
> Se per noi par non ebbe il tuo martire,
> Senza misura sien tuo' cari doni."[2]

God will forgive him. The quarrel is made up: the conflict of love and violence resolved. He had been robbed by his nature of natural and fruitful love, but through supernatural love he can bear the fruit of his salvation. It was the only marriage possible for him, and he prayed for its consummation:

> "Manda 'l predetto lume a noi venturo,
> Alla tua bella sposa, acciò ch'io arda,
> Il cor senz'alcun dubbio, a te sol senta."[3]

Hope was born of that marriage, and his exaltation is expressed in the triumphant leap upwards of the *Resurrection* (Plate VIII, p. 247)

[1] *Rime*, LXXVIII: " O nott', o dolce tempo . . . "
[2] *Rime*, CCLIV: " Mentre m'attrista e duol . . . "
[3] *Rime*, CCXXXVIII: " Vorrei voler, Signor, quel ch'io non voglio . . . "

LOVE AND WAR IN SHAKESPEARE'S "TROILUS AND CRESSIDA"

D. A. Traversi

THE CLOSE relationship between the values of love and war, which is one of the most interesting—and, as some critics would add, one of the most " modern "—aspects of Shakespeare's *Troilus and Cressida*, corresponds to a conception of dramatic unity which was, at the time of writing, new in his work. The novelty consists in uniting, for the first time and in a manner mutually illuminating, a personal theme and its public, " social " extension. Instead of a political conflict objectively studied and commented on by a character (such as Falstaff) who stands, in a sense, outside it, we are presented with a personal issue—the story of Troilus and Cressida, two lovers of opposed parties—set in the context of the Trojan war. The situation of the lovers is variously connected with the cleavage between the warring parties to which they respectively belong; and the connection thus dramatically established is further strengthened by the pervasive presence of imagery which suggests disruptive tendencies barely contained within a single way of feeling. The result, in terms of poetic drama, is less a finished and coherent creation than a statement of emotional ambiguity, the reflection of an experience deprived of order and seeking clarification through its own expression.

This ambiguity, in so far as it affects the personal action, is clearly connected with themes that found expression, perhaps almost sim-ultaneously, in the Sonnets. Taking as his point of departure the conventional subject of so many Renaissance sonneteers—the union with his mistress desired by the poet—Shakespeare's most individual sonnets convert this theme, which is applied to a variety of human relationships, into an apprehension of the parallel fulfilment and destruction of human values by time. Time, which brings passion to its consummation, implies equally its decline; for the union of love, the very desire for which is inconceivable apart from its temporal setting, demands, as a necessary condition, an unattainable eternity. The desire for unity is inevitably preceded by a state of separation, and to this tragic separateness it equally inevitably, in the flesh, returns:

> "Let me confess that we two must be twain,
> Although our undivided loves are one."
>
> (Sonnet XXXVI)

The action of time, which is at the same time creative and destructive, which both makes love possible and destroys it, is the unavoidable flaw at the heart of passion. The dramatic presentation of this contradiction, in the setting of a political situation which in some sense reflects it, is the theme of *Troilus and Cressida*.

The flaw thus introduced by time into human experience is represented dramatically in the separation which overtakes the two lovers, a separation foreseen from the beginning and implicit in the logic of events. Of the spirit of this separation, Troilus' leave-taking is probably the clearest expression:

> CRESSIDA: And is it true that I must go from Troy?
> . . . Is it possible?
> TROILUS: And suddenly: where injury of chance
> Puts back leave-taking, justles roughly by
> All time of pause, rudely beguiles our lips
> Of all rejoindure, forcibly prevents
> Our locked embrasures, strangles our dear vows
> Even in the birth of our own labouring breath;
> We too, that with so many thousand sighs
> Did buy each other, must poorly sell ourselves
> With the rude brevity and discharge of one.
> Injurious time now with a robber's haste
> Crams his rich thievery up, he knows not how;
> As many farewells as be stars in heaven,
> With distinct breath and consign'd kisses to them,
> He fumbles up into a loose adieu,
> And scants us with a single famish'd kiss,
> Distasted with the salt of broken tears.
>
> (IV. iv)

The peculiar verbal intricacy of this speech is highly characteristic of the play and helps to throw light upon the nature of its inspiration. The experience reflected in it is, verbally at least, tremendously rich, endlessly elaborate, but the ordering of it is not equal to the complexity. The adverse action of time upon the parting lovers is represented by an astonishing number of verbs—" puts back ", " justles roughly by", " rudely beguiles", " forcibly prevents ", " strangles "—but the emotion does not *develop*, does not acquire added coherence in the expression. It remains simply a long and acutely-sensed effort to express a state of conflicting feeling. It belongs, in short, to a period in Shakespeare's development in which the keenness of his apprehension of certain elements of experience was not accompanied by a corresponding sense of order and significance; for the attainment of that order and significance in his love-poetry we shall have to wait until *Antony and Cleopatra*.

None the less, although unsatisfactory, the experience behind these lines is highly individual. In each of the verbs of parting which we have just collected there is an element, sharply and vividly realized, of harsh and hostile physical contact. This laboured feeling is balanced by the poignant thinness of the positive love-imagery which so inadequately accompanies it. Troilus, whose awareness of separation is so acute, so tangibly conceived, can only express his passion in images as intense as they are airy and essentially bodiless. Love is indeed " rich " in his estimation, fit to be mentioned with the " stars of heaven "; but it can only be expressed in " sighs " and " laboured *breath* ", in the hurried breathlessness of " distinct *breath* and consign'd kisses ", and in the intensely palated but transitory delicacy of " Distasted with the salt of broken tears ". Opposed to this " airy ", pathetic passion, the full brunt of the senses is felt in every phrase that stresses parting. " Roughly ", " rudely ", " forcibly ", time and hostile circumstances undermine the tragic " brevity " of love, so that the " locked embrasures ", which should normally convey the intensity of physical union, are felt to be only an effort to snatch a moment's identity in the face of events which are forcibly drawing the lovers apart. The parting imposed by external circumstance, indeed, is subsidiary to a certain weakness inherent in passion itself. The ideal, which is perfect union, is desired intensely, but is as light as " breath " or " air "; and the bodies through whose union alone this intensity can be enjoyed are always, while they are united, " labouring " against a tendency to separate. Their " labour ", irrevocably frustrated, issues in nothing tangible or permanent. Throughout *Troilus*, as at this, its moment of deepest emotion, the elements in love making for separation are too strong for those which desire union; and " injurious time " is the process by which separation is born out of desired consummation.

Troilus and Cressida, then, in so far as it deals with the central pair of lovers, projects a metaphysical situation into the evocation of a personal relationship. The play is, in this as in other respects, the product of a profound uncertainty about the value of experience. The personal consequence of this uncertainty, as it affects more particularly the love-poetry of Troilus, is the corruption of romantic sentiment. Once more, we are taken back to the Sonnets. The sensation conveyed by some of the most individual of these poems turns upon a combination of conventional Petrarchan devices with an intense, and normally disturbing, sensual quality; the familiar image of the lily, to take an obvious example, with its associations of beauty and purity, is transformed by a magnificent juxtaposition of convention and immediacy into the potent corruption of " Lilies that *fester* smell far worse than weeds " (Sonnet XCIV). A somewhat similar effect, dramatically presented, is apparent in Troilus' first account of Cressida:

> " I tell thee I am mad
> In Cressid's love; thou answer'st ' she is fair ';
> Pour'st in the open ulcer of my heart
> Her eyes, her hair, her cheek, her gait, her voice,
> Handlest in thy discourse, O that her hand,
> In whose comparison all whites are ink
> Writing their own reproach; to whose soft seizure
> The cygnet's down is harsh, and spirit of sense
> Hard as the palm of ploughman."
>
> (I. i)

The underlying convention here is clearly Petrarchan, romantically abstracted from common reality. It makes itself felt in the assertion that Troilus is " mad " for love, in the strained use of " pour'st " and " handlest " to describe Pandarus' speech, in the comparison of Cressida's hand to the " cygnet's down ", and in the introduction of " ink " to bring out by contrast its superlative whiteness. But the conventional imagery is transformed, as it were, from within in a manner so closely bound up with the convention that it acts as a corrupting agent, intimately related to the surface sentiment. By giving deep sensuous value to the Petrarchan images, it conveys simultaneously an impression of intense feeling and an underlying lack of content. " Handlest in thy discourse " is, as I have said, a far-fetched, an intensely literary image; but it brings with it a notable keenness of touch which is developed in the contrast between harshness and the " soft seizure " of the cygnet's down and in the almost unnatural immediacy of " spirit of sense ". Yet the conventional note remains, and with it the feeling that Troilus' passion, for all its surface intensity, has an inadequate foundation, is vitiated by the strained self-pity which allows him to refer to " the open ulcer of my heart ", and by the weakness to which he confesses in the course of the same speech—" I am weaker than a woman's tear".

It is important to realize why this weakness, which Cressida after her own fashion shares with her lover, does not produce a tragedy of

PORTRAIT OF THE ARTIST (DETAIL)
Durer: Louvre

character, but of situation. The tragedy, indeed, consists less in the personal suffering of the lovers than in the overriding influence exercised by time upon all human relationships and feelings. In *Antony and Cleopatra*, at least while the lovers are united by their feeling for one another, personal emotion has become strong enough to override mutability; in *Troilus*, the supremacy of time is never really questioned and so a consistent status as persons inevitably eludes the lovers. Their weakness reflects the uncertainty of mood in which the play was conceived and to which they owe the peculiar poignancy, more than sentimental and less than tragic, with which they meet their personal fortunes. Antony and Cleopatra, as lovers, are fully-drawn human beings because their love, while it lasts and within its own clearly-defined limitations, is valid and confers upon their emotions a full personal value; and, conversely, the complete realization in evil of Regan and Goneril in *King Lear*, with the sensual ferocity that characterizes their behaviour, proves that Shakespeare, when he wrote that play, felt himself able to distinguish between the various elements in his moral experience without falling into ambiguity and confusion. Antony and Cleopatra, Regan and Goneril, have full reality as characters precisely because they proceed from a clear understanding in their creator of the value of human emotion as distinct from the evil implied in it. *Troilus and Cressida*, however, with its intuition of passion as vain and transitory, is compatible with no such individuality of presentation; for time, as it is understood in this play, destroys personal values and makes them invalid.

This limiting observation can be applied with equal force to the behaviour of both the lovers, and through the entire action. Cressida's falseness does not spring from a deep-seated perversity, or even from a strong positive attraction for Diomed, but from the mere process of events, from a flaw inherent in the human situation. Her tragedy, such as it is, derives from awareness of her helplessness. We feel it in her pathetic appeal when Troilus prepares to leave her after the night they have spent together:

> " Prithee, tarry;
> You men will never tarry,"
> (IV. ii)

and in the moment of self-knowledge in which she tells him:

> " I have a kind of self resides with you,
> But an unkind self that itself will leave
> To be another's fool."
> (III. ii)

There is something in the expression of this uncertainty, half punning and conventional, which makes it difficult to conceive of Cressida as a fully realized being. At most, she lives for us only in the mood of the moment, with barely a sign of that responsibility and consistency which is involved in the very conception of character. Any attempt to subject her inconsistency to a moral, of the kind which the medieval elaborators of this legend had in mind when they denounced her " faithlessness ", is out of place because the spirit in which Shakespeare created her made it impossible for her to be shown as really responsible for her actions; and without responsibility there can be no moral evaluation. When she comments, in the early part of the play, on her refusal to reveal her feelings for Troilus:

> " Yet hold I off. Women are angels, wooing;
>   Things done are won; joy's soul lies in the doing,"
>
> (I. ii)

her aphoristic lines are not a revelation of wantonness, but simply an impression of the sense, which constitutes the only true tragedy of this play, of the impossibility, the meaninglessness of constancy in a world where time dominates human relationships, and where attraction and separation seem necessary and connected aspects of a single situation.

This impossibility also dominates the poetry of Troilus himself and is there further developed from its original basis in romantic sentiment. Troilus' passion, even before it is faced with the necessity for separation, is strong only in anticipation. The intensity of its sensations is conveyed in a refinement of physical feeling, in an attempt to embody in terms of the senses an insubstantial and incorporeal emotion:

> " I am giddy: expectation whirls me round.
>   The imaginary relish is so sweet
>   That it enchants my sense; what will it be,
>   When that the watery palate taste indeed
>   Love's thrice repurèd nectar? death, I fear me,
>   Swounding destruction, or some joy too fine,
>   Too subtle-potent, tuned too sharp in sweetness,
>   For the capacity of my ruder powers:
>   I fear it much, and I do fear besides
>   That I shall lose distinction in my joys . . ."
>
> (III. ii)

The sensations of this passage are intense enough, but only on the palate and through the senses; like the corresponding emotions of Cressida, they scarcely involve any full personality in the speaker. Troilus' emotions are concentrated on " expectation ", on " the *imaginary* relish ", and he feels that the " watery palate " will be too weak to sustain the actual consummation. The whole speech turns upon this contrast between the refined intensity of feeling which he seeks, self-consciously and with a touch of indulgence, in " Love's *thrice repurèd* nectar", and the giddiness, the " swounding destruction ", which would follow its impossible consummation. The experience of love, it is suggested, is so fine, so " subtle-potent ", that it surpasses the " ruder powers " of the body and remains an incorporeal aspiration which the senses strive vainly to attain.

Yet, by a strange contradiction, it is precisely because fulfilment in love is sought by Troilus exclusively on the sensual level that it proves unattainable. We can see now why the poetry of this play makes such extensive use of the imagery of taste, why Cressida, for example, says before she leaves Troy for the Greek camp:

" The grief is fine, full, perfect, that I taste."
(IV. iv)

Taste is a sense at once luxurious, delicate, and transitory; also, it can be connected, in gross opposition to Troilus' bodiless idealism, with digestion and the functioning of the body. For the weakness of Troilus' passion, as we have already suggested, implies that it is patient of corruption; and that corruption—it can now be added—is the logical consequence of an effort to extract from the refinement of the sensual a substitute for spiritual experience. Immediately before the speech just quoted there is a striking turn of phrase in his appeal to Pandarus:

" O, be thou my Charon,
And give me swift transportance to those fields
Where I may *wallow* in the lily-beds
Proposed for the deserver." (III. ii)

The ideal aspirations of Troilus remain abstract, intangible; such intensity as they achieve derives from their subjection to time, from their awareness of their own transitory nature. But this impermanence makes them bodiless, so that the sensual instincts, unable to associate themselves fully with the insubstantial ideal of union in a mutual passion, express themselves both weakly and basely, " wallowing " in what would be, if it were more forceful, a corrupt satisfaction.

This special use of the contrasted implications of sensual experience, indeed, is extended in the course of the play from the personal to the public action, and contributes thus to the unity of its conception. The refined imagery of taste given to the Trojans, and especially to Troilus, reflects a bodiless ideal which becomes, in the mouths of the scurrilous Thersites and the Greek cynics, a series of clogged, heavy references to the digestive processes. Thersites has " mastic jaws ", and Achilles calls him " my cheese, my digestion ", whilst Agamemnon tells Patroclus that Achilles' virtues:

> "like fair fruit in an unwholesome dish
> Are like to rot untasted."
>
> (II. iii)

In fact, the very sense which expresses the related intensity and lightness of Trojan passion becomes, in the Greeks, a symbol of inaction and distemper out of which issue the boils, " the botchy core ", of Thersites' disgust.

In this way we pass from the individual to the public action, from the love of Troilus and Cressida to the war between the Greeks and Troy. This connection between the private and the public theme is, indeed, the most original feature of the play. The two parties, like the two lovers, are differentiated by divergences within a common type of feeling. The Trojans share the fragile intensity of Troilus. They are deeply concerned with the value of " honour " and with a view of love which claims to be idealistic, whilst Hector shows the virtues of war which are so noticeably absent from the bulky Ajax and the graceless Achilles. Typical of them is the speech in which Troilus explains the case for continuing the war:

> " But, worthy Hector,
> She is a theme of honour and renown;
> A spur to valiant and magnanimous deeds,
> Whose present courage may beat down our foes,
> And fame in time to come canonize us."
>
> (II. ii)

Yet the lightness and grace of this idealism obviously covers a certain artificiality. The verse itself is unsubstantial and the expression vague and highflown. It reads, at this stage in Shakespeare's development, like a survival from earlier plays set against the contortions and in-volutions of so much of *Troilus*. This impression is neither accidental nor isolated. Hector's reasoning in the same scene shows clearly that the arguments advanced by Troilus are as flimsy in content as their expression is tenuous. For all this " honour ", for which Troilus has announced his readiness to fight and, if need be, to die, is directed to the defence of Helen, whose worth has been destroyed by the manner in which she has been stolen from Menelaus. Even Paris can only argue that the original dishonour of her rape should now be redeemed by the heroism shown in her defence. The tone of the Trojan references to Helen contrasts strangely with the idealism of their declared intentions. Paris pleads that he

> " would have the *soil* of her *fair* rape
> Wiped off in honourable keeping her,"

and Troilus, conveying a slight but unmistakable twist to conventional imagery, declares that Paris:

> ". . . brought a Grecian queen, whose youth and *freshness*
> Wrinkles Apollo's and *makes stale* the morning."

The juxtaposition of " fair " and " soil ", " freshness " and " stale ", touches the basic weakness of Trojan idealism, and points to the way in which that idealism is organically connected in its expression with the sluggish inertia that prevails in the Greek camp.

The true nature of this Trojan weakness is perhaps most explicitly stated by Troilus when he sets forth, in an attempt at reasoned expression, his argument for the continuation of the war:

> " I take to-day a wife, and my election
> Is led on in the conduct of my will;
> My will enkindled by mine eyes and ears,
> Two traded pilots 'twixt the dangerous shores
> Of will and judgement: how may I avoid,
> Although my will distaste what it elected,
> The wife I chose? There can be no evasion
> To blench from this, and to stand firm by honour."
>
> (II. ii)

Troilus' terminology is indefinite and the expression of his argument, like so much of what passes for discussion in this play, far more complicated than its content. There seems at one point to be an opposition of " will ", which we may associate with the satisfaction of sensual impulse, and " judgement ", by which this impulse should normally be restrained and directed: the opposition, in short, of sensuality and moral control which became a little later the central theme of *Measure for Measure*. In that play, however, the moral conflict is explicitly stated, and—what is more important—takes shape in a dramatic clash of clearly defined personalities; in *Troilus and Cressida*, there is only an uncertainty, a sense of uneasiness, which the notable incoherence of the expression reflects. The conclusion reached by " judgement " is that affirmed by Hector—" value dwells not in particular will ", but rather in a weighing of alternatives in the light of the principles of reason—but the whole trend of Troilus' reply is to annihilate, or at least wilfully to confuse, the distinction between " will " and " judgement " themselves, to show that " judgement " is powerless and irrelevant once the sensual will has impelled man towards action. In other words, the basis of Troilus' honour is simply sensual impulse, and its weakness lies largely in its unwillingness to recognize this fact, and in the abstraction and lack of content which follows in the train of this evasion.

Hector, indeed, is sufficiently outspoken on the subject of Troilus' infatuation:

> " Is your blood
> So madly hot that no discourse of reason,
> Nor fear of bad success in a bad cause
> Can qualify the same? "
>
> (II. ii)

The argument—although Troilus rejects it and Hector himself fails to follow it to its conclusion in the field of practical application— once more binds the personal love-theme to that of the justification of public action. Troilus—and in this he is typical of all the Trojans—refuses to admit the weakness of his conception of honour, which is, however, implied in the very situation which brought the war into being; for the reality of Helen, as Hector points out, does not correspond to Troilus' embroidered and Marlovian conception of her:

> " Brother, she is not worth what she doth cost
> The holding."
>
> (II. ii)

But this same lack of solid foundation is apparent, as we have seen, in the undertones of Troilus' own poetry, where the unacknowledged sensual basis of his idealism refuses to be entirely suppressed. Underlying the light and " poetical " quality of Troilus' emotional flights, there is a distinct strain of coarseness and inertia. It appears in the references, so typical of this play, to the " soiled silks " and the " remainder viands " which are thrown away " because we now are full ". Most typical of all, in the determination to hide its own weakness which it implies, is the Trojan reaction to reason:

> " Nay, if we talk of reason,
> Let's shut our gates, and sleep: manhood and honour
> Should have hare hearts, would they but *fat* their thoughts
> With this *crammed* reason: reason and respect
> Make *livers pale* and *lustihood deject*."
>
> (II. ii)

This insistence upon mental inertia and the obstruction of physical processes, as applied to reason, stands in significant contrast to the lightness and artificiality of Troilus' idealistic outbursts; but they are organically related to them. The Trojan devotion to honour, Shakespeare would seem to say, is devotion to an abstraction that has no sufficient basis in reason—to something that is, in fact, in itself, no more than an empty justification of impulse; but—it is equally important to realize—to abandon honour for its lack of rational foundation is to expose oneself to the danger of lethargy, to a rooted disinclination to act at all.[1] Once more we are faced with the split between motive and impulse, moral *value* and sensual substitutes, which dominates this play without a real glimpse of resolution.

The analysis of this important scene suggests how the contrast between the Greek and Trojan parties, which most critics of the play have noted, is modified by significant points of contact. The Trojans, for all their concern to defend " honour" , as they conceive it, against the Greeks, are strangely related to their enemies. This relationship, of course, is openly " symbolized " in the combat between Hector and Ajax (IV. v), when Hector refuses to carry on the duel with his " cousin-german " and Ajax agrees to call a truce. But the contacts established by a common type of imagery are still more important for an understanding of the play. In the Greek camp, we find fully explicit the staleness which Trojan " honour " had tried to ignore. Where the Trojans reject reason in favour of ill-considered action, the Greeks accept it and are reduced to inaction. Agamemnon's very first speech, as the head and corner-stone of Greek unity, shows how inconclusive are the intellectual processes so painfully followed by the leaders who accompany him, and how closely related they are to the views expressed by Troilus on " crammed reason ":

---

[1] The relation of this to *Hamlet*, and in particular to such a soliloquy as " How all occasions do inform against me " (IV. iv) is worth careful attention.

"Princes,
What grief hath set the jaundice on your cheeks?
The ample proposition that hope makes
In all designs begun on earth below
Fails in the promised largeness; checks and disasters
Grow in the veins of actions highest reared,
As knots, by the conflux of meeting sap,
Infect the sound pine and divert his grain
Tortive and errant from his course of growth.
Nor, princes, is it matter new to us
That we come short of our suppose so far
That after seven years' siege yet Troy walls stand;
Sith every action that hath gone before,
Whereof we have record, trial did draw
Bias and thwart, not answering the aim
And that unbodied figure of the thought
That gave it surmised shape."

(I. iii)

Agamemnon's thought proceeds not from point to point according to a definite logical sequence, but by a series of indeterminate digressions which reveal his incapacity to come to a conclusion. His laboured illustrations and the theoretical observations which accompany them destroy the coherence of an argument which they do nothing to further; as so often in this play, there is no recognizable development of thought to justify the complexity. The repeated doublings of words— "checks and disasters", "tortive and errant", "bias and thwart"— all lay emphasis upon obstruction, upon the speaker's struggle against obscure impediments which hinder the Greeks from successful action; and the use of unusual and unassimilated Latinized words, such as "conflux" and "tortive", produces a similar sense of resistance and difficulty. More significantly still, these obstructions are associated with disturbances and interruptions in organic growth. The prospects of hope "fail in the promised largeness", do not grow to their proper and anticipated stature. "Checks and disasters" are indissolubly intertwined with natural growth, and the very rising of the sap in the "sound pine", which is so eminently a natural process, produces infection and distortion in the growth of the tree. Most important of all, because it corresponds clearly to the spirit most fully expressed by Troilus, though it is "unbodied" and its processes, separated from the actual course of events, are equally cut off from the sensual immediacy which finds irresponsible expression in the comments of Thersites. The keen nervous quality which is so noticeably lacking in the theoretical observations of the Greek leaders breaks out significantly in Thersites' sweeping affirmation of anarchy and disorder; in a similar manner, Troilus' disembodied idealism covers a sensual impulse which he refuses to recognize.

It is only natural that this discrepancy in the Greeks between thought and action should be expressed in terms of physical disorder; and here the link with the Trojans becomes even more explicit. Thersites' boils and plague-spots are related to Agamemnon's laborious thoughts on authority just as Troilus' contempt for " crammed reason " and his insistent sense of soilure and physical obstruction are connected with his abstract idealism. The vital point in Shakespeare's presentation of the Greeks is this association of continual ratiocination with a complete overthrow of " degree " in their ranks; they are entirely unable to turn council into united action. The position in the Greek camp is briefly summed up by Thersites, whose clear-sightedness can produce nothing but stagnation: "Agamemnon is a fool to offer to command Achilles; Achilles is a fool to be commanded of Agamemnon; Thersites is a fool to serve such a fool; and Patroclus is a fool positive" (II. iii). Whilst Agamemnon, Nestor, and Ulysses scheme and discuss, Ajax and Achilles " fust " (the word is typical) out of action; the hand that executes is out of touch with the " *still and mental* parts " that contrive the conduct of the war. Perhaps the point is most clearly made by Ulysses in his account of Achilles' pride:

> " imagined worth
> Holds in his blood such swoln and hot discourse
> That *'twixt his mental and his active parts*
> Kingdom'd Achilles in commotion rages
> And *batters down himself*."
>
> (II. iii)

The conflict in Achilles between personal pride and duty to the Greek cause is stated here in terms of " blood ", of sensual passion; the implications of " swoln and hot ", suggesting feverish disorder due to extreme intemperance, are unmistakable. The adjective " kingdom'd ", like so many of the words which characterize the poetry of this play, is not fully explicit; but it clearly refers the personal issue back to the general theme of " degree ". The individual warrior, like the Greek polity at war, should be a unity founded upon " degree "; and " degree" in the individual is an ideal correspondence between thought and action, between impulse and control, between " blood " and judge-

ment.[1] On both sides, this balance is profoundly disturbed. The
" cunning " of the Greek leaders is manifestly out of touch with practical
considerations and expends itself in an activity completely disproportionate to the desired end: " it will not in circumvention deliver a
fly from a spider, without drawing their massy irons and cutting the
web " (II. iii). On the Trojan side, the infidelity of Cressida finally
undermines Troilus' faith in " honour " as a basis for action and leaves
him dimly aware of the incompatible and contrary elements which
underlie what he had assumed to be the indivisible simplicity of human
passion:

> " Within my soul there doth conduce a fight
> Of this strange nature, that a thing inseparate
> Divides more wider than the sky and earth;
> And yet the spacious breadth of this division
> Admits no orifex for a point as subtle
> As Ariadne's broken woof to enter.
> Instance, O instance! strong as Pluto's gates;
> Cressio is mine, tied with the bonds of heaven:
> Instance, O instance! strong as heaven itself;
> The bonds of heaven are slipp'd, dissolved and loosed:
> And with another knot, five-finger-tied,
> The fractions of her faith, orts of her love,
> The fragments, scraps, the bits and greasy relics
> Of her o'er-eaten faith, are bound to Diomed."
>
> (V. ii)

All the characteristics of the love-poetry of Troilus can be recognized
here—its tenuous and unnaturally refined expression, its subtlety in
dealing with vast distinctions within an apparent unity, its sensuous
thinness balanced by the imagery of disgust and repletion which connects it with the verse given to the Greeks and indicates the unifying
factor in this play. For the ambiguous attitude towards experience
which so deeply exercised Shakespeare in many of his Sonnets is the
determining factor in his presentation of both parties. Proceeding
from his sense of the disharmony introduced by their subjection to the
temporal process into the love of Troilus and Cressida, it expands to
embrace the two parties in their fantastic and unreasonable conflict.
The Trojans follow a false idealism, which deceives itself with talk of
" honour ", but is really based on " blood " and ends in a pathetic

---

[1] Compare *Hamlet*:

> "... blest are those
> Whose blood and judgement are so well commingled
> That they are not a pipe for fortune's finger
> To sound what stop she pleases."
>
> (III. ii)

and helpless realization of its own insufficiency; the Greeks elaborate endlessly a " judgement " that is out of touch with the instinctive sources of action, until Agamemnon's chaotic reasoning finds its proper counterpart in the distorted bitterness of Thersites' diseased sensibility.

The fundamental impulse of this play, and the link which binds personal cleavage to political disorder, is now clear. Ulysses' argument on " degree " reduces itself finally to an intuition of self-consuming passion:

> " Then everything includes itself in power,
> Power into will, will into *appetite*,
> And appetite, an universal wolf,
> So doubly seconded with will and power,
> Must make perforce an universal prey,
> And last *eat up himself*."
>
> (I. iii)

The speech is saved from the charge of abstraction by this relation of " degree " to the disorder introduced by passion or " appetite " into the human organism. This disorder, present on both sides in the conflict between Greeks and Trojans, is the theme of the play. The Trojans sought to ignore the limitations of passion in a bodiless " idealism "; the Greeks, quite incapable of idealism, are weighed down by all that the Trojans try to forget. Both sides are bound together by the occasion of their quarrel; as Thersites says—" all the argument is a cuckold and a whore ". Troilus, in one magnificent phrase, sums up the crux from which the subtle contradictions of this play draw their interest:

> " This is the monstruosity in love, lady, that the will is infinite and the execution confined, that the desire is boundless and the act a slave to limit."
>
> (III. ii)

The " infinity " sought by the will is the idealistic love of Troilus, which neglects the wearing action of time and the related inability of passion to live up to ideals of love and honour which can only be redeemed from abstraction by an adequate spiritual integration; and the very " boundlessness " of the desire, when it encounters the limits imposed by time and the body to which, in the absence of such an integration, it feels enslaved, turns to the clogged inertia of Achilles and the endless self-scrutiny of the Greek camp.

LOVE AND AGGRESSIVENESS IN DOSTOIEVSKY

JACQUES MADAULE

ONE OF the commonest themes in Dostoievsky is that of the " double ". This theme is the subject of one of his earliest novels and he returned to it again with the character of Versilov in *A Raw Youth*. Versilov is an aristocrat who has fallen into ruin and disrepute, and all his actions are characterised by an essential duplicity. Even at the end of the book it is very difficult to decide whether his character is low and despicable or whether he is an idealist whose actions have been misunderstood. His heart is torn between two women: the former serf Sonia, with whom he has been living for years, and Katerina Nicolaevna Akhmakova, a woman of society. Versilov respects Sonia, who is to him the very symbol of the Russian people, just as he respects her husband, the old wandering pilgrim Makar Ivanovitch. But he has nevertheless grievously insulted Makar by taking his wife away from him, and in the early stages of his relationship with Sonia he has shown no respect for her virtue either, for he has simply seduced her. Sonia seems intended to represent a certain kind of beauty, whose contemplation has the effect not of arousing passion but of calming it. Versilov returns to her after his queer escapades as the prodigal son returned to his father, and Sonia never fails to forgive him.

Akhmakova is perhaps no less innocent than Sonia, but her innocence is accompanied by a kind of ingenuous perversity. The main thing about her is, however, her beauty, which is utterly different from Sonia's. Versilov is ill with love of her, and capable of any kind of villainy to possess the body and soul which are withheld from him. As soon as Akhmakova is involved, all his reason seems to desert him, and the " double " takes the place of the real person. This is the meaning of the dreadful letter that he sends her, for example:

" Depraved as you are in your nature and your arts, I should have yet expected you to restrain your passions and not to try your wiles on children. But you are not even ashamed to do that. I beg to inform you that the letter you know of was certainly not burnt in a candle and never was in Kraft's possession, so you won't score anything there. So don't seduce a boy for nothing. Spare him, he is hardly grown up, almost a child, undeveloped mentally and physically—what use can you have for him? I am interested in his welfare, and so I have ventured to write to you, though with little hope of attaining my object. I have the honour to inform you that I have sent a copy of this letter to Baron Buring."

Anyone who remembers the plot of the novel will find it difficult to imagine a greater mass of infamy gathered together into so few lines. Can it be explained by the fact that Versilov is torn by a double kind of jealousy? He shudders at the thought that Akhmakova is on the point of marrying Buring; and he is also jealous of his own son, the shy young man whom he hypocritically takes it upon himself to defend. But it would be a misunderstanding of Dostoievsky's real thought to explain such an outburst as a result of jealousy only. In Dostoievsky the apparent reasons are never the real ones. The truth is that Versilov both loves and hates Akhmakova, and his hatred of her is the exact measure of his love. Love and hatred go hand in hand in him, so that it might not be far from the truth to see the above letter as a striking declaration of love.

Akhmakova represents for Versilov the impossible, the beauty which confronts one like a challenge. He takes up the challenge. If Akhmakova cannot be his, she will at least not be anyone else's, and certainly not that fool Buring's—he will kill her first; not in a sudden fit of despair, but with the same savage joy with which he shatters Makar Ivanovitch's ikon. To understand Dostoievsky properly one must never forget that injury and insult are one of his most constant themes: his first novel was called *The Insulted and Injured*. I wonder whether it has been sufficiently observed how large a place affairs of honour occupy in his work? It would be a mistake to see this as a mere literary convention. It goes much deeper. The human person is made in the image of God. Any insult he receives is an insult to God Himself. At the same time, not everyone is in a position to insult or to be insulted: some are beneath insult, others above it. For there to be any insult there must be a certain equality between giver and receiver. But insult, once experienced and remaining unforgiven, introduces into the soul of the receiver an absolute division. It is this which gives rise to the phenomenon of duplicity which we are here attempting to analyse. Moreover, the insult does not only act upon the receiver; it reacts upon the giver, and in the same way. There exists a kind of reciprocity of insult. Why did this thoughtless young aristocrat seduce his servant-girl and thus insult the pious Makar Ivanovitch? It was because he was himself grievously insulted by their virtuousness. It was a matter of the utmost necessity for him to do something to besmirch their purity. He has been forgiven by both of them. It was impossible that he should not be forgiven, for they both, by their very nobility, stand above insult. All Versilov has to do is to become their equal. But this is just what he is unable to do, despite all his efforts, and that is why he goes on insulting them to the very end in spite of himself. He imagines that he will recover his integrity by inflicting on them a final insult, this time of so serious a nature that it will be absolutely unforgivable. When he died, Makar Ivanovitch left behind him an ikon, to which he was greatly attached. Versilov, engrossed in his desperate love for Akhmakova, has come back for a moment to Sonia. The ikon is standing on a table. Here are Versilov's words:

" ' I really don't know, Tatyana Pavlovna dear, what's the matter with me. Don't be uneasy, I still remember that you are Tatyana Pavlovna, and that you are dear. But I've only come for a minute, though; I should like to say something nice to Sonia, and I keep trying to find the right word, though my heart is full of words, which I don't know how to utter; yes, really, all such strange words somehow. Do you know I feel as though I were split in two.' He looked round at us all with a terribly serious face and with perfectly genuine candour. ' Yes, I am really split in two mentally, and I'm horribly afraid of it. It's just as though one's second self were standing beside one; one is sensible and rational oneself, but the other self is impelled to do something perfectly senseless, and sometimes very funny; and suddenly you notice that you are longing to do that amusing thing, goodness knows why; that is you want to, as it were, against your will; though you fight against it with all your might, you want to. I once knew a doctor who suddenly began whistling in church, at his father's funeral. I really was afraid to come to the funeral to-day, because, for some reason, I was possessed by a firm conviction that I should begin to whistle or laugh in church, like that unfortunate doctor, who came to rather a bad end. . . . And I really don't know why, but I've been haunted by the thought of that doctor all day; I am so haunted by him that I can't shake him off. Do you know, Sonia, here I've taken up the ikon again ' (he had picked it up and was turning it about in his hand), ' and do you know, I have a dreadful longing now, this very second, to smash it against the stove, against this corner. I am sure it would break into two halves—neither more nor less.' "

A few moments later Versilov does in fact put his words into action, and the image breaks in two—into two pieces exactly. Doubtless in this breaking of the ikon we are meant to see a symbolic meaning which does not concern us here. But it is also an insult to the memory of Makar Ivanovitch, a kind of repetition, in another form, of the earlier insult involved in the seduction of Sonia. And this time Makar cannot forgive him, for he is dead. Again, it was at the dictate of this same " double " that Versilov wrote the letter to Katerina Nicolaevna quoted above. What insult, then, has he received from Katerina Nicolaevna? It lies in her beauty, a beauty accompanied by innocence but which nevertheless rouses the passions instead of calming them. The innocence must be a feigned innocence, then, and the virtue false. Hence the letter, which raises the unresolved question of Akhmakova's profound perversity; for there is nothing more perverse than vice masquerading as virtue. On the real personality of Akhmakova *A Raw Youth* does not enable one to dogmatize with any certainty. Right to the end, like Versilov himself, she remains an enigma.

But what there is no doubt about is the fact that Versilov, because he loves Akhmakova, and to the very extent that he loves her, tries first to dishonour her and then to kill her. This is the last scene in the book, and also the most extraordinary. For the last time, by getting a most odious blackguard to try to blackmail her, Versilov endeavours to force Akhmakova to humiliate herself. As she triumphantly resists this attempt, spitting in the blackmailer's face, Versilov, who has been hiding behind a tapestry, steps forward. The first thing he does is to dismiss the unforunate Lambert, who has been threatening Akhmakova with a revolver; for it is for Versilov, and Versilov alone, to do the killing, if there is to be any. But let Dostoievsky speak for himself:

" She saw Versilov, turned suddenly as white as a sheet, gazed at him for some moments immovable with indescribable horror, and fell into a swoon. He rushed to her. It all flashes before my eyes as I write. I remember with what terror I saw his flushed, almost purple face and his bloodshot eyes. I believe that though he saw me in the room he did not recognise me. He caught her as she fell unconscious, and with amazing ease lifted her up in his arms, as though she were a feather, and began aimlessly carrying her about the room like a baby. It was a tiny room, but he paced to and fro from corner to corner, evidently with no idea why he was doing so. In one instant he had lost his reason. He kept gazing at her, at her face. I ran after him; what I was most afraid of was the revolver, which he seemed to have forgotten in his right hand, and was holding close to her head. But he pushed me away, once with his elbow, and the second time with his foot. I wanted to shout to Trishatov, but I was afraid of irritating the madman. At last I drew back the curtain and began entreating him to put her on the bed. He went up and laid her down on it, stood over her, and gazed at her face; and, suddenly bending down, kissed her twice on her pale lips. Oh, I realised at last that this was a man utterly beside himself. He suddenly waved the revolver over her, but, as though realising, turned the revolver and aimed it at her face. I instantly seized his arm and shouted to Trishatov. I remember we both struggled with him, but he succeeded in pulling away his arm and firing at himself. He would have shot her and then himself, but since we would not let him get at her, he pressed the revolver against his heart; I succeeded, however, in pushing his arm upwards, and the bullet struck him in the shoulder."

It will be observed that according to the narrator Versilov has lost his reason when this scene takes place. But what does this mean? Is it not a fact that Versilov's reason has always been unstable, even when he has appeared at his most lucid? that he has been continually threatened by his double, who in the end gains such a shattering victory over him? Now Versilov's mental sickness is not physiological, or even psychological; it is spiritual. The thing that is affected in him is the spirit—the *pneuma*, in the most comprehensive and most elevated sense of the word. Every sane man is able to endure the sight of virtue or beauty; Versilov is unable to do this, because he has sinned against Sonia and Makar, that is to say, against the Russian people. It must not be forgotten that we are concerned with an aristocrat, one of the most brilliant representatives of that Russian nobility which had given so much to Russian civilisation and to human civilization as a whole, but which, unfortunately, had alienated itself from its people, and thus given itself up to destruction and death. Versilov is the typical uprooted Russian nobleman, endlessly oscillating between Europe, the land of miracles, and holy Russia; just as he oscillates between Sonia and Akhmakova. He cannot possess the one without betraying the other. This is the reason why he would like to crush Akhmakova under his heel, for her mere existence prevents him from regaining his equilibrium and finding peace with himself. What Versilov has forgotten is that one sin is not washed away by another.

But it is necessary to go down deeper still, into an abyss of human turpitude that Dostoievsky is the only person, or at least the first, to have explored with such unflinching courage. I have said a great deal about humiliation and insults. But the worst humiliation of all is the one we inflict on ourselves when we become conscious of how despicable we ourselves are. In some cases it may happen that this consciousness

comes to us from outside, that a humiliation inflicted upon us by someone else reveals to us our own essential despicableness. But however
it may come to us, as soon as we become conscious of this fundamental
truth, that we are creatures of sin, we can only react to it in one of two
ways: either, like Sonia in *Crime and Punishment*, like Prince Myshkin,
Chatov, Makar Ivanovitch, like the *staretz* Zossima and Alyosha
Karamazov, we accept this humiliation and make it the cornerstone
of our salvation—because, through humility, we have discovered
within ourselves the disfigured image of Christ: then all is well, and
all is grace. Or we revolt: and then we see only one way of reacting
against our depravity, and that is to accept it with bravado, and
humiliate others as we ourselves have been humiliated. From that
moment on, any kind of beauty or nobility is both desirable and hateful
to us. The receiver of the insult becomes the giver. His love has a
curse upon it. He cannot touch anything he loves without spoiling it.
He both wants and does not want to spoil it. He wants to spoil it,
because then he would stop loving it, and he imagines that he would
then be reconciled within himself. But he does not want to spoil it,
to the extent that there remains within him something resembling the
divine. It is because he is unable to transcend this division within his
soul that Versilov succumbs to madness.

He is not the only one of his kind; and if I have begun with him,
this is because he is the most enigmatic, the most difficult to understand,
of Dostoievsky's characters. But we have previously seen this madness
of Versilov's break out on the magnificent, tragic countenance of
Nastasia Philippovna in *The Idiot*. She too is mad, and acts like a
mad woman right to the very end, to that death at the hands of Rogozhin which she knows she will not escape. Nastasia Philippovna is
the proud daughter of a ruined nobleman, raised amidst all the refine-
ments of elegance and the best education; but when her guardian
finally discloses the intention behind all this care, she receives a blow
from which she never recovers. In vain Prince Myshkin endeavours,
to the last, to save her and reconcile her to herself. Although in fact
she loves him more than he loves her, she knows herself unworthy of
his love and does everything she can to escape from him. She implores
him to marry Aglaya Ivanovna. No other woman, perhaps, has ever
sacrificed herself to such an extent as Nastasia Philippovna.

For her there is Rogozhin, and the dagger that Rogozhin has hidden
in the pages of a " History of Russia ". I will omit the account of the
actual murder, though it contains some of the most perfect writing
Dostoievsky ever achieved, since this concerns the art of the novelist,
which it is not my intention to discuss here. But the character of
Rogozhin is extremely interesting. He loves Nastasia Philippovna with

a love that is hopeless and veritably insane, though he knows that she will never return his love—is indeed incapable of loving him. At first he tries to entice her by parading his wealth and giving her presents. Nastasia accepts the presents, but remains unimpressed. It seems that her humiliation is so profound that she has been taken beyond the reach of any earthly gratification. Rogozhin's irresistible fascination for her is that he brings death with him. He himself knows this; from the beginning he is never for a moment in doubt about it. If he has no power over Nastasia's heart, he has power over her life. This it is that brings that queer light into his eyes which Myshkin perceives so clearly. But the final explanation of Rogozhin must perhaps be sought in the following passage from *The Brothers Karamazov*:

" There is a remarkable picture by the painter Kramskoy, called ' Contemplation '. There is a forest in winter, and on a roadway through the forest, in absolute solitude, stands a peasant in a torn kaftan and bark shoes. He stands, as it were, lost in thought. Yet he is not thinking; he is ' contemplating '. If anyone touched him he would start and look at one as though awakening and bewildered. It's true he would come to himself immediately; but if he were asked what he had been thinking about, he would remember nothing. Yet probably he has hidden within himself the impression which had dominated him during the period of contemplation. Those impressions are dear to him and no doubt he hoards them imperceptibly, and even unconsciously. How and why, of course, he does not know either. He may suddenly, after hoarding impressions for many years, abandon everything and go off to Jerusalem on a pilgrimage for his soul's salvation, or perhaps he will suddenly set fire to his native village, and perhaps do both."

This applies to Smerdyakov, but it would be equally true of Rogozhin. The son of a merchant, brought up in an atmosphere of religious gloom, he might have worked hard and made money, like his father, and worked out his salvation in the old faith, just as easily as he becomes the murderer of Nastasia Philippovna. All that this would have required would have been for her tragic, beautiful face not to have caught and riveted his attention one day. And I sometimes wonder whether Rogozhin is not in a sense the most perfect lover to be met with in the whole gallery of Dostoievsky's characters. For in him love is absolute, with just enough admixture of hatred to make the final murderous act possible. As soon as he sees Nastasia Philippovna he knows that she is his. A kind of predestination unites them. When, on the very day she is to marry Myshkin, she is suddenly abducted by Rogozhin, she does not attempt to make the slightest resistance. She knows that this is her destiny, and that he is taking her away, not from love of her, but to her death. And it is death that she has chosen, because she has been unable to forget her humiliation, and Myshkin has been unable to reconcile her divided soul with itself. Rogozhin takes her to his house as though she were something infinitely precious. She lies down gravely on the bed that was to have been her marriage-bed and is to be her death-bed. It seems that she falls asleep, and for a long time Rogozhin watches her lying there peacefully. Then he takes hold of the sacrificial dagger and inflicts upon her heart the tiny wound of death. There is a faint trickle of blood. The whole scene is enacted with the majestic simplicity of classical tragedy. Whereas Versilov's predicament was infinitely complicated (this being the essential weakness of the novel), the situation between Rogozhin and Nastasia Philippovna has all the clarity of a silhouette. Love and aggressiveness are here reduced to their essential elements. In Rogozhin's own soul there seems hardly a trace of conflict. He knows as well as Nastasia does that things cannot happen any differently. As for Myshkin, he remains shattered by a disaster that he has been unable to prevent. If one attempts to discover the secret weakness that brings Myshkin's efforts to nought, I believe it to lie in his sensuality. Like the later Karamazovs, Myshkin is a sensualist, and only if he had been able to overcome his own sensuality would he have been able to prevent this tragedy.

This, as we have seen, was Versilov's weakness and had brought tragedy to Katerina Nicolaevna. For Dostoievsky, sensual love is a love that leads to death. I believe that with this we reach the heart of the matter. You can read every one of Dostoievsky's novels and not come across a single case of happy love. Perhaps it would have been Alyosha's vocation to find such a love, but Dostoievsky had neither the time nor the strength left to write the concluding part of *The Brothers Karamazov*. His entire work may be taken as a commentary on the words of the Apostle: " The flesh wars against the spirit ". The flesh is essentially impure, and its impurity reaches its height when it is clothed in beauty. For beauty is of the spiritual order, but it is traduced and betrayed by the flesh. Herein lies woman's power and weakness. She presents us with an image of the highest aspirations of our soul, and at the same time she arouses our lowest instincts. She is thus at once an object of adoration and of scorn, of love and hatred. Her beauty evokes in our minds the beauty of the angels, but we cannot possess this beauty except by embracing the flesh. Our highest and lowest powers are moved under the same impact. The spirit would subdue the flesh, but the flesh aspires to humiliate the spirit. Woman is thus at once stronger and weaker than man. From this feeling of strength and weakness grows the modest pride, the aggressive savagery, of so many of Dostoievsky's heroines.

It will be observed that in several novels the hero seems to be divided between two loves: between a woman of the utmost purity, and a courtesan; as though he is trying to satisfy the aspirations of the spirit and the aspirations of the flesh separately. Thus in *The Idiot* Myshkin finds himself torn between Nastasia Philippovna and Aglaya Ivanovna. He cannot raise the first out of her abjection and at the same time marry the second. He has to choose between them; and the whole drama centres round the fact that he is unable to do this. Superficially, he seems to side with Nastasia. But she herself knows quite well that this is not so, and that if he were to marry her it would be out of pity, still in his heart of hearts loving Aglaya. Nastasia is too proud to be able to accept anything less than perfection; she prefers Rogozhin's savage integrity. Nor can Aglaya accept such an equivocal situation; and the dramatic encounter between the two women, in the course of which the girl of ill repute insults the young society woman and mocks at her, is one of the great scenes in the book.

There is a similar, if not an identical situation in *The Possessed*. Here too is a girl—Elisabeta Nicolaevna—in love with a man—Stavrogin—whom, despite her devotion, she is unable to cure, because he is beyond all possible cure. We learn from his " confession" the reason for this: having once given way to his animal passions and seduced some poor girl, he then allowed her to hang herself without making any attempt to stop her; just as, later, he allows his wife, the woman with a limp, to be killed by the blackguard Feoka Maria Timophoievna. Here, unfortunately, I cannot give Stavrogin's character all the attention it deserves, since it is not directly connected with our subject. In *The Possessed* the key to the drama is not love. Three women, all very different from each other, gravitate round Stavrogin, trying in vain to save him. The reason for their failure is that he has passed beyond their power and lives immured in a kingdom that seems closed even to the angels. There has never been so purely spiritual a tragedy described in any other literature. My intention here has merely been to recall briefly that sensuality is not absent from it.

Whereas in *A Raw Youth* Dostoievsky attempted several themes at once, without fully working out any single one, in *The Brothers Karamazov* there is one dominant theme—sensuality; and it is here that we find Dostoievsky's ultimate thought on the subject with which we are concerned. The father, Fyodor Pavlovitch, is a pure sensualist. There is no division in this character's heart, for he never seems to have felt the slightest breath of any spiritual love at all. Dostoievsky had already sketched this sinister kind of character several times: there is Svidrigailov in *Crime and Punishment*, for instance. How low a man may descend through boredom and self-disgust—a disgust fully acquiesced in, and arousing no reaction in its subject—is revealed in the character of Fyodor Pavlovitch. He accepts the fact that he is a sinner. He is sin itself. A woman has no need of beauty to attract him. He finds hidden charms in the ugliest. On one of his orgies he has got the innocent Smerdiachtchaia with child—the child who is one day to be his mother's avenger. As for his two wives, one the mother of Dmitri, the other the mother of Ivan and Alyosha, the first used to beat him, and finally left him, the second, the " possessed ", as he calls her, is his drudge. Through her, if he had been accessible to it, he could have known a woman's tenderness. But Fyodor Pavlovitch is nothing but a perverse, evil buffoon. Others may be above humiliation; he is beneath it. He enjoys being contemptible, and heaps more contempt upon himself than anyone else does. But occasionally during the night he has strange fits of anguish, and then his old servant Grigori has to come and calm him down. He is torn between avarice and sensuality—which are, in fact, simply two aspects of the same vice. Sensuality proves to be the stronger, and to possess Grushenka he is prepared to lose three thousand roubles. These roubles are the pivot on which the whole drama turns: they lead Fyodor Pavlovitch to his death.

To this degraded creature have been born four sons, who all to some extent or other share the Karamazov sensuality. Three are legitimate: Dmitri, Ivan and Alyosha. The fourth is the illegitimate Smerdiakov, poor, innocent Smerdiachtchaia's son. Dmitri, or Mitya, the eldest, is not only violent but sensual as well. This character is undoubtedly one of the most vivid of Dostoievsky's creations, and he is of the utmost importance for our present discussion. He belongs to a type, several examples of which we have already met in the earlier novels: I need only refer here to the unfortunate Prince Sokolski in *A Raw Youth*. These people are not so much misguided as uncontrolled. They throw themselves into life violently, with an extraordinary appetite for it. They find everything good. They make love to any woman who will let them, they gamble, marry, they squander their money, and in the end resort to dishonest practices. Fyodor Pavlovitch's avarice is transformed in his eldest son into reckless prodigality. The sensuality is still there, but in Dmitri it has not destroyed a genuine attachment to higher values.

All this appears clearly in Dmitri's relationship with Katerina Ivanovna, a girl of great beauty, proud and haughty like others we have already met. Dmitri is both attracted and repelled by her.

"I saw her eyes taking my measure one evening at the battery commander's, but I didn't go up to her, as though I disdained her acquaintance. I did go up and speak to her at an evening party not long after. She scarcely looked at me, and compressed her lips scornfully. 'Wait a bit. I'll have my revenge,' thought I. I behaved like an awful fool on many occasions at that time, and I was conscious of it myself. What made it worse was that I felt that 'Katenka' was not an innocent boarding-house miss but a person of character, proud and really high-principled; above all, she had education and intellect, and I had neither. You think I meant to make her an offer? No, I simply wanted to avenge myself because I was such a hero and she didn't seem to feel it."

The whole drama lies in these few lines. Dmitri Karamazov never thinks of asking Katerina Ivanovna's hand in marriage, because he considers himself unworthy of her, and also because marriage with her would mean changing his style of life. Nevertheless she attracts and interests him, if only by her obvious disdain for this barrack-room Don Juan. He longs to humiliate her and have her at his mercy. Now it so happens that he knows that Katerina's father is unable to balance his accounts, and that some day he is going to need four thousand five hundred roubles. Dmitri tells Katerina's sister: "When they demand that four thousand five hundred roubles from your father, and he can't produce it, he'll be tried, and made to serve as a common soldier in his old age, unless you like to send me your young lady secretly. I've just had money paid me. I'll give her four thousand if you like, and keep the secret religiously."

Here it is necessary to reproduce in full the scene that unfolds a few days later between Dmitri and "Katya":

"She walked in and looked straight at me, her dark eyes determined, even defiant, but on her lips and round her mouth I saw uncertainty.

"'My sister told me,' she began, 'that you would give me four thousand five hundred roubles if I came to you for it—myself. I have come . . . Give me the money!'

"She couldn't keep it up. She was breathless, frightened, her voice failed her, and the corners of her mouth and the lines round it quivered.

"My first idea was a—Karamazov one. Once I was bitten by a centipede, brother, and laid up a fortnight with fever from it. Well, I felt a centipede biting at my heart then—a noxious insect, you understand? I looked her up and down. You've seen her? She's a beauty. But she was beautiful in another way then. At that moment she was beautiful because she was noble, and I was a scoundrel; she in all the grandeur of her generosity and sacrifice for her father, and I—a bug! And, scoundrel as I was, she was altogether at my mercy, body and soul. She was hemmed in. I tell you frankly, that thought, that venomous thought, so possessed my heart that it almost swooned with suspense. It seemed as if there could be no resisting it; as though I should act like a bug, like a venomous spider, without a spark of pity. I could scarcely breathe. Understand, I should have gone next day to ask for her hand, so that it might end honourably, so to speak, and that nobody would or could know. For though I'm a man of base desires, I'm honest. And at that very second some voice seemed to whisper in my ear: ' But when you come to-morrow to make your proposal, that girl won't even see you; she'll order her coachman to kick you out of the yard. " Publish it through all the town," she would say, " I'm not afraid of you." ' I looked at the young lady, my voice had not deceived me. That is how it would be, not a doubt of it. I could see from her face now that I should be turned out of the house. My spite was roused. I longed to play her the nastiest swinish cad's trick: to look at her with a sneer, and on the spot where she stood before me to stun her with a tone of voice that only a shopman could use.

" ' Four thousand! What do you mean? I was joking. You've been counting your chickens too easily, madam. Two hundred, if you like, with all my heart. But four thousand is not a sum to throw away on such frivolity. You've put yourself out to no purpose.'

" I should have lost the game, of course. She'd have run away. But it would have been an infernal revenge. It would have been worth it all. I'd have howled with regret all the rest of my life, only to have played that trick. Would you believe it, it has never happened to me with any other woman, not one, to look at her at such a moment with hatred. But, on my oath, I looked at her for three seconds, or five perhaps, with fearful hatred—that hate which is only a hair's-breadth from love, from the maddest love!

" I went to the window, put my forehead against the frozen pane, and I remember the ice burnt my forehead like fire. I did not keep her long, don't be afraid. I turned round, went up to the table, opened the drawer and took out a banknote for five thousand roubles (it was lying in a French dictionary). Then I showed it her in silence, folded it, handed it to her, opened the door into the passage, and, stepping back, made her a deep bow, a most respectful, a most impressive bow, believe me! She shuddered all over, gazed at me for a second, turned horribly pale—white as a sheet, in fact—and all at once, not impetuously but softly, gently, bowed down to my feet—not a boarding-school curtsey but a Russian bow, with her forehead to the floor. She jumped up and ran away. I was wearing my sword. I drew it and nearly stabbed myself with it on the spot; why, I don't know. It would have been frightfully stupid, of course. I suppose it was from delight. Can you understand that one might kill oneself from delight? But I didn't stab myself. I only kissed my sword and put it back in the scabbard."

The reader will, I hope, excuse this excessively long quotation, since it is of absolutely crucial importance. In it are found some of Dostoievsky's essential themes. In the first place, there is the anxiety that grips the individual who is a prey to an ambivalent emotion——this is regarded by contemporary psychology as a standard phenomenon. Dmitri longs to humiliate Katya; but he realises quite clearly that she will not be humiliated, whatever he may do. The same thing is true of Versilov when he overhears the conversation between Akhmakova and Lambert. Secondly, there is the image of the tarantula, or the centipede, which occurs again in connection with Svidrigailov and Stavrogin. The former imagines hell as a bath-house in the country, overrun with spiders' webs. As for Stavrogin, it was through watching a tiny red spider crawling up the stalk of a geranium that he wilfully lost the chance of saving the girl he had betrayed from hanging herself. But these are simply external, and in a sense superficial, aspects of Dmitri's predicament. Fundamentally there is a conflict within him between two natures, almost two spirits. One, the devil that he inherits from his father, appears now as sensuality and now as utter depravity. But both rouse the same longing—to inflict a decisive humiliation on Katya. The second temptation was infinitely more perverse than the first. In it there reappears all the ghastly buffoonery of Fyodor Pavlovitch. Dmitri is on the brink of giving way to it, and that is why he hates Katya. She seems to be there simply to present him with a challenge. The question is, will he be able to accept it? Her beauty is in itself a challenge, beauty that can even come to him and ask for money without being sullied.

The feel of the frozen window seems to have put an end to his anxiety. A good angel was watching over Dmitri at that moment, doubtless the same angel that at the last moment stays his hand from the murder of his father. It would be a mistake, however, to interpret this scene in purely psychological terms. The invisible powers of which the Apostle speaks are involved here too. The man of honour who turns round and proffers the note for five thousand roubles, then himself opens the door for his visitor, is a màn in whom the spirit has triumphed. But this victory is not final. Mitya needs further trials, like Raskolnikov, before he can reach the haven of salvation. What he has done for Katya she can never return. She will offer him her hand in vain, for he cannot accept it. It is at this point that he meets the other woman, Grushenka. It is not fitting, in fact, that a man like Dmitri Karamazov should be saved by the generosity of a woman. What he needs to do is to save a creature who has sunk even lower than himself.

It is possible to see a romantic influence, coming from *La Dame aux Camélias*, in the part played by courtesans in Dostoievsky's work. There is a straight line from Sonia in *Crime and Punishment* to Grushenka in *The Brothers Karamazov*, by way of Nastasia Philippovna in *The Idiot*. Nevertheless Grushenka is distinguished from the other two by the fact that she seems at first sight to be, to a far greater extent than they are, an absolute demon of sensuality, sent to the Karamazovs to ruin them all. She has loved only one man in all the world, and he was not worthy of her love; and it is when she is blinded by his unworthiness that she throws herself at Dmitri. There has to be a certain equality between two people before they can help each other. Sonia would have been no use to Raskolnikov if he had not been a murderer and she a prostitute. Prince Myshkin, on the other hand, was too pure for Nastasia Philippovna; so was Katya for Dmitri. That was why he sent his brother Alyosha to bow down before her when dismissing her.

But it is necessary to penetrate still deeper into the reciprocal feelings of Dmitri for Katya, and of Katya for Dmitri. The truth is that they are never in love with each other. Dmitri admires Katya's beauty and purity, but he is repelled by her pride. The only woman he loves, and who remains with him to the end, is Grushenka. Similarly, Katya sees in Dmitri a generous soul who could be saved by love, but the only person she loves is Ivan, the second of the Karamazovs.

> " ' That's what I loved you for, that you are generous at heart! ' broke from Katya. ' My forgiveness is no good to you, nor yours to me; whether you forgive me or not, you will always be a sore place in my heart, and I in yours—so it must be.' "

The torment which Ivan experiences is of a different kind from Dmitri's. Set between the violent Dmitri and the gentle Alyosha, the second Karamazov endures all the lacerations of intelligence and pride. This is why he can love and be loved by the proud Katya. But what concerns us at the moment is not so much the relationship between Ivan and Katya, as that between Ivan and Dmitri. Katya, who is not completely blinded by her love for Ivan, says, for example, " If you knew how he talked! If you knew how he loved that wretched man at the moment he told me, and how he hated him, perhaps, at the same moment." Ivan knows that to win Katerina Ivanovna he must surpass Dmitri in generosity. Now, Dmitri has carried abnegation to the length of voluntarily allowing his brother to pay court to Katya. It is true that he hopes in this way to get rid of her. His generosity is, in a sense, simply a kind of contempt for them both. The result is that though they are attracted to one another by love, they are kept apart from each other by pride. It is a bitter thought for them that they can only love each other through the disdainful generosity of the " unfortunate ", and because in any case he has a personal preference for Grushenka. Hence the mixture of love and hatred which we find in both of them towards Dmitri. True, Ivan behaves with the utmost generosity towards his brother; but at the same time he hates him. Likewise, Katerina Ivanovna would belong entirely to Ivan if it were not for the irrepressible jealousy which she feels towards Grushenka and which in spite of herself draws her to Dmitri. Here we have a conflict between pride and sensuality, and the proud are much further from salvation than the sensual and the violent. We know what will happen to Dmitri and Grushenka. It is much more difficult to imagine the fate of Ivan and Katya . . . But it is time to seek the resolution of the discord in Alyosha.

He too is a Karamazov, a sensualist in whom there appears, as he says to his fiancée Lise, " the primitive force of the Karamazovs ". The problem is whether the spirit of God will triumph over this force. We know that it was Dostoievsky's intention that it should. But that was to be at the end of the drama, which was never written; and before that Alyosha was to experience many reverses. But how is it that wherever Alyosha goes he brings peace, being unable either to injure or be injured? The answer is that he has triumphed over pride and violence within himself. Pride ruins Ivan, and also his hideous double Smerdyakov. Violence ruins Dmitri. The earth-force can only be chained down by meekness and humility. Now it is ultimately this mysterious and all-too-real earth-force—what might be called the spur of sin—that unleashes amongst men the ambivalent complex of love and aggressiveness from which all their lacerations arise.

Man does not demand to be loved so much as to be treated according to his essential dignity. This, indeed, means being loved, but with a different kind of love. Love of the violent and sensual kind can be an insult, and the worst kind of insult, to the person who is made its object. Such, for example, at the lowest rung of the ladder, is Fyodor Pavlovitch's love for Grushenka. But the feelings which Katya and

Dmitri have for each other are, too, not without an insulting element. Katya cannot forgive Dmitri for the fact of having one day humiliated herself before him, and then been overcome by his generosity. Dmitri cannot forgive Katya for having humiliated him in return by having been prepared to forgive him for embezzling three thousand roubles. To all appearances they are even. But it is only in appearance. No two people are ever even until they deliberately abandon the field of opposition and hostility on which love is merely another form of the everlasting conflict between human beings.

" ' I must make you one confession,' Ivan began. ' I could never understand how one can love one's neighbour.' " This, in fact, is the whole mystery, to which the life of Christ gives us the one key that exists; and we thus find ourselves brought back to the central problem in Dostoievsky, which is, as Père de Lubac has so clearly seen, the problem of atheism. Men cannot love each other without God. What they call love is simply an uneasy search for themselves by means of another. The person they choose to help them in this grim voyage of discovery is at once victim and executioner, enduring as much suffering as he causes, and suffering as much from the pain he inflicts as from the pain he receives. To the question posed by the one, no answer is made; instead, another question comes back to him as an echo. The passionate lover will not accept the fact that the other person exists as a person. He longs to destroy the other as a person and force him to be nothing more than a mock-double of himself. This is no doubt the mysterious reason why Akhamakova loves Versilov for one moment and then turns away from him. For she does not want to die, but to live. If she had surrendered to Versilov's love it would have annihilated her more surely than the revolver he brandished at her in his fit of madness. Nastasia Philippovna on the other hand, because she wants to die, elopes with Rogozhin.

But besides this love of death there is in Dostoievsky a love directed towards life, a love in which tenderness triumphs over aggressiveness, and this is only to be a found in a kind of love whose principle lies not in man but in God. But God made Man. And this is the myth of the Grand Inquisitor, in which we see the restless, tormented soul of Ivan Karamazov clearly delineated. He had intended to make this legend an indictment of Christ, but, as Alyosha points out to him, his story is a eulogy of Jesus, not a condemnation, as he intended. Christ's silence in the face of the Grand Inquisitor's accusations, and the kiss which at the end burns the Inquisitor's heart, are precisely the reply, and the only possible reply, to the cry which goes up to Him from all the insulted and all the injured who have suffered on earth since the beginning of the world. It is thus not only true to say that if God does not exist, everything is allowable; it must be added that if God had not been made Man, all love between human beings would have had a curse on it, and could only have ended in the death of the lovers at each other's hands. It is through their failure to appreciate this attitude of Dostoievsky's towards love that some critics—Chestov, for example—have managed to assert that the great novelist was fundamentally a Nietzschean in disguise.

Indeed, though the crucial question for Dostoievsky centres round the existence of God, it only arises for him as the result of another question that had scandalised him from the days of his youth: the shocking problem of evil, of the suffering that is gratuitously inflicted upon the innocent. Just before he relates the story of the Grand Inquisitor to his brother, Ivan refers to this problem. To it there is no answer except Christ. Now Christ is really only to be met with in insult and injury. Raskolnikov has to cross the door of shame into the house of the prostitute Sonia to find the Gospel, just as Dostoievsky could only discover it by being sent off to prison and spending many years there, himself one of the insulted and injured, amongst others who were insulted and injured; who were doubtless great sinners too, but amongst whom there were some who, having accepted their sinfulness in all humility, had thereupon entered into the order of peace. To such humility the proud Raskolnikov is called by the humble Sonia. And in the same way it is in humility and humiliation that Dmitri and Grushenka meet and finally achieve communion.

The Brothers Karamazov, of course, is unfinished. As far as one can judge, Dostoievsky intended to write two further novels to bring the work to completion. In this truly eschatological work he would ultimately have shown the reconciliation of the sinners and their final pardon. It seems likely that Ivan and Katya too would have found salvation, and that Alyosha, after a long period of trial, would have finally fulfilled the mission which the *staretz* Zossima had laid upon him when he advised him to leave the monastery and live in the world. This was the very mission that Dostoievsky assigned to the Russian people, whose vocation, he believed, was to bring Christ to the other peoples of the earth. However, even in its present form, the book ends with an apotheosis, the burial of Ilusha, the young boy who had been insulted and injured in the person of his father. It was clearly impossible to go any further, and Dostoievsky's plan was unrealizable otherwise than in this form.

What, in the forward march of humanity towards the *Parousia*, of which the burial of Ilusha is simply a humble pre-figuring, is the role of love, the love that, unlike the love of charity, is a matter of personal choice? Why should it seem to be inevitably accompanied by aggressiveness, and even hatred? The reason is that all beauty is a provocation, a challenge, an insult. When it appears, it awakens within us all our powers, the lowest and the highest together. Under its rays man's inner nature seems to be illuminated with an implacable light. Everything noble in us, and everything vile, emerges with perfect clarity. If pride and sensuality triumph, catastrophe is inevitable. For pride shuts us in upon ourselves and obstructs our self-giving. The man of pride crouches over the insult he has suffered, and watches over it as though it were his dearest treasure. And sensuality is strangely mixed up with pride. Its one aim is to take, but at the same time it longs to sully beauty and destroy it, and thus annihilate its unbearable provocation. If it realizes its aim, pride is avenged by the elimination of every obstacle, and man dies in the solitude of despair.

Only the charity of Christ, because it is a love from which no one is excluded, can save us from this abyss. Thus the whole of Dostoievsky's work is based on an opposition between sacred and profane love—portrayed for all time in the famous work by Titian and sometimes described by the moderns under the terms of Eros and Agape. But it would be a falsification to present this opposition as the thing of primary importance in Dostoievsky. It has been observed that feminine characters play only a secondary part in his novels. Women, and the love they inspire, form the pretext for the drama; they are never the subject of the drama itself. In some of the most important novels, such as *Crime and Punishment* and *The Possessed*, the love conflicts are explicitly relegated to the background. The thing that unites Raskolnikov and Sonia is certainly not love in the ordinary sense of the word. Stavrogin has long been beyond love. Amongst the victims of love one may come across the figures of two or three women, but they are not of the same stature as Chatov, Kirilov or even Verkhovenski. The part played by love seems superficially much greater in *The Idiot*, *A Raw Youth* and *The Brothers Karamazov*. But is this more than superficially so? The enterprise on which Myshkin embarks when he decides to leave Switzerland and return to Russia would doubtless have failed, even if he had not come across Nastasia Philippovna and Aglaya on the way. The same may be said of the problems raised for, and by, Versilov. And if sensuality seems to be the devil that torments the Karamazovs particularly, it is nevertheless quite clear that the murder of Fyodor Pavlovitch by Smerdyakov, and the fate of Dmitri, and the private sufferings of Ivan, and the vocation of Alyosha, are none of them determined by the presence or absence of Lise, Katya, Grushenka. What a difference there is in this respect between Dostoievsky and Tolstoy! The reason is that Tolstoy is immersed almost entirely in the world of the flesh; whereas for Dostoievsky the supreme questions are of such a kind that sexuality is never essential to them.

Our concern here is the conflict between love and aggressiveness. It is this which has been at the root of our nature ever since the first sin was committed; we find it installed at the very heart of love. We love for good or for evil reasons, and here in this context they appear more indistinguishable than anywhere else. Each man is brother to all other men, but at the same time he is their implacable enemy. We pass from love to hatred and from hatred to love without any transition, for they are two complementary aspects of one single movement. Thus we saw Katya and Dmitri, and Ivan and Katya, constantly seesawing from one passion to the other. Only Alyosha, who in spite of his doubts and weaknesses has received from the *staretz* Zossima the message of Christ, shows· himself truly able to wipe out injuries, to bring peace to little Ilusha, to gather around him in a real brotherhood the boys who had been Ilusha's tormentors.

The meaning of all this seems clear enough. This ambivalence of love and aggressiveness is the sign of a nature deeply rent and divided against itself. If the lovers fail to conjure up between them the presence of a third Person who is at once the foundation and the object of their joint love, it is impossible for them to regard each other in any other way than as irreconcilable enemies. The man will be victimized by the woman, the woman will be victimized by the man; both linked in an infernal series of insults and injuries whose end will be Rogozhin's murder of Nastasia, and the ultimate collapse of Myshkin's reason, or else the sordid rope with which Stavrogin hangs himself in spite of all the efforts of his guardian angel Dasha. Dostoievsky's entire work thus appears as a long indictment of Eros—it being impossible for us to recreate Paradise Lost by our own efforts—and as a pathetic aspiration towards Agape, which alone can open the gates of the Kingdom of Heaven to us. We are not allowed to see the absolute triumph of Agape in Alyosha: Dostoievsky died with no strength to lead us into the Promised Land. But his cry of mingled distress and hope has resounded throughout the world, and his labour has surely not been wasted—if through it we have been reminded once again of the greatness of our misery and the misery of our greatness.

ARE SYMPATHY AND AGGRESSIVENESS MATTERS OF INSTINCT?

JEAN LHERMITTE

EVERY time the tragedy of war recurs, bringing in its wake material and moral havoc, unleashing those most cruel instincts and passions that inevitably accompany its cataclysms, the question arises in the minds of many, whether the aggressive or combative instinct is to be found in the furthest depths of man's nature; whether there is an instinct in man which exists as the foundation and source from which this tendency inexorably derives, or whether, on the contrary, the violent conflicts by which humanity is rent are the result of social forces or economic laws that have been badly understood or badly applied.

In short, the problem which faces us is to decide whether the tendency towards aggression which is, unfortunately, all too often revealed in the conduct of men, can be legitimately equated with a fundamental instinct—whether this lust for war really corresponds to the structure of our mind in its most essential characteristics.

Now it is well known that ever since man began to philosophize— i.e. to reflect on the motive-forces of his own activity—nothing has ever been found to exist without its opposite, whether the thing be material or spiritual; there is no thesis without its antithesis, no heat without cold, no black without white, no repulsion without attraction, no sympathy without antipathy, no love without hatred.

Love and hatred are words that I shall avoid in this article, the reason being that they are connected with feelings of considerable complexity which have a high intellectual content, and cannot therefore be considered as principles of our instinctual life, or of the primitive tendencies of our moral nature.

As Ribot has said:

" It was a recognised teaching amongst the ancients that all the passions could be reduced to love and hatred: this is repeated again and again. They seem to have reached this conclusion by comparing and contrasting the various passions, appropriating the resemblances, eliminating the differences, and so by a process of reduction abstracting from all this multiplicity characteristics of the most general kind.

" If by love and hatred are meant the movements of attraction
and repulsion which exist at the root of the emotions, there is
nothing wrong in this; but it should be realized that what we get
in the end are simply abstractions, theoretical concepts. This kind
of statement is misleading and has no practical value whatsoever. If
love (and what kind of love?—for there is nothing vaguer than this
word) and hatred are meant in a more concrete sense, to be regarded
as the original source from which all the other emotions arise, this
is a mere point of view, an assertion that has never been proved."

I have thought it worth while to quote these words at the beginning because, like Ribot, I shall try to get away from all purely verbal
academic psychology. It has been in existence for so long and it has
managed to give us nothing better than empty shadows, things without
life and devoid of all concrete reality. No doubt it is true that man is
distinguished from the animals by the qualities of his mind, his creative
intelligence, his faculty of judgment, his moral perception, by his inner
life and by that capacity for reflecting upon himself which enables him,
with the help of grace, to apprehend the divine; but it must not be
forgotten that animals, too, are capable of a definite psychic activity
and that in both the highly-civilized man and the humblest of animals,
apparently, we find instincts at the root of their activity—or, to use
a more modern word, their comportment. We must not be afraid,
therefore, of taking a glance at the animal world if we wish to try to
understand the elements that lie behind all our behaviour, individual,
family and social.

But before we get to grips with our subject we find ourselves obliged
to determine the meaning of terms used not only by philosophers but
by psychologists, educators, biologists and " doctors of the spirit ".
What exactly is meant by the words " instinct", " tendency",
" need", " inclination", " emotional disposition "? The word " instinct " has often been defined, of course; but fundamentally all the
definitions seem to lead to the same conclusion: instinct appears in the
light of any unbiased observation as an innate, hereditary aptitude,
manifesting itself, in every individual of a species, as a power to do
certain things automatically and inevitably, without previous apprentice-
ship, without forethought, without any possibility of progress, without
any knowledge of what is being aimed at or of any relationship between
the aim and the means necessary to attain it (Roger).
Thus, from this point of view, instinct and intelligence seem to be
absolutely opposed, since intelligence is a matter of penetration, com-

THE CRUCIFIXION

Grünewald: Colmar Museum

prehension, knowledge, foresight, anticipation and judgment, whilst instinct seems to be essentially conditioned, spontaneous, unchanging, complete in itself and blind as to the aims it is pursuing. From the evolutionary point of view, instinct finds its most perfect manifestation in insects, whereas in man—i.e. the being who has reached the highest stage of evolution, and is the most recent to be organised—instinctive activity tends increasingly to be dominated and restrained by conscious intelligence. Bergson's views on this point are well known: in his *Creative Evolution* there is a splendid development of the idea of a division of life into two separate streams throughout the whole range of being—on the one hand the creative, inquiring intelligence, and on the other the activity of instinct. Nevertheless, although Bergson did not go to the extent of claiming that instinct excludes intelligence completely—far from it, for he maintained that every instinct has its fringe of intelligence—it must be confessed that he drew too sharp a line between these two kinds of activity which lie behind the conduct of living creatures, and that today biologists are far less categorical, endeavouring to find tracks of intelligent activity in the components of the play of instinct. We have also learned that before any instinctive activity can come into operation, it needs to be preceded by what is called a preparatory phase, characterized by a particular attitude and also by the expression of feelings of disquiet or anxiety, without which it could never develop. Unlike the " mechanists ", for whom instinct was closely correlated with the structure of the organism, particularly the nervous system, we realise today that instinctual activity is not quite as blind as it was thought to be, that it is capable of amelioration and can experience anticipation; in short, that its behaviour cannot be looked upon as the unfolding of a chain of reflexes, but rather as a reaction involving an adaptation by the whole organism. In the same environment different creatures will develop different kinds of conduct and behaviour; again, the same individual is capable of different kinds of activity without any changes taking place in his environment, if for one reason or another his physiological and psychic condition undergoes any alteration. And it is here that there come into play those determining inner elements of instinct which I have already mentioned, and which have been so often described by psychologists in such unsatisfying terms as " emotional dispositions ", " tendencies ", " feelings ". These elements are simply the dark side of instinctual activity, and if they seem to be much harder to define, this is because they are subjective, whereas instincts behave in such a way that it is possible to keep all their variations under close observation.

As Guillaume has shown in his recent *Traité de Psychologie*, the analysis of the internal factors of instinct is made difficult and hazardous by the arbitrary use of the terms employed, and by insufficient attention to the finer shades of the meaning of words, so that there is often confusion between the words " tendency ", " inclination ", " leaning ", " feeling ", " affection ", " appetite ", " need ", " disposition ", " aptitude ", " faculty "; whereas each of these words should be reserved for one particular differentiated quality. On one point, however, all are agreed, and that is that the psycho-physiological activity of instinct has two sides to it, one objective and concrete, appearing in its external form in behaviour, and the other remaining to a great extent subjective—the emotional state, the feeling, the appetite, the need, the inclination, the tendency—in short, the depressing or stimulating emotion.

All this helps us to realise the variations and vicissitudes in the life of the instincts—how sensitive they are to change, and to different times of life in the psycho-physiological condition of the individual; and also how certain instincts which have been perfectly organised are inclined to degenerate and even to die out altogether.

There are, of course, many varied lists suggesting how instincts should be clasified: William James, for example, recognises no less than twenty-two modes of instinctual activity, MacDougall reduces the number to fifteen, whilst in his latest book Henri Roger maintains that all the instincts can be put into two groups only, one covering those whose aim is self-preservation—i.e. the instinct for food and the instinct of self-defence, which reaches its highest point in the aggressive tendency—the other, the instincts which aim to protect the species. In this latter group are found the gregarious, family, social instincts, whose corresponding tendency is easily seen in the feelings of sympathy, reconciliation, solidarity, human brotherhood.

As I said at the beginning, a comparison of the instinctive activities of animals and men can be highly instructive. There is the defensive instinct, for example: we know that, like a human child, a young animal is obsessed by the fear of anything that is strange to it, whilst at the same time it is driven by a contrary tendency, corresponding to the instinct of curiosity analysed so thoroughly by the Russian physiologist Pavlov. But besides this instinctive " global " fear, which applies to the whole range of things that are unknown and consequently charged with mystery, there are more specific fears which are remarkable in this sense, that the only reason for their existence must lie in some kind of hereditary transmission. Thus, a dog which has never seen a wolf will relapse into a condition of the utmost terror if it scents the tiniest shred of the skin of that animal; young chicks become terrified when they see a hawk for the first time (Spalding-Preyer). More remarkable still—when some animals live together they develop such feelings of hatred and hostility and aggressiveness towards each other that the weakest of them can become the worst of tyrants.

In animals, as in man, the defensive instinct can manifest itself externally in either a passive or an active form. As regards passive defence, an animal that finds itself, or imagines itself, to be in danger, will hide, burrow into the ground, conceal itself in a tree or furrow, run away, or take advantage of the cover of a leafy tree to steal out of sight. Some creatures, moreover, have a remarkably powerful gift for being able to change the colour of their coat or plumage or skin, according to circumstance, so that they harmonize perfectly with the surrounding conditions and are thus difficult to make out and capture. Moreover, along with this natural mimicry there is sometimes a more complicated kind analogous to that of civilised man—it was seen during the recent war. What I am thinking of here is the tendency which drives animals to cover their bodies with bits of plants in their efforts to avoid danger or enemies who may pursue and kill them. There is the crab, for instance, which covers itself with seaweed, choosing its own assortment until it becomes indistinguishable from its marine environment. More remarkably still, Minkievicz has even shown that if pieces of differently-coloured silk are put near to this creature it will choose pieces which have colours like the bottom of the aquarium, and cover itself with them. During the war, the various armies developed exactly the same methods of concealing themselves from the enemy. There is no fundamental difference between the so-called instinctive camouflage adopted by animals and the highly conscious camouflage devised by men.

If instinctive passive defence manifests itself in the ways I have described, active defence appears in the struggle waged against an enemy on the attack, or who seems likely to attack. Animals can engage on a defensive war just like men; and on this point, too, we must endeavour to be modest, for we have introduced nothing new. In this field the varieties of instinctual activity are infinite, and there are many authors who have described at great length the different ways in which the fighting and aggressive instincts manifest themselves. This point, however, is a little remote from our present intention, which is to discover whether aggressiveness can, in fact, be regarded as a pure manifestation of instinct.

In his classic work on the psychology of the feelings, Ribot remarks that aggressiveness is sometimes present in animals in a pure state because in some creatures it is not restrained by any contrary instincts: it really does appear like a force of nature, released and liberated from every kind of constraint. By way of example, we may mention the carnivores, the voracious beasts of prey; the attack which they develop comes like a whirlwind; it is brutal, sudden, violent, devastating, cruel, ungovernable and, so far as one can judge, irresistible. The reason is that in this case the fighting instinct sends its roots down into an appetite which is absolutely essential for the maintenance of life—the appetite for food—and thus there appears in all its nakedness Darwin's "struggle for existence", the struggle for the life of the individual and the species: the need for food demands to be satisfied. The violence with which this instinct is released is so great that it is hard to believe that it is accompanied by any feeling of pleasure.

The instinct for food is not, however, the only instinct that releases activity of this surprising violence; the sexual need, too, can be charged with such a high emotional content that the reactions which result from it, setting male against female, can be no less violent. There should be no astonishment at finding it proved by experiment and observation that the two instincts, for food and sex, should manifest themselves with such irresistible force: for if these two tendencies were not endowed with such savage energy not only the individual but the whole race would die out—whereas life must inevitably tend towards its own perpetuation.

When we come to analyse the behaviour of man, we find a great variety of instinctive impulses, often indistinguishably involved with each other; but the thing which gives man's instinctive activity a much higher complexity than that of animals is the fact that in man instinct is, to a greater or less extent, bound up with consciousness. In reality, in fact, it is only in special circumstances, particularly those of a pathological nature, that instinct appears in the pure state conceived by Ribot. Whereas in animals tendencies and instincts only appear to be restrained and governed by impulses and needs and repressed cravings, in man the instinctive activity seems to be under the control of one sovereign force—reason, intelligence. No doubt it is true, as may be seen only too often, that this controlling force can be overcome by the blind impetuosity of instinct; nevertheless, it is generally true to say that in ordinary life the activity of the instincts is governed and controlled and canalised by superior forces which are in fact the feeling of moral obligation and conscious intelligence. And thus we discover that it is precisely when, under the pressure of pathological or other conditions, intelligence, reason and moral sense give way, that the instinctive activity, freed from all restraint, manifests itself as ungovernably, savagely, irresistibly and dangerously as it does in animals. Another thing we discover is that feelings normally regarded

as manifestations of a particular instinct can undergo such a development that behaviour is profoundly affected by them. Thus the need
for food and drink, whose satisfaction is accompanied by a feeling of
pleasure, can be completely perverted when this feeling predominates,
and the individual begins to eat and drink merely for the pleasure of it.
The same is true of the sexual instinct, which can be deflected from its
proper aim of procreation, and become simply a means of personal
pleasure and satisfaction, utterly egoistic and utterly remote from
what it would be if the instinctive activity was expressing itself
normally.

But we can go still further; in certain deviations of instinct we find
that a feeling normally associated with a particular instinctive impulse
becomes involved with a kind of behaviour absolutely different from
what we should logically have expected.

Sadism, cruelty, the pleasure derived from another's pain—these
are examples of feelings which have formed an abnormal connection
with the aggressive or combative instinct. Although it is true that
such deviations are met with, at least as far as we can see, in humans
more frequently than in animals—perhaps because it is easier to
analyse humans—they are no less striking in animals, who can take
a perverse pleasure in torturing their victims before killing them. And
then again they are to be found in almost a pure state in children, who
delight in making innocent animals suffer. " At that age there is no
pity," says Lafontaine, and only too often the facts prove him to be
right. What are we to say of parents who, instead of restraining their
children in this matter, are amused by them? As Montaigne wrote:
" It is one of their mothers' pastimes to watch their children wring
the neck of a chicken or enjoy hurting a dog or cat."

There is no need to remind anyone that this cruel or sadistic instinct
—which is no different from the aggressive, fighting instinct, except
in its contents—is capable of being released with unbelievable
violence when wars, revolutions and social upheavals descend upon
the world. Then all the tendencies opposed to the destructive instinct,
all the reasons which man's intelligence or moral sense has put up
against it, are obliterated, and the spirit of war appears—pitiless,
savage, merciless; and through the cracks of a fragile, superficial civilisation bursts the most rudimentary instinct that is to be found even
amongst animals.

I have already indicated how closely instinctive tendencies can be
associated in animals, and there is a great deal more that could be said
about this association in man, particularly about the connection between the aggressive instinct and the sexual impulse. It is a commonplace that some people look upon love as a battle in which two forces

are opposed to each other, in which the victory of one means the defeat of the other. No less obvious is the fact of sexual jealousy, bringing conflict, duels, battles and even wars in its train.

But at the back of this sombre picture a light shines, and this comes from an instinct that is at the opposite pole from that of aggression, combativeness and cruelty—the social instinct, reinforced by the feelings of solidarity, sympathy and affection. And it should be noticed in the first place that the social tendency towards mutual help and co-operation is to be found, not only in every human race, but also in the animal world, even though there it has not been studied so much. I should like to mention a few of the facts that prove this. Romanones relates that one day three crows banded together to steal a piece of meat that a dog was eating. One of them bit the dog's tail so that the dog turned round with a yelp of pain; then the other two seized the meat, and the little trio of robbers calmly flew off and had a good feast on the top of a nearby wall.

Henri Roger also relates that his friend, Professor Hartmann, told him that on his farm he had two turkeys, each of which looked after its own little brood without paying any attention to the other's. One morning both turkeys hustled their little ones into the same corner of the meadow, then went and hid side by side near the opposite corner, where they had seen a snake lying. This snake they chased off and killed. After the exploit the two mothers came back, took charge of their offspring again, and went their own separate ways without paying the slightest attention to each other. This seems to be a farmyard picture of the kind of associations of which we humans have also had experience, in which, after the defeat of the enemy, allies go off on their own and return to their own private occupations.

The sympathetic instinct of mutual co-operation, which is at least suggested by the preceding examples, is found fully developed in the insect world, where it appears in a state of purity, because here there seems to be not the slightest trace of reason or abstract intelligence or moral sense, at least in the way we understand these things. But the insect category seems rather too remote for the evidence that could be drawn from it, about the instinctive activities of collective warfare and social organisation, and the connected tendency towards mutual help, to be applicable to human beings, except at the cost of falsifying the resemblances. Much more relevant are the observations that have been made of the higher apes quite recently by a number of biologists, especially Koehler and his followers. In general, monkeys which live in groups go out looking for food together and entrust one or two of their number with the job of looking after their collective security. At the first cry of danger all the monkeys make off together, and then come back and fetch any one which has lagged behind, or is in danger. Occasionally they will band together and be emboldened to attack a powerful enemy. Thus, a group of apes has been seen to rush furiously upon an eagle which had one of their young ones in its claws, tear its feathers from its body and bite it, to make it let go of its prey. Apes have such a feeling of solidarity when they feel that an enemy is about that they have been known to attack a panther and drive it off. It is not until one gets down to the cynocephalus that monkeys are not dangerous to humans, and according to Henri Roger they have been observed on the top of a hill throwing stones at these creatures— which they rightly considered to be their enemies.

Amongst humans the instinct and tendency and feeling of sympathy and co-operation seems so general and so highly developed that any attempt to describe it would be a waste of time. What is more difficult is to define the extent to which behaviour which seems to us to be governed by sympathy has its origin in instinct, and to decide whether what we take to be instinct should not rather be looked upon as an expression of intelligence. Of course, this problem has existed for a long time, but it must be confessed that it has received far deeper consideration lately as a result of the research made by psycho-analysts, particularly the investigations of Adler and his followers. Adler, it will be remembered, bases his whole method of moral education for children on the development of the co-operative instinct, and he has proved that it is indeed an instinct that is involved, because its first manifestations appear within the first few days of life. If you watch a child soon after it is born, you will find that it hardly opens its eyes and begins to move its limbs—of which it has only the vaguest conception—before it turns towards its mother's breast and co-operates with her to take its first food. Soon this first feeling of sympathy appears in movements more expressive than this—in its smile, for example; " Incipe, parve puer, risu cognoscere matrem," says Virgil. Later this feeling of sympathy grows stronger and wider, expanding outwards from the mother to the rest of the family circle and then spreading amongst society generally. And it is to the extent that this instinct of solidarity and active co-operation develops that first the child, then the young man, is transformed into the social being that he is meant to be. And it is also in the absence of any proper development of this co-operative instinct that the origin of many cases of psycho-neurosis is to be found.

Final proof of the instinctive quality of this disposition has come from the observation of patients whose intellectual and moral development has been arrested or deflected under the burden of sickness. Many individuals suffering from debility or psychic insufficiency show not only a deficiency of the higher functions but an apparently excessive development of the instinctive functions. These are not, of course, all of the same quality, but if there are some which have a harmful effect in family or social life, there are others which are very precious because they are characterised by a burst, a sudden current, of sympathy, a desire for co-operative activity and mutual help. The same thing happens in the animal world, in which this tendency sets itself up in opposition to the anti-social tendencies and thus gives the individual a kind of equilibrium, which may be precarious, but which is nevertheless compatible with a family life that does not suffer too much from upset.

Although I am far from imagining that I have fully discussed the subject proposed, I nevertheless hope to have shown that human nature reveals a dual instinctive tendency which appears in our social behaviour: the aggressive fighting tendency, and its opposite, which consists in human brotherhood, active co-operation and mutual help, fed by the feeling of sympathy.

All the evidence goes to show that it is the latter disposition which, if they were wise, men would do their utmost to develop, in their endeavour to realise that ideal of human concord which lies in the hearts of all who imagine a better state for mankind, one more in harmony with human destiny. But this does not mean that the aggressive fighting instinct is a bad thing " in itself "; on deeper consideration it emerges as a source which can be most fruitful in producing the highest kinds of virtue.

For man, in fact, fighting does not necessarily mean engaging in physical violence; transposed on to the spiritual plane, the fighting instinct can lead to the highest peaks of morality.

By destroying the evil passions, by systematically removing the weeds and brambles that invade the garden of the soul, aggressiveness can help man to approach the sublime, becoming the most efficacious motive-force of spiritual progress.

" Violenti rapiunt illud," says St. Matthew: surely by these words Christ meant the most heroic aspect of the fight for those moral and spiritual values which are of the utmost importance if mankind is ever to be regenerated.

THE PROBLEM OF AMBIVALENCE

GEORGES PARCHEMINEY

THE SCOPE AND AIM OF THIS ESSAY

THE WORD " ambivalence " appeared in the literature of psychiatry for the first time in 1911 in an article by Professor Bleuler of Zürich, who used it to mean a paradoxical unity composed of contrary tendencies which had been found, nevertheless, to exist in some sort of association with each other. The unification of these tendencies, however, only existed in the delirium of schizophrenia or in the oniric thoughts of the normal person. Leaving aside these two psychic conditions, which lie outside the scope of the present essay, I shall discuss ambivalence as it appears when these two opposed tendencies appear together in the field of consciousness, either directly or indirectly, whenever any sort of psychological activity has been aroused.

The idea of ambivalence can be studied in different modes of this psychic activity; I shall here confine myself to a consideration of it from the point of view of the two main streams of human affectivity, love and aggression.

The question arises, whether these two affective poles are always intimately associated in the human personality and whether, as a result of this, affective ambivalence forms part of the normal structure of psychic life, or whether, on the contrary, ambivalence is entirely a psycho-pathological phenomenon to be found only in the neurotic or the delirious. Does psychic life bear in the profoundest depths of its structure an indissoluble bond between this twin pair, love and violence?

By conceiving the problem in this way we shall be obliged to refer principally to those psychological ideas which are based on the theory of psycho-dynamism. This theory, first enunciated by Ribot in his conception of tendencies, found its fullest development in the work of Janet and Freud.

It is above all in Freud's work that the idea of ambivalence can be discerned in its most logical and coherent form: we know, moreover, how deeply the thought of Bleuler was inspired by the ideas of psycho-analysis.

There is no need to emphasise that Freud's ideas make no claim to be exhaustive. At every stage of his work Freud emphasises their speculative side; nevertheless, in the field of clinical facts and experimental research the scientific value of Freud's work has been proved and continues to be proved by experience.

THE ORIGIN OF THE PSYCHO-DYNAMIC THEORY OF IMPULSES

The theory of psycho-dynamism involves two ideas—on the one hand, the idea of psycho-genesis, psychic causality, and on the other, an idea of energy: psycho-analysis bases its explanations on the action of primitive vital energies. The science of psycho-analysis is therefore at once psychological and biological, the psychic reactions of the individual being integrated with the laws and behaviour of living things. One result of this, as Odier has observed, is that the biological psychologist refrains from formulating value-judgments.

The psychic representants of these vital energies are made up of "impulses"; a word which seems more satisfactory than "instincts", because it gives a better idea of the dynamic element in the German word *Trieb*.

Impulses are therefore the psychic representations of an excitation whose source lies in the human organism.

"The instinctive impulses," says Freud, "and their transformations, form the ultimate limit of psychoanalytical investigation: beyond this limit they give place to biological research."

How are these primitive impulses to be defined and isolated?

If one consults the various works that have dealt with the idea of instinct (excluding the study of animal behaviour) one is struck by the diversity of the instincts that each author attributes to the individual. It seems as though as many instincts are created as there are needs (the play instinct, the imitative instinct, the social instinct, the religious instinct, and so on), or that the idea of instinct is confused with that of physiological function.

From the very beginning Freud objected to this way of looking at the matter. "We had felt for a long time", he wrote at the age of seventy-three, "that behind this mass of smaller instincts there lay something powerful and serious, something that could only be approached with great caution."

In a first attempt at classification Freud isolated two fundamental impulses, one of self-preservation and the other of the preservation of the species; to which corresponded two primordial needs, hunger and love.

Instead of basing his classification on the study of behaviour, Freud adopted the theoretical principles of biology, principles which are primarily energistic in essence.[1]

The first principle he called the pleasure-displeasure principle (*Lust-Unlustprinzip*). This is a regulative mechanism essentially dynamic in nature, which in fact controls the life of the impulses. When the impulse is subject to some kind of psychic tension, we endeavour—instinctively—to put an end to this tension, because it is accompanied by a sensation of pain; the destruction of the tension produces a feeling of pleasure, which is called the satisfaction of a need. In other words (Odier) we are impelled to replace the displeasure created by the tension by the pleasure which is created by release. This theory derives from a suggestion made by Fechner.

But as the satisfaction of the instinct cannot be achieved because of the exigencies of the external world, and because it would prove dangerous to the individual, this principle gives way to a principle known as the reality-principle, which serves the self-preservation instinct. It signifies, in fact, what is known in biology as adaptation to the environment.

We thus have a schema composed of the two main fundamental impulses; the self-preservation instinct, based on the reality-principle, and the sexual instinct, based on the pleasure-principle. There is no need to remind the reader once again that in Freud's mind the word sexual was never restricted to its narrower meaning: it includes in fact a whole series of partial impulses, emanating from a variety of organic sources which may exist in the first place quite separately from each other, and each aiming at a particular organic pleasure. It is only much later that a synthesis may take place that gives one the right to speak of the reproductive instinct, and it is only then that the whole becomes recognisable as a specific sexual instinct.

What characterises these partial impulses is the fact that they can be subject to displacement, change of aim, inhibition, repression; in a word, like physical forces, they obey the laws of the displacement of energy.

Freud gave the name " libido " to the energy possessed by the tendencies connected with what we sum up in the word love, an energy which he looked upon as being of a certain specific quantity which is not, however, measurable. In justification of this broad use of the term " love ", he invoked his own researches as indicating that all the different kinds of " love " are really different symptoms of one and the

[1] It is because I wish to stress the importance of the idea of energy in psychoanalysis that for the next few pages I shall take the reader through Freud's successive theories which, though no more than temporary structures, are necessary for a deeper understanding of the facts. I hope the reader will pardon me for leading him by such a roundabout route to Freud's ultimate ideas.

same totality of tendencies, which in some cases tend toward sexual union and in others away from it, but at the same time preserve enough characteristic features to make their identity unmistakable. He argued that ordinary language was fully justified in giving " love " this multiplicity of meanings, and that a synthesis of that kind should form the basis of our theories on this subject.

If this be accepted it clearly follows that emotional states are subtended by a specific energy existing at the biological level. This energistic hypothesis, as we shall see later, has been most fruitful, and if the conception of the libido has been misunderstood or adversely criticised, I for my part am in entire agreement with Jung when he says that the idea of the libido is one of the most important acquisitions in psychology, equal in importance to Robert Mayer's principle in physics.

In his first reflections on the facts, then, Freud set up the impulses of love or *aimance*, to use the term suggested by Pichon, against the self-preservation instinct, and in this latter he included a whole series of aggressive impulses to which, in the beginning, he did not grant their full importance.

However, a deeper study of neuroses, of certain impulses which had as their object the ego, and which he grouped together under the general heading of narcissism, the increasing importance of the aggressive tendencies which appeared in the forms of sadism and primary masochism—subjects which lie outside the scope of the present essay—all this mass of observed fact led Freud to ask himself whether there might not exist in psychic life tendencies which obey a different principle from the pleasure-principle, and exist above it.

The question centred round the existence in the species of a tendency to repetition, to a kind of stability which appeared more elementary, more fundamental, than the pleasure-principle, which would lead to this latter's being supplanted by a more powerful force.

By a process of reasoning whose speculative character he particularly emphasised, Freud attempted to discover the nature of the connection between the impulses and this tendency to repetition.

An instinct, he argued, would be the tendency possessed by an organism to re-establish an anterior condition: it would be bound up with the idea of the inertia of organic life. Pushing this theory to the extreme—and having established by experiment that everything that lives returns to an inorganic condition—it could be said that the end towards which all life tends is death, or, conversely, that the non-living is anterior to the living.

It would be a contradiction to put the self-preservation instincts into this group; and so Freud was led to postulate the existence of independent elementary impulses called death-impulses or destructive impulses.

Although Freud endeavoured to support his theory by arguments borrowed from biology (Weissmann), and although some of his followers have claimed to find a parallel between these death-impulses based on a stability-principle and the physical idea of entropy, in reality Freud was led to adopt this idea primarily through his clinical experience, and in particular through his experience of the bio-psychological processes, still so puzzling, of masochism and auto-destruction.

However this may be, we here reach Freud's definitive idea, which was always based on a fundamental dualism, and which connects up at this point with our problem of ambivalence. The idea is that of an original dualism between life-impulses and death-impulses.

The life-instinct includes the primitive sexual instinct, which in the author's mind takes on a wider significance, approximating to the Platonic " Eros ": it thus comprises all the vital impulses that are directed outwards, and the self-preservation instinct to which it was originally opposed.

Eros is a vital instinct in the widest sense, and its function is to ensure the union of the parts of the living substance; it is opposed to the death-instinct, which evolves secretly. The mystery of life is to be found in the struggle from birth onwards between these two instincts, to each of which corresponds a physiological process (Construction and Destruction). Sadism and masochism are psychic representants of the death-instincts, according to whether these are directed outwards or turned in upon the individual.

I must insist on the speculative nature of this theory, which, in Freud's own words, " is an artificial construction made from hypotheses which could quite easily collapse like a pack of cards".

What remains as ascertained fact in the psychological and psychopathological field is the existence of two groups of opposed impulses, libido-impulses or life-instincts, aggressive impulses or death-instincts.

This brings us back to the idea of ambivalence. It is a fact that psychological observation regularly reveals that in the most unexpected ways violence accompanies love, and often precedes love in human relationships; that love can be transformed into aggressiveness, and vice versa. According to the theory of a fundamental dualism of impulse, there cannot be a real transformation, a change of sign, but only succession in time under the given influences of these joint impulses.

Before concluding these theoretical considerations, it must be asked whether other scientific ideas give a more satisfactory solution of the problem of ambivalence.

In opposition to Freud, who, as we have shown, adopts a dualist position, stands von Monakov with his essentially monistic theories, who derives all instincts, primary or secondary, hormic or neo-hormic, from an original *horme* which he considers to be the matrix of the instincts. There is a different idea in MacDougall, who divides instincts into primary and secondary or pseudo-instincts. Again, in the work of Kurt Goldstein, which is similar to that based on the *Gestalt* theory, the idea of instincts disappears and the author regards life as a series of structurations bound up with an external world conceived as a source of continual danger.

If, again, one refers to animal biology, it becomes clear how much more difficult it is to say exactly what an instinct is. Some (Verlaine) deny the theory of instincts absolutely; others describe instincts under a variety of aspects and often confuse them with reflexes or tropisms.

Recent books (Cuénot's, for example) on this question of instincts are concerned chiefly with the fundamental question of finality or non-finality in biology and throw no real light on our problem.

The Development of the Impulses and their Integration in Psychic Life

It now becomes necessary to describe briefly the fate of these two impulses in the development of the personality. We know, indeed, that the psychic life of the adult is not formed all at once, but is the resultant of successive integrations before it becomes capable of the higher mental operations; in Janet's words, there exists a hierarchization of psychic functions.

This progressive development from a childish to an adult mentality takes place parallel with the biological, psychological, and indeed social problem of adaptation. It has become an accepted fact today that there are profound resemblances between the psychic life of the child and the behaviour of the primitive, resemblances which are found again in the oniric thought of adults and, finally, in the mechanisms of unconscious psychic life, as proved by the study of neuroses.

In its earliest years the child lives entirely under the sign of narcissism, it is still incapable of feeling any objectal emotion: there is no question yet of any libidinous instincts. Nor can there really be any question of ambivalence. Everything seems to be reduced to assimilative functions centring round the digestive apparatus, and here there can already be seen a destructive component, an absorption or devouring of the object, involving destruction. This initial phase has been compared with the cannibalistic attitude of the primitive, and it is also found in certain kinds of regressive delirious behaviour in the schizophrenic.

Then the child begins to have to give way to certain educative forces; and as it is still not capable of real oblative feelings this phase is characterised by the prevalence of aggressive impulses (the need to bite, to tear up, etc.). The analytical school has emphasised the importance of these impulses at this stage of development.

How does the psychic life of the child behave during these early stages? Besides the teachings of the psycho-analysts we may mention here the works of the genetic psychologists, especially Piaget, the authority on this matter, and we shall soon see the importance of studying how psychic life and the development of the impulses converge.

In the first years there is no reflective consciousness. The child speaks its thought, experiences it, but does not socialize it. " In the beginning," says Piaget, " it serves immediate satisfactions long before it is devoted to the search for truth. It is an imagination bordering on hallucination which enables desires to be no sooner entertained than they are realized." Here we see clearly that the child lives under the exclusive domination of the pleasure-principle.

The reality-principle is imposed progressively: Jones says that it is certain that in the first phases of life there is no consciousness of the self as a thing distinct from the world.

Piaget sums up the characteristics of the childish mentality in the following terms: absence of reflective consciousness, non-socialization of thought, incapacity for mental synthesis or syncretism, symbolism, pre-logical mentality.

As a result of this psychic life, there begins to take place an adaptation to the environment, which is determined at this stage by the idea that the child has developed of the world.

Piaget concludes by saying that in the child the sense of reality only grows up slowly, by the progressive elimination of thought-realism and subjectivity, the progressive elimination of feelings of magical participation and animism. "We believe," he adds, "that a day will come when the thought of the child will be put on the same level as regards the thought of the normal adult as the primitive mentality described by Lévy-Bruhl and the autistic and symbolic thought described by Freud."

This seems to me to be a matter of the utmost importance, for if the thought is governed by the feeling of magical omnipotence, and is invested with this power, the impulses which are integrated into it will share in this power.

Now we have seen that at this first stage the aggressive impulses alone seem to come into action, the childish ego living under the sign of narcissism. The result is that we find these feelings of magical omnipotence, domination and destruction, appearing in the human being. The child identifies itself with the rest of the world: all its surroundings are simply a prolongation of itself: it *is the world*. " One

gets the impression when studying the child's joy at being the world,"
says Piaget again, " that it experiences all the joy of a god governing
the movements of the stars."

There is no need to emphasise the importance of this first emotional
grouping in the human being. It is found again in the neurotic and
in certain cases of delirium; moreover, it lies at the very foundation of
the human soul, behind all daydreams—and also, it must be said, it
is the commonest motive-force behind human action.

I shall endeavour later to show the part played by these first tendencies
in the neurotic.

It is only round about the third or fourth year of life that we can
properly speak of ambivalance. At this period the child exteriorises
its first libidinous impulses, naturally directing them towards its
parents. Here we have the typical schema of the Oedipus adventure,
whose importance can no longer be doubted, and whose solution can
be decisive for the individual. This ambivalence manifests itself in
an exclusive love for the mother (in the boy), with feelings of hostility
and jealousy towards the father. This is the theoretic schema: in
actuality, emotional reactions of much greater complexity arise.

But these first manifestations of ambivalence find themselves opposed
by the reactions of the parents, and the first manifestations of moral
consciousness appear—in particular, the first feelings of guilt, which
are bound up with the satisfaction of these impulses.

We here find ourselves face to face with another aspect of the problem
of impulses, not from the point of view of their integration into psychic
life, but as so many tendencies to be satisfied, standing in opposition
to the first elements of moral prohibition—i.e. the problem of the
impulses experienced as feelings, as emotions.

Whether this primitive moral force (the " super-ego " of the psycho-
analyst) is considered as an introjection of the first parental prohibitions,
or whether there is held to be some kind of hereditary super-ego as
well, any development of the theoretical side of this question lays itself
open to a good deal of speculation and criticism. But the important
point to remember is that this first moral consciousness is in its essence
absolutely different from that of the adult. It obeys, in fact, the very
laws of regressive psychic life that were briefly sketched above.

Piaget has shown clearly that one can speak of the existence of a
moral realism in the child—i.e., the child considers moral laws to
be absolutes, like words. Just as there is no distinction between the
ego and the non-ego, subjective and objective, in the same way moral
duties exist by themselves and impose themselves obligatorily. The
child only admits an automatic kind of justice in which the sanction
is in keeping with the action, and takes the form of expiation, effacing

the actual misdeed by the efficacy of pain. The law of retaliation is the rule. " At this stage," says Baudouin, " we can speak of a primitive super-ego and say that already we can see—as later we see it persist-ing in the adult unconsciousness—the collective unconscious wholly existent in the psyche, primitive humanity coming to life under our very eyes."

The fate of the impulses is therefore bound up with the problem of adaptation, the demands of the environment, and the first moral consciousness. It has already become a social problem. This means that the function of the moral force will be to hold in check the asocial side of these primitive impulses.

Repression (a normal mechanism and by no means pathological, as is often mistakenly said) will therefore mean neutralising the erotic impulses when they are directed towards objects and aims prohibited by the group and the collective consciousness (incest, perversions, etc.), and the aggressive impulses in the form in which they are most dangerous to civilised society—sadism. " This last," says Odier, in his recent magnificent book,[1] " is the supreme revenge of civilised man against civilisation ". Or in its inverted form of masochism: we can see in the psycho-pathological clinic how this strange destructive activity turns against the individual—suggesting the theory of death-impulses which we have already discussed.

Here it must be said again that in the problem of the normal existence of the individual, as in the problems of the collectivity and civilization generally, the most dangerous element does not arise from the erotic impulses, but mainly from sadism, from the aggressive impulses. It is in the intensity of this unrepressed or incompletely repressed sadism, invested with the feeling of magical omnipotence, that the mystery of most neuroses lies, and it is perhaps in the persistence of these factors in man at a certain degree of intensity that the whole drama and future of civilisation are to be found. We are here, obviously, very far from agreeing with those somewhat old-fashioned critics who insist on bringing against analytical science the charge of a kind of pan-sexualism.

However that may be, the problem of ambivalence arises from the fact that the two forbidden impulses are henceforth intimately con-nected by a common link, the feeling of guilt, and thus erotic and sado-masochistic impulses are joined together—in a sketchy state in the so-called normal person and in their fullest intensity in the pervert.

There is no need to attempt to trace here the main lines of the development of the personality, the progressive movement from a

---

[1] Charles Odier, *Les deux sources, consciente et inconsciente, de la vie morale,* in the series " Cahiers de Philosophie ", Neufchâtel, Editions de la Baconnière.

pre-logical mentality to the rationality of adult psychic life, from the primitive moral consciousness to that of the grown-up.

We shall simply say that the solution of the problem of impulses— or rather, of the problem of the fate of the impulses—lies in the successful repression of their amoral and asocial parts and, with the progressive development of the ego, in the full consent of the individual to the renunciation of the satisfaction of these impulses. This seems to be in agreement with what Allers, in a remarkable work, has described as the sacrificial finality of instinct.

Again, the ascending evolution of the person will mean the fullest possible abandonment of the narcissistic power with which these impulses have been invested, and consequently the increasing import- ance of oblativity, the gift of self.

It is only through the possibility of a libido exteriorized to the maximum that the displacement of libidinous energies, and above all sublimation, can take place.

If we assume the hypothesis of an instinctual dualism (Eros and Thanatos) between life-impulses and death-impulses, we then see that everything that comes under the general heading of affectivity will correspond to the life-impulses, and our working hypothesis is that this impulse-energy constitutes the motive-force of human activity. Confirmation of this point of view is to be found in numerous authors. We have already shown that it forms the essence of Ribot's and Janet's ideas. Other psychologists such as MacDougall express themselves in identical terms. " Directly or indirectly," says the latter, " the instincts are the first motive-forces of human activity: it is through the conative force of certain instincts that any thought-sequence, however cold and passionless it may be, is impelled towards its end, and that any corporal activity is sustained." Affectivity, in its positive value, is to be found at the basis of every psychic and organic activity, and in the field of speculative thought, no matter how abstract.

I am in full agreement with Pichon when he says: " Knowledge is not something passive; on the contrary, the linguistic genetics of logic and psychoanalysis agree in teaching that it is an active effort of libido."

If, then, we look upon affectivity as the positive value (representing the life-impulse), is there any opposite condition in which the negative value appears isolated in any way?

It seems relevant here to refer to a work of Heidegger's. After showing that it is an affective tonality that puts us in the presence of the existent as a whole, Heidegger asks whether there may not be another tonality which can put us in the presence of the void, and he comes to the con- clusion that this is realised in anxiety, which, he says, reveals the void.

There is no need here to follow Heidegger through all his metaphysical speculations, but we can ask whether the word " void " may not perhaps be replaced by the "feeling of death". Anxiety çould then be looked upon as an inhibition of the positive values of libido and as the appearance in the foreground of the negative values, those hypothetical death-impulses which according to Freud develop secretly.

These ideas are, of course, absolutely theoretical: they raise another problem, the problem of anxiety. For what it is worth, I have found in my clinical treatment of certain patients a remarkable confirmation of Heidegger's theory.

THE THEORY OF NEUROSES: AMBIVALENCE IN NEUROSIS

Though the psychic personality develops by achieving integrations of a more and more complex kind, it does not necessarily follow that at each new stage the previous stage is reduced to nought. Psychic activity must not be reduced to the field of consciousness only: it is necessary to envisage the reality of unconscious forces. The unconscious is not inactive or merely residual in character, nor again is it necessarily pathological; on the contrary, as has been clearly shown by Baudouin, the unconscious is synonymous with activity.

But the characteristic thing about this activity is that it appears as a closed system, in this being diametrically opposed to the creative activity of the conscious ego, which is capable of being enriched and acquiring new values. Similarly in the field of morals one has to take account of an unconscious morality (the super-ego) which, as Odier has shown, constitutes a closed system, whilst the moral consciousness of the evolving ego represents a system open to the world of values.

But it would be inaccurate to maintain that this archaic unconscious morality merely represents something pathological as, according to his great work, Dalbiez seems to think.

The human personality is in truth in a perpetual state of becoming; it is a system in which the finest acquisitions, those which have reached furthest into the world of intellectual values, are the most fragile and the most susceptible to inhibitions and regressions. The laws of psycho-dynamism are closely connected with the principles formulated by Jackson, and may be summed up in this general law enunciated by Kretschmer: When at the very centre of the psycho-motivating field of expression a superior force suffers a functional weakening, the force immediately below it recovers its independence and begins to function according to its own fundamental laws.

The model of this rhythmical, regressive dissolution is found, devoid of all pathological features, in dreams. When for a moment conscious psychic life becomes inhibited, we see the resurgence of a whole form of thought obeying definite psychological laws that reproduce in their main lines the laws of thought of the child or the primitive. Similarly, in the moral field we discover the same archaism.

It can be asserted that human psychic life contains a considerable amount of activity in a potential state, the normal ideal being that in which, during waking hours, the lower activities do not come into action. It is hardly necessary to point out that this ideal is a pure abstraction and that if the neurotic represents the typical schema of a dualism between conscious and unconscious activities, the difference is frequently only one of degree between the neurotic, the " nervous " person in the ordinary meaning of the word, and the genuine normal type.

It now becomes necessary to discuss the manifestations of ambivalence in their relationship with unconscious psychic life and consciousness.

The study of neuroses supplies us with an immense field of psychological exploration and it is here that they can be most easily grasped and understood in all their importance.

People often speak about neuroses without giving any precise definition of the word, and indeed it eludes definition. For neuroses are not morbid entities but reactional functions in which variable factors of an impulsive, moral or social kind appear, under certain conditions, in a naturally fragile constitution. Neuroses must therefore be studied from the anthropological point of view.

If we attempt to give an approximate definition of neurosis, and indeed of normality, we immediately find ourselves faced with the problem of adaptation and its success or failure.

As one stage succeeds another in the course of the progressive adaptation which we have already described, the ego may be said to be constantly finding itself faced with vital problems which it must resolve, situations which it must dominate and which, when this is successfully performed, are experienced by the ego as successful, and thus mark a stage in its enrichment. On the other hand, when there is failure these situations are experienced by the ego as catastrophic, to use Goldstein's word, and they give rise to anxiety.

Briefly, it can be said that the dangers which the ego may come up against in the course of its adaptation are, on the one hand, of an external kind, bound up with forbidden impulses (it being felt that there is something dangerous in satisfying them—hence the fear of a threat or punishment) and, on the other hand, moral (introjection of external prohibitions). The normal is ideally that which best effects this work of adaptation, whose main lines I have already indicated.

It seems that an alarm signal may be utilised by the ego to put it on the alert against any danger that may threaten it. This biological reaction manifests itself as anxiety. And in the normal person anxiety is limited to the perception of an external danger; it is a kind of necessary safe-guard. But (and here we have the essential point about neurosis) if in the course of his development—and especially during the period of infancy, when the problem of adaptation is at its most delicate, the infantile ego still being fairly fragmentary—the individual lives through situations which are felt to be dangerous—catastrophic situations, as Goldstein calls them—the infantile ego will not be able to get beyond this stage and will remain, from the affective point of view, fixed there.

Later, this anxiogenous situation will be interiorized, but it will maintain its energy-potential in the unconscious, and every vital situation that comes afterwards will cause it to vibrate in harmony with the original situation, will be invested with the repressed energy and, in certain conditions, will reactivate the original situation. That is why, when we are faced with the neurotic, we find ourselves in the presence of a whole series of anachronistic reactive formations deriving from the primitive mental stage to which I have already alluded; in a word, obeying the regressive psychological mechanisms of the unconscious, and hence inaccessible to, and irreducible by, the will and rational logic.

To return to the question of ambivalence. I have tried to show that the two main groups of life-impulses and death-impulses each have a double aspect; one, the more primitive, is amoral and asocial and con-sequently should submit to repression, the other (as far as the life-instinct is concerned) being that of libido—the desexualised Eros, as it might be called. The integration of this impulse into non-sexual aims is essential for the human being. But whilst the erotic impulses as a whole are remarkable for their plasticity, their faculty for displace-ment and sublimation, the same thing is not true of the aggressive impulses. One may certainly speak of these tendencies being diverted to social objects or to the affirmation of self (ambition, competitions of a sporting or intellectual kind, for example), but the problem of aggressiveness is in fact more complicated than this, for it is directly related to the problems of adaptation and anxiety, as I shall show later.

The chief characteristic of neurosis is the failure of repression, and since, as a result of regression, we find in the neurotic a reactivation of the whole of his infantile psychic life, we can more easily study the reactions of ambivalence in him, for we find them nearer to their impulsional origin, in a more naked state.

But the chief point seems to be that regression takes place at all levels of psychic life and consequently reactivates in the unconscious the magical omnipotence of thought which is bound up with the badly-repressed impulses. This gives us the key to the patient's behaviour, which is in fact the subjection of a conscious personality to an inner demon.

The neurotic appears as a person incapable of oblativity, objectal love, unable to renounce narcissistic satisfactions. Just as, in its early years, the child imagines itself to be the centre of the world, so the neurotic (in his unconscious activity) experiences phantasms of power and domination, allied to the aggressive impulses, which develop to the maximum extent. The idea of complexes has undoubtedly been greatly misused in our day, and it is therefore with some trepidation that I venture to suggest that there may be a veritable " Lucifer complex " in the neurotic's unconscious, and even, perhaps, to some extent, in the unconscious of every human being.

Freud suggested a theory of the highest value when he pointed out that in neurotics, and particularly in the very frequent cases of obsessional neurosis, one finds oneself in the presence of an absolute separation of impulses (*Triebentmischung*). This means to say that there is no saturation of the negative values by the positive ones, each value appearing in isolation. This, of course, is simply an analogy between psychic dynamism and the laws of chemistry, and consequently its value is only metaphorical.

The classical example is supplied by what is known as obsession by contrast. As soon as any individual suffering from this obsession has a certain idea or thought, with a certain positive value (direct or transposed libido) he is immediately assailed, despite himself, with an opposite thought of a sadistic character. This is a constant fact, and I for my part have never come across any patients who have not shown signs of this morbid kind of behaviour.

For instance, a person may wish to go into a church or say his prayers; immediately every word, every thought is deformed, associated with images that are not only highly sadistic but often of the filthiest character. This causes him to feel guilt and incessant remorse, and an obsessive compulsion to keep on praying until his guilty thoughts disappear. Obviously, this conflict has no end, for we have here two different levels of the psychic life : the sadistic image is simply the emergence into the field of consciousness of badly repressed aggressive impulses.

Another manifestation of ambivalence appears in the psychic mechanism known as simultaneity. This is characterised by the fact that any thought connected with a particular emotional condition is immediately annulled by a thought of the opposite kind. This annulment can develop to extreme lengths, until it causes a complete loss of

Heidegger's " emotional tonality " and brings the individual face to face with the total anguish of the void. We also find ambivalence in the familiar mechanism of the taboo. The individual projects a magical value on to some external object, this value being at once sacred and prohibitive. This is the typical ambivalence behind primitive taboos.

There is no space here for further discussion of these questions, whose further development belongs to the sphere of psychiatry.

Nevertheless, I should like to draw attention to the puzzling behaviour of many neurotics, which raises more directly the question of the theory of death-impulses.

I often find in treating serious cases of neurosis, in which the individual suffers cruelly, that the symptoms disappear as though by magic when an organic affection intervenes.

In one case I know of, the obsession that tortured the patient consisted in an ever-renewed impulse to kill somebody (to throw somebody under a train, and so on). This person lived in a state of constant anxiety at the thought that his watch over himself might relax. Then, as a result of a change of conditions, all these various homicidal obsessions disappeared, and the patient immediately became a victim of an obsessive preoccupation with himself, and lived perpetually haunted by the fear of death. In this case there was simply a displacement, a return of sadism upon the individual himself.

In more complex cases that I have observed patients have been subject to an increasing tendency to commit suicide, and from my observation of them after they have attempted this, and incurred serious bodily harm, I have found that instead of suffering from these self-inflicted wounds—which should have seriously affected them—they lived in a state of radiant happiness.

It is true that many different theories and arguments can be built up on such cases: all I wish to do here is to emphasise the fact that the problem of the aggressive instinct behind the primary death-impulses remains highly mysterious.

One last word about neuroses. Our subject is ambivalence, and this assumes a certain equilibrium between contrary impulses; it would be more correct, however, to speak of one impulse's prevailing over another in the case of the aggressive impulses.

The fact is that the more such patients are analysed, the more striking becomes the almost total absence of true libido, of any warm feeling of affection or enthusiasm. And this is usually camouflaged by an attitude of the most uncompromising virtue. I could give many examples of this.

I remember a case of obsession which I followed in collaboration with Professor Lhermitte, whose competence in these matters is well

known; the person concerned said something which is logical enough
from the analytical point of view, but no less frightening for all that:
" I don't understand what is meant by this word ' love ': it's a word
without any meaning for me." It would need many pages to show the
kind of emotional void in which this person lived; and yet he was all
the time obsessed with religious ceremonies, especially praying, which
he did endlessly, the theme of the Last Judgment being uppermost in
his mind. Weeks in which plenary indulgences could be gained were
a matter of the utmost importance to him, for he used to calculate with
mathematical precision how many days in purgatory he would have
remitted for them; but unfortunately all the prayers that he said with
this intention were always being annulled by images of impurity.

It would have been vain to look for the slightest genuine movement
towards God in all this apparent piety: he had never felt any such thing.
It was necessary to say all these prayers like a Tibetan Lama: that was
the important thing. God was simply the introjection of an abstract
punitive power.

In the same way, women were by definition impure creatures to be
avoided, and also hated. It was strange to see how, indirectly, his
sadism exteriorised itself so triumphantly. For he knew by heart,
and in the utmost detail, all the torments undergone by the Christian
martyrs, and could describe with endless satisfaction all the most
refined kinds of torture, particularly those that had been directed against
women. It will not be surprising if we add that he went regularly to
Confession and Communion, apparently in all good faith.

One of the components of his narcissism that had remained intact
was rather peculiar. He had had made for himself and for a certain
number of his relatives a burial place of cement, strong enough to
resist anything; " for," he said, " it is essential for my bones not to be
moved out of position, for how would they be able to be found all
together on Judgment Day if they were mixed up with others? "

There is no point in giving any further examples; I have simply aimed
at showing briefly how ambivalence manifests itself in neurosis, camouflaged behind the symptoms but always recognizable, and remarkable
for the intensity of its expression.

The treatment of neurosis derives directly from the idea of ambivalence. We have already said that the neurotic is absolutely incapable
of oblativity, objectal love, and that in him repressed aggressiveness
stifles love. The chief directives given by psychoanalysis involve
mainly the following operations: liquidating the charges of repressed
aggressiveness (hence the importance of transference); making the
individual capable of love by liberating him from the guilt attached to
all the libido impulses; substituting a rational adult moral consciousness

for an archaic moral one (unconscious super-ego); helping him to renounce narcissistic satisfactions; and increasing his capacity for objectal love. Such, briefly condensed, are the aims of psychotherapeutic medicine. It is immediately apparent that the part played by the doctor involves, willy-nilly, a certain moral attitude.

Acceptance and renunciation are the key to normal emotional development, as Pichon has justly pointed out.

This means that the object of the treatment of neuroses is to go back behind the individual's psycho-emotional development, and then, on the basis of acceptance and renunciation, enable him to develop it anew.

There is one point, to which the study of neuroses draws attention, which is of the utmost importance in the future of the individual. It concerns the relationship between anxiety and the aggressive impulses.

I have already dealt at length with the adaptation-processes which necessitate from the individual the abandonment of the pleasure-principle and submission to the reality-principle. These first stages already contain the possibility of psychic conflict, the child reacting aggressively against the constraints imposed upon him either by the external world (parents, teachers) or by his first moral consciousness, which seems to be the introjection of external prohibitions.

But as this aggressiveness cannot exteriorize itself, because it would mean the threat of danger, it is repressed by means of anxiety, which thus acts as a kind of safeguard. Such repression does not mean liquidation; on the contrary. By following this schema one would arrive at an inter-reaction of anxiety and aggressiveness, one conditioning the other and vice versa.

When in fact we find ourselves faced with the great adult syndromes in which anxiety is predominant—in phobias, for example—we get some idea of the enormous importance of potential aggressiveness.

One seems to be faced with a vicious circle, the child's education necessarily involving submission to constraint or moral obligation. Nevertheless, it is only here that renunciation and acceptance, which go hand-in-hand with love with all its oblativity, can and should operate to the maximum.

It can therefore be said that one of the criteria of health, of moral and physiological equilbrium, lies in the quantitative connection between these two antagonistic impulses.

A REPLY TO SOME CRITICISMS

The preceding observations will enable us to discuss briefly some of the passages in the remarkable studies by Thibon and Allers which appeared in the April 1936 volume of *Études Carmélitaines* (*Psychologie et Mystique de l'Amour*). These highly instructive essays, which deal to a great extent with the subject with which we are concerned here, include a number of severe criticisms of Freud's psychology which do not seem to be entirely justified. Thibon's work, for instance, gives the impression that he is dominated by value-judgments which tend to interfere with the objectivity of his criticism.

Let us take a few sentences by way of example. " Freudianism dethrones man and slanders the spirit . . . Freud's explanation of sublimation has a vulgar character, based on a mere system of economy."

Like many other critics Thibon imagines that psycho-analysis is an explanation or reduction of the higher by means of the lower. Many writers have already refuted this way of regarding it—for example Baudouin (*Découverte de la Personne*, Alcan): " It must be said again that though psychology discloses relationships between higher phenomena and primitive phenomena, it never pretends to reduce the former to the latter, nor to lump the two together. The reader must familiarize himself with the continuity which the idea of the unconscious enables us to realise in psychology, but he must not take it to mean identification . . ." and later: " It will never mean reducing one thing to another, art to sexuality, love to instinct, the person to the individual, but seeing the continuity between these things."

I, for my part, have aimed to show throughout this essay that impulses never explain any psychic phenomena or any of the humblest or most elevated feelings in art or religion, but constitute their motivating form, their energy, and give them their efficiency-capacity.

With these reservations we can fully subscribe to Thibon's conclusions, particularly his explanation of the psychological phenomenon of sublimation (although he dislikes the word itself). I fully agree with him that sublimation takes place with the co-operation of instinct and not by means of instinct.

As regards Allers's conclusions, these seem to call for a number of reservations. Allers says that instinct is an abstraction, and on the basis of this principle he consigns to oblivion all psychological systems that derive from the idea of instinct. When he says that psychoanalysis depends on results ascertained by biology, he misrepresents Freud's thought, for Freud showed that biology has no criterion or absolute certitude, and we have already emphasised the hypothetical element in Freudian theory, which Freud himself admitted was to be found in his work. Allers goes on to insist that the idea of instinct cannot be applied to every manifestation of love (the love of nature, of country, of God, etc.). In this he seems to misunderstand Freud's most important work, for what Freud saw in impulses was Eros, everything that can be included in the idea of libido. I have already discussed this point.

A few pages further on Allers mentions conflict and neurosis and states that in the Freudian scheme the repression of instincts is looked upon as the sole cause of neurosis. But Freud always maintained that the cause of neuroses was not repression, but on the contrary the failure of repression. Again, in his account of neurosis, Allers speaks of conflicts between instincts, whereas we speak of conflicts between impulses and the super-ego (the primitive moral consciousness).

There are some splendid pages in which Allers shows how the neurotic is in a state of inner revolt against his destiny, because he has failed to accept the human condition. " For thousands of years Satan's words have gone on echoing in the deepest recesses of our ego: *eritis sicut Dei.*"

There could be no more eloquent or exact description of the behaviour of the neurotic on the level of psychic regression and at the stage of the magical power of thought, when an all-powerful domination is associated with the primary aggressive impulses.

With these reservations we can say that the above-mentioned studies by Allers and Thibon shed valuable light on the problem with which we are concerned, the relationship between love and aggression.

AMBIVALENCE IN NORMAL PSYCHOLOGY

A study of ambivalence in present-day psychology offers considerable analogies with what I have said about neuroses. Where is the exact line to be drawn between the neurotic, the nervous and the normal? For instance, when somebody is always washing himself we say that he has a " mania " for cleanliness; a more extreme case of the same thing we should describe as an obsession. The same laws of psychic life apply throughout the whole of psychology. As Kretschmer used to say, the psychology of neuroses is the same as human psychology in general.

I shall here do no more than give a brief explanation of the conditions in which ambivalence appears in normal psychology.

In a rough and ready way, we can distinguish three aspects of any individual's behaviour. The first includes all the acts or thoughts or behaviour-attitudes in which one of the values is conscious and the other unconscious. Typical of this are all those lapses of memory and oversights which are so common in everybody's everyday life. For a more complete description of these I recommend the excellent account given by Dalbiez in his well-known work on the subject.

By way of example we may mention one young man who seemed greatly inhibited in his behaviour and who learned of the death of one of his professors, a man for whom he had a special liking and esteem. During a conversation which I had with him about the dead man before the burial service, he said to me: " I must leave you and go and congratulate the family ". Confirmation of his unconscious aggressiveness came later when I was able to reveal to the young man the aggressiveness that lay hidden within him against this professor and against the whole system of authority which he embodied. The same ambivalence was present in his religious attitude.

In the second group ambivalence is latent, and the individual remains ignorant of it as far as its instinctive emotional root is concerned: in reality it forms an integral part of the individual's character.

To show what I mean I will assume two opposite cases, in each of which one of the impulsive poles is dominant. I can imagine, for instance, the type of individual who can be described as having enthusiasm, zest for life, a creative spirit. At the other extreme we have the sceptical negative type of person who possesses the critical faculty to a maximum degree.

The first type manifests the activity and predominance of all the libido impulses, the Platonic Eros. In the Gospels it is said that faith can remove mountains. But faith is an act of love, and it is this creative dynamism which makes the individual capable of the most sublime flights of thought, spiritual creation and spiritual acquisition.

The second attitude corresponds theoretically to the predominance of the aggressive impulses, absolute criticism and negativism being the work of death and destruction.

Of course this is only an abstraction, and I certainly have no wish to seem to reduce the critical spirit founded on logic and reason to the level of a destructive instinct.

We often meet a type of person in whom ambivalence can be discerned in its pure state, in an endless alternation between these two impulsive tendencies. This kind of person has a " mania " for doubts and scruples. Freud has shown with the utmost clarity the ambivalent emotional root of this kind of psychological behaviour—which seems objectively to be devoid of any emotionality, evolving in the sphere of logic and the most abstract reasoning.

In the third group we find all the attitudes or kinds of behaviour in which ambivalence is conscious in both its opposed terms. I mean those emotional states which have been described at such length throughout literature, the transformation of love into hatred. Is this a case of a reversal of impulse, a mere change of sign? For my part I do not think so: I believe that the highest love, in the absolute sense of the word, must correspond to a maximum of oblativity, a total gift of self to the object, and an absolute condition of this is the renunciation of every kind of narcissistic satisfaction. Love of this kind is incapable of any reversal.

But this sublime kind of love is very rarely met with: only in the behaviour of the great mystics do we find any suggestion of such absolute perfection.

On the less lofty level of everyday life, passionate love is always associated to some extent or other with certain narcissistic components, and it is the privation of these satisfactions that causes the appearance of aggressiveness. This is due to the perseverance of an infantile mechanism: a child, who is capable of renunciation on only a small scale, reacts to any privation by bad temper.

A human psychology must take full account of the importance of the first inclinations that appear in childhood: in this connection we may mention Montaigne's remark in his book *On Custom*: " I have found that our greatest vices receive their character in our earliest days, and that our chief government lies in the hands of our nursemaids."

I shall not proceed any further in my study of ambivalence— otherwise I should need to review the whole field of psychology; instead, I shall end this paragraph with a quotation from Baudouin which expresses my point of view perfectly: " One has to descend into the region of the instincts to understand anything about the psychology of opposites. There are no real opposites in the object, they only exist in ourselves in the form of reversible dual tendencies, tendencies demanding action, movements going in two opposite directions. This is basic to any understanding of the ambivalence of feelings and even for an understanding of association by contrast. This latter does not explain the reversal of tendencies; it is on the contrary an expression of this on the level of images."

AMBIVALENCE IN THE COLLECTIVE UNCONSCIOUS

I have discussed ambivalence as it appears in the behaviour of primitives and in the structure of the child's psychic life, and tried to show that it lies at the root of psychic life in general. My hypothesis is supported by the conclusions reached by Jung in his recent books. Jung gives the name of archetypes to original images existing in the unconscious (" genuine innate complexes," he calls them) but these images are not merely virtual; they are centres charged with energy and as such able to cause fundamental modifications in human life. In his description of this in terms of *animus* and *anima* there is a double polarisation which could be interpreted as a funda- mental ambivalence—on another level, it is true. According to Jung these are by no means mere abstractions but absolutely existential truths.

AMBIVALENCE IN COLLECTIVE PSYCHOLOGY

The fate of any individual, judging simply by the play of impulses and moral elements, could theoretically be reduced to one of three possibilities. First, moral censorship could succeed in repressing the impulses (on their asocial or perverse side); the energy derived from them would be devoted to the service of the ego, and thus the personality would be able to develop happily.

In the second case, as a result of various etiological factors, repression would not take place. A conflict would then be set up between impulses and moral censorship and appear in the form of symptoms: this would give rise to neurosis.

In the third case the moral censorship would be lacking: we should find ourselves faced with perversion.

It is tempting to make similar deductions in collective psychology, but here we come up against problems of still greater complexity and we must be content to note a few analogies.

The profound modifications of an individual's psychic life as a result of his being an element in a collectivity, modifications connected with a regression of the ego, have often been described—by Le Bon and Freud, for example.

The same regressive processes might possibly be discerned in the psychic life of most of the leaders of men, and this would enable one to see the element of narcissistic regression in their desire for absolute power. But this lies outside the scope of our present purpose.

In one of his books, *Civilization and its Discontents*, Freud suggests that the individual already suffers from a conflict between his longings for happiness, his " pleasure-principle ", and his desire to belong to an aggregate, a community. There is, from an early stage, an antagonism between the individual and society. The individual looks to society to satisfy this search for happiness; but contrariwise society and civilization insist on a renunciation of the instinctive impulses and erect a morality, a repressive collective censorship.

To Freud aggressiveness means a primitive, instinctive, autonomous disposition of the human mind, and civilization finds in it its most redoubtable obstacle.

This aggressive impulse, man's fundamental feeling of hostility, represents the death-instinct, which shares its dominion over the world with Eros. The meaning of the development of civilization, he says, is no longer obscure. It reveals the struggle between Eros and Death. This struggle is the essential content of life.

If it is asked, to what means can civilisation have recourse to prevent aggression, the answer is neither more nor less than the formation of a moral consciousness, a strict super-ego which manifests itself in the individual as a feeling of guilt. But then, if this feeling of guilt becomes the main problem in the development of civilization, the progress of the latter must be paid for by a loss of happiness, the consequence of the growth of this feeling. Freud ends with these lines which, though written in 1926, seem as though they might have been written today: " The fateful question of the human species seems to me to be whether and to what extent the cultural process developed in it will succeed in mastering the derangements of communal life caused by the human instinct of aggression and self-destruction. In this connection, perhaps the phase through which we are at this moment passing deserves special interest. Men have brought their powers of subduing the forces of nature to such a pitch that by using them they could now very easily exterminate one another to the last man. They know this—hence arises a great part of their current unrest, their dejection, their mood of apprehension. And now it may be expected that the other of the two ' heavenly forces ', eternal Eros, will put forth his strength so as to maintain himself alongside of his equally immortal adversary."

The problem of ambivalence thus leads to the problem of the future of civilization, which lies outside the limits of this essay and could only be properly discussed in a much wider perspective. I shall confine myself here to a few remarks prompted by the play of the two antagonistic impulses which have formed the subject of the present essay.

I have mentioned the directives suggested by psychotherapists in the treatment of neuroses—saturation of the negative values by the positive values and the dominance of the libido impulses; the search for oblativity and the renunciation of narcissistic satisfactions; the utilization of sublimation; the disappearance of the feeling of guilt that is bound up with a false, neurotic, moral consciousness.

Can such data be transposed into the field of collective psychology?

Libido impulses can be polarised either round an individual or round a group. Can this individual or group, whose job is to ensure the maximum amount of happiness to the collectivity, justify the hope placed in it? What means has it at its disposal? For a discussion of this subject we refer readers to the authoritative work by Professor de Greeff: " Drame humain et mystiques humaines " (Études Carmélitaines, 1937). But, in the first place, the submission of the individual or society to a leader or an abstraction like the anonymous State raises the question of the restraint and reinforcement of aggressiveness.

In the second place the relationship between the leader and the collectivity which he controls, and vice versa, involves a certain regression—the successive reactions are no longer, or only partially, submitted to the laws of reason.

Is it possible to speak of sublimation in collective psychology? The truth is that what we most often see is a diversion of the aggressive currents on to certain specific objects. If this is so, then the art of politics consists in a tactful displacement of collective emotions that are in a state of tension; but this is a very different thing from a process of sublimation.

There are some people who find a solution of this problem in scientific mysticism. In my opinion there is no mysticism in science. Freud, it will be remembered, refused to find any hope for the happiness of mankind in science. He did not make the mistake of confusing science with its applications, which are subject to the emotional reactions of the people who make use of them.

It may be objected here that the question of happiness has nothing to do with impulses, but the fact is that, in the case of the neurotic, who forms the permanent subject of our research and therapy, we find the cure indissolubly bound up with happiness.

This leads me to remark—now that I have emphasized the decisive importance of the individual's spiritual ascension, his capacity for renunciation and acceptance and for *aimance* (in the most oblative sense of the word), which condition his feeling of happiness, his joy in living in the highest sense of the word—that these very mechanisms will play an important part in the future destiny of the collectivity; and in these conditions it may be said—as a matter of strictly objective fact and in accordance with the main ideas outlined in this essay—that the Christian ideal remains the only possible solution of the problem of the destiny of man.

I shall leave it to others better qualified to discuss this crucial question—but I believe that in the main the ideas presented here will be found to agree with those to be found in the remarkable essay by Professor Lhermitte in which he describes the classical theory of instincts.

THE RÔLE OF THE PRIEST AND THE DOCTOR: CONCLUSION

Finally, I should like to draw attention to two points which concern both the doctor and the priest as directors of souls. The first concerns the connection between anxiety, guilt and aggression. There is no need to discuss here the comparative value of leniency and strictness in educational methods, but I should like to emphasize the following point: in the vast majority of cases of serious neurosis that I have seen, I find myself faced with people who have transferred to religion a

THE CRUCIFIXION
Antonello da Messina: Antwerp Museum

THE CRUCIFIXION

restraint and fear which have generated more hatred than can easily be described. In other words, for these people God has become a threatening figure, always ready to punish. This neurotic attitude, which represents the exact opposite of true religion, can be aggravated or reinforced by too strict and absolute an attitude on the part of directors of conscience.

If the patient, faced with a growing feeling of guilt, has no other resource except one that accentuates his neurosis, he may be tempted to reject all constraint, and then his aggressiveness breaks through his defences with an iconoclastic rage that knows no bounds.

My final point concerns the joint action of psychotherapist, doctor and priest. The fact is that the problem of neuroses and their cure can no longer be considered from any other point of view than that of general anthropology. The doctor who attacks the therapeutic problem becomes a spiritual doctor whether he likes it or not: neurosis, illness, moral guilt and sinfulness form one whole. Similarly, the priest, whose spiritual activity may resolve the individual's moral conflicts, will often find that his action goes beyond the limits of psychic life and helps to cure disturbances and morbid symptoms appearing on the bodily level.

This means inevitably that we must abandon the old idea of a separation between mind and body and consider the existent in its totality; and this—apart from any metaphysical speculations—means maintaining, as far as the doctor is concerned, a purely empiricist position.

THE DYNAMISM OF LOVE

Père Lucien-Marie de St.-Joseph, O.C.D.

IS LOVE the contemplative's concern, and aggressiveness more characteristic of the active type, so that there is an absolute antinomy between the two things? If this were so, then love would be essentially the sign of a somewhat feminine, rather weak nature, of the kind that tends to wait in silence for the outpouring of the intimate life of God; whereas the quality that would reveal a strong masculine nature would be the aggressive power of a being always in movement, impatient for new achievements in the practical order. The first would point to the Magdalene in the perfect silence of her abandonment to the divine love—though she is not represented in the Gospel as being always at Our Lord's feet—the second to St. Paul, even though St. Paul's own writings do not manifest an unqualified adherence to this point of view.

If this were the case, it would be easy to understand the impression gained from a hasty reading of the works of St. John of the Cross which was summed up in the following disillusioned remark, " When you get to the bottom of them, they're all about love "—the implication being that the gentleman in question was anxious to get on with the apostolic business and had found very little in the way of principles for immediate all-conquering action in the *Ascent* and the *Dark Night*.

But perhaps there was a bit too much simplification in such an outlook. The kind of antithesis that can easily be stated in an extreme form on the plane of natural psychology may not be quite valid on the level of supernatural reality with which St. John of the Cross is concerned; the truth may lie rather in a living synthesis, in which love is the fountain-head of a dynamic force, whose capacity for achievement is endless. The results reached by objective inquiry (by Bergson, for example) confirm the apparently theoretical data supplied by St. John of the Cross (the fact is that St. John of the Cross advances no ideas except those founded on experience: it is thus not surprising that his teaching coincides with that of modern philosophers).

On this point, as on many others, there are to be found in the works of St. John of the Cross materials for a synthesis as yet unmade, whose immediate consequences would be extremely important for the direction of souls.

We must not succumb to the temptation to make pure speculation out of the writings of one who was above all things a practitioner. We must respect his method. Since the object of his inquiry is always the progress of the soul towards God—spiritual movement—it will suffice to turn quite objectively to the passages in which he shows the development of love in the soul, and we shall not be surprised to find at the end of this development such a living union between love and triumphant activity that not even the greatest of the Apostles ever imagined anything finer.

I

" To attain to the Divine light of the perfect union of the love of God ":[1] such is the ambition by which, from the very first lines of the Prologue to the *Ascent of Mount Carmel*, St. John of the Cross assumes his reader to be animated. This is sufficient to put him into the category of an exotic plant—in plain terms, he is considered to write only for people who have leisure enough to think about other things besides immediate action. But as soon as you look into the matter, you find that he writes " for all alike ". And when he reaches one of the climaxes of his teaching he declares, in words which seem to suggest a sort of grim resolution to silence those who would discourage us from ideals: " and since it is very necessary, not only for those souls that achieve prosperity, but also for all the rest who seek their Beloved . . ."[2]—which very neatly describes the state of every Christian on earth in his pilgrimage heavenwards.

The splendour of the ultimate end to which he aims to lead the soul that confides itself to his care he describes with a passion that is intended, no doubt, to inspire the requisite amount of enthusiasm in the heart of his disciple, but also to reduce to silence the critics who can easily be sensed lurking in the background: "And there is no need to wonder that the soul should be capable of aught so high; for since God grants her the favour of being deiform and united in the Most Holy Trinity, how is it a thing incredible that she should perform her work of understanding, knowledge and love in the Trinity, together with It, like the Trinity Itself, by a mode of participation, which God effects in the soul herself? "[3]

[1] All references to the works of St. John of the Cross are taken from *The Complete Works of St. John of the Cross*, translated and edited by E. Allison Peers, Burns, Oates & Washbourne.
[2] *The Living Flame of Love*, stanza iii: vol. iii, p. 74. (Hereinafter referred to as *Living Flame*.)
[3] *Spiritual Canticle*, stanza xxxviii: vol. ii, p. 176.

Only lack of faith could make us hesitate: "And there is no reason for marvelling . . . if we consider that He bestows them [favours] as God, with infinite love and goodness."[1]

When God bends over one of His creatures, and the latter gives its full consent, who can prevent Him from taking entire control of it and transforming it and making it a shining witness to His love on earth?

The truth is—but we are not sufficiently acquainted with it—that before such heights we are simply children, very small children. To try to insist on reaching the end by ourselves means behaving like any obstinate little brat that tries to walk on its own when its mother wants to take it up in her arms: it hardly makes any progress at all, and nullifies its mother's love.[2] Let us have no illusions about it— by ourselves we shall never be able to travel along this road as we should, " howsoever good thou mayest be as a walker ".[3]

Here we have a metaphorical but nevertheless a quite clear description of the powerlessness of even the finest human virtues. Loving union with God is the kind of end that demands, even more than reason enlightened by faith, a different motive-force from the human will, no matter how supernatural the virtues by which it is aided, a different " style " of relationship with both God and man.

Unless we are content, then, to relapse—like more than one of St. John of the Cross's contemporaries—into a disillusioned scepticism that may be of inestimable danger to souls, we are obliged to have recourse to something better than human goodwill, even when this is enriched by the supernatural virtues. God must " take thy hand and guide thee in the darkness, as though thou wert blind ".[4] And since we shall never succeed " completely—very far from it " in out-growing this childishness,[5] obviously the Holy Spirit Himself will have to intervene directly, to get rid of our puerile way of judging and thinking of God,[6] to strip our will of its old affections and its human predilections, its mean way of loving, " the soul being clothed with a new supernatural attitude according to all its faculties ".[7]

This is a necessary intervention, but it is not by any means due to the supernatural resources of a few initiates or (and it is a perpetual temptation to think this) souls with enough leisure to think about other things besides immediate action. The gifts of the Holy Spirit

[1] *Living Flame,* prologue: vol. iii, p. 16.
[2] *Ascent of Mount Carmel,* prologue. (Hereinafter referred to as *Ascent.*)
[3] *The Dark Night of the Soul,* bk. ii, ch. xvi: vol. i, p. 451. (Hereinafter referred to as *Dark Night.*)
[4] ibid., bk. ii, ch. xvi: vol. i, p. 451.
[5] ibid., bk. i, ch. vii: vol. i, p. 370.
[6] *Ascent,* bk. ii, ch. xvii.
[7] ibid., bk. i, ch. v: vol. i, p. 33.

are to be found throughout the works of St. John of the Cross, even though he may rarely name them.[1] They constitute a supernatural power to be found in everyone who has been baptised, requisite for all here on earth and sufficient to enable anyone to attain the ideal—as set forth, for instance, in the sublime passage on the priestly prayer of Christ in St. John:[2] " Wherefore this Divine breath of the Holy Spirit is greatly to be desired, and likewise that every soul should pray that He may breathe through its garden so that the Divine odours of God may flow. And because this is so necessary, and of such great glory and good for the soul, the Bride desired it and prayed for it in the songs[3] in the same terms as here, saying: Rise up hence, north wind, and come, south-west wind, and breathe through my garden; and its fragrances and special spices shall flow."

We have said elsewhere that the entire work of St. John of the Cross is simply an account of this re-adoption by the Holy Spirit of the weak and impure creature, with the aim of transforming his doubly deficient activity and leading him to a divine manner of thinking, loving and acting. Like all true optimists the saint is not afraid of disclosing the height of the ideal to be attained and the redoubtable difficulties to be overcome. He knows that the strength on which he relies can never be exhausted. This in fact seems to be his entire theme.[4]

If we can grasp this, seeing beyond the mere material words of his treatises, beyond his particular literary and theological idiom, and beyond his imagery, which is highly characteristic of its period, we shall be able to get inside his thought and make contact with the simplicity of his original intuition.[5] One of the best ways of expressing this intuition seems to be by way of the following question: how can we summon the Spirit of God, who is all-powerful and infinitely pure, receive Him into our souls, and allow Him utterly to transform our being and our human way of behaving, with all their impurities and infirmities?[6]

[1] Jacques Maritain, *The Degrees of Knowledge*, trans. Bernard Wall and Margot R. Adamson, Geoffrey Bles, p. 442, n. 3.
[2] *Spiritual Canticle*, stanza xvii: vol. ii, p. 295.
[3] iv. 16.
[4] Jacques Maritain says: " An attentive consideration of these things proves that the basic features, the prime character of the spiritual doctrine of St. John of the Cross, belong more than all else to the practical explication of the theology of the gifts of the Holy Ghost " (*The Degrees of Knowledge*, p. 423).
[5] Bergson, *La pensée et le mouvant*, p. 137.
[6] A practical intuition, if such a self-contradictory way of putting it may be allowed: St. John of the Cross might be described as the Doctor of the science of the ways leading to God.
The best image the saint found to express this intuition was that of the log set burning by fire. This is doubtless why the *Living Flame* seems to be the

This is a problem if ever there was one! To participate in the life of God, to realise this fantastic dream of enabling a mere human to tap the infinite resources of the divine activity, putting at our poor human disposition the coefficient of the divine power, breathing into our soul the very breath of God so that we really live—and therefore act—like children of God, sharers in the divine nature! Nor does St. John of the Cross restrict himself to mere speculation; he is concerned with one thing only—to *realize* his experience, and to help all who come to him to realize it too and, each in his own way, to share it.[1]

One thing is clear and recurs again and again in different forms in the saint's writings, and that is that if we are to reach the ideal he sets before us God Himself must take control of our inner life. As soon as the first sign of the divine initiative appears, the soul is obliged to adopt a receptive attitude that is quite different from the kind of personal activity that went on before. In the human dynamism an active change of principle takes place the moment God takes hold of the soul.

This is a pity for those who imagine that perfection is gained by " the strength of the wrists ". There comes a time, or rather normally there should come a time, when " it is God Who is now working in the soul ".[2] He " is the Master and Guide of this blind soul ".[3] " God Himself feeds and refreshes the soul, without mediation, or the soul's active help."[4]

The *Spiritual Canticle*, despite its imagery, is just as emphatic in its insistence on our helplessness and the sovereign power of the

---

summary and synthesis of his whole teaching, because of the unity of this image, which lies at its very heart. The *Dark Night*—which, as regards the means to be adopted, is more fruitful in images—does not suggest quite so aptly the simplicity of the Mystical Doctor's central intuition.

[1] This determination to deal with living realities only no doubt determines his particular style as a writer. He is closely acquainted with the classical division of the gifts of the Holy Spirit and is not afraid to allude to it in more than one place (*Spiritual Canticle*, stanza xvii). But he is not concerned with any classification of essences according to their specific differences. Do the gifts of the Holy Spirit, in any case, act in us in a pure state, steadily? Or rather is it not true to say that the life of any soul normally involves a whole complex of supernatural influences in which several gifts, not to mention the virtues, act simultaneously? For this reason it seems to me to be difficult—not to say a mistake—to try to turn St. John of the Cross's slices of life into flat surfaces, the essences of speculative theology. (I refer the reader to my remarks on this point in *Études Carmélitaines*, October 1938, p. 267, n. 2.)

The saint never mentions explicitly the various gifts of the Holy Spirit, though he certainly knew the order of their classification. He was not interested in classifying them, but in exercising them . . . Is it quite certain that the Wisdom he so often mentions is exactly what is usually meant by the gift of Wisdom?

[2] *Dark Night*, bk. i, ch. ix: vol. i, p. 376.
[3] ibid., bk. ii, ch. xvi: vol. i, p. 452.
[4] ibid., bk. i, ch. xiv: vol. i, p. 394.

divine initiative. Happy is the soul who has "invoked and obtained the breeze of the Holy Spirit . . . which is the proper disposition and means for the perfection of this estate ".[1] Not only the Spirit of God " guides her in this solitude but . . . He does it alone, communicating Himself to her without other means ".[2] Why should this be surprising, since " those great and supernatural favours which God grants in this estate . . . belong not to the ability and natural working and diligence of the soul "?[3]

As for the *Living Flame*, the emphasis on the all-powerful nature of God's initiative is repeated so often that I cannot possibly quote every case. Like wood entirely penetrated by fire, " the soul can perform no acts, but it is the Holy Spirit that moves it to perform them ".[4] " God is the principal agent in this matter, and the guide of the blind self, He will take it by the hand and lead it where it could not of itself go."[5] And still more absolutely: " God is the agent, and . . . He is secretly speaking to the solitary soul while the soul keeps silence."[6] " The Holy Spirit is the principal agent and mover of souls and never loses His care of them."[7] " In every soul, in the manner that seems good to Him, He will build a supernatural building."[8]

Thus seized by the Holy Spirit, who " never loses his care "[9] for the souls He occupies, the whole attitude of the soul must be to receive what she cannot create and follow what she can only receive. On certain pages of the *Ascent* and the *Living Flame* the word " receive " occurs like an obsession. What else can the soul do, indeed, except " receive . . . that which is given to it "?[10] " Its chief care will be to see that it sets no obstacle in the way of the guide."[11] " One that receives " must be inspired by "God as one that gives",[12] and model himself on Him. But this does not take place without a great deal of preparation on the part of the soul.

For no one has taken more care to avoid the dangers of Quietism than St. John of the Cross, despite his determination to bring out the full value of the partial truth that had been revealed—and corrupted—in the teaching of the *Alumbrados*. The whole of the

---

[1] *Spiritual Canticle*, stanza xxvii: vol. ii, p. 138.
[2] ibid., stanza xxxiv: vol. ii, pp. 160–1.
[3] ibid., stanza xxxiv: vol. ii, p. 162.
[4] *Living Flame*, stanza i: vol. iii, p. 21.
[5] ibid., stanza iii: vol. iii, p. 74.
[6] ibid., stanza iii: vol. iii, p. 82.
[7] ibid., stanza iii: vol. iii, p. 82.
[8] ibid., stanza iii: vol. iii, p. 83.
[9] ibid., stanza iii: vol. iii, p. 82.
[10] *Ascent*, bk. ii, ch. xv: vol. i, p. 128.
[11] *Living Flame*, stanza iii: vol. iii, pp. 74–5.
[12] ibid., stanza iii: vol. iii, p. 76.

Ascent of Mount Carmel is simply an extended explanation of what is involved in this receptive attitude to the graces of the Holy Spirit. And God knows, the requirements are not negligible. For " the soul has within itself, through this recollection of itself and this forgetfulness as to all things, a preparedness to be moved by the Holy Spirit and taught by Him ".[1] In this sense—and superficially this seems almost to contradict the previous assertions—it is not the Beloved alone who creates the virtues in the soul but " the Beloved and I ". The nosegay is a dual achievement.[2] The heroic renunciation of all things creates in the soul a kind of solitude that becomes a positive virtue, " whereby she is now moved and guided to the Divine things of the Spirit of God."[3] Even when the soul is at its most passive under the touches of the Holy Spirit, and all its movements are divine (having the Spirit of God as their motivating power and rule), even then, " although they come from Him, they belong to the soul likewise, for God works them in the soul, with its own aid, since it gives its will and consent thereto."[4] According to the old physics a flame was simply burning air: therefore the movement and brightness of the flame belong wholly, neither to the flame nor to the air, but to both air and flame together, and it is the fire that causes them to exist in the air by maintaining it alight.[5]

Obviously in this case passivity does not by any means signify the renunciation of all activity; it means submitting oneself to the source of an activity infinitely richer than any kind of human activity whatsoever.

The interval between the time during which the soul—still very human, even though it is under the influence of grace—preserves its own control over its activity, and the moment when the Holy Spirit, having taken it entirely into His own hands, moves it Himself to do whatsoever He wills, contains a long series of transformations, both painful and pleasurable, which are described in the *Dark Night*, the *Spiritual Canticle* and the *Living Flame*. For the change from one moving principle of human activity to another is connected with a change in the way in which this activity itself is exercised. The divine way goes with passivity. But the Kingdom of God does not come in a flash.

God's action is sweet despite its strength, for He begins " to work from the lowest and extreme end of the senses of the soul in order

---

[1] *Ascent*, bk. iii, ch. vi: vol. i, pp. 239–40.
[2] *Spiritual Canticle*, stanza xxv: vol. ii, p. 132.
[3] ibid., stanza xxxiv: vol. ii, p. 160.
[4] *Living Flame*, stanza i: vol. iii, p. 24.
[5] ibid., stanza iii: vol. iii.

that He may gradually lead it, according to its own nature, to the other extreme of His spiritual wisdom, which belongs not to sense."[1] Each act of generosity increases the faith and love in the soul and hence brings it more light and a greater share in the gifts of the Holy Spirit. For is not love the cause and the means through which God communicates these gifts?[2]

From both the moral and the psychological point of view our soul is sick and needs curing. The health of the soul is God Himself. Hence the severity of certain kinds of treatment.[3] The poultice used in the hospital at Medina inspired one of the finest and also one of the most comforting passages in the *Living Flame*.[4] It is not only intelligence and will that have to be transformed, but all the powers and affections of the soul. The night does not spare a single one.[5] All the sufferings of the Dark Night simply reveal the progress that is being made, the change of manner—of mode, to use the old word—of our psychological dynamism, the remoulding of our activity, both interior and exterior.[6] The tears, the cries, the sparks from the log thrown on the fire, are simply feeble images of the torments felt by the soul subject to the inner flame that is eating away its thick human substance and gradually bringing it towards the divine. This loving knowledge is received passively into the soul according to the supernatural mode of God, not the natural mode of the soul itself.[7] There is much comfort in knowing that the earliest and humblest sufferings experienced by the soul on its way to this inner transformation are caused by a flame that will enable it in the end to know the ecstasy of perfect compliance with the divine will. However dark, at times, may be the road up which they lead the soul, the ten steps of the secret ladder by which the soul rises symbolize a progressive ascension, or rather the slow transformation of a human activity, at first uncertain because of its native infirmity, towards its total assimilation by God in the beatific vision.[8]

It is not necessary to wait for the beatific vision, however, to know the riches of the dynamic life of God. Even here below some souls have felt themselves possessed by the Spirit of God. All their inner activity and all their external behaviour have been transformed by it.

---

[1] *Ascent*, bk. ii, ch. xvii: vol. i, p. 139.
[2] ibid., bk. ii, ch. xxix: vol. i.
[3] *Dark Night*, bk. ii, ch. xvi: vol. i.
[4] *Living Flame*, stanza ii: vol. iii.
[5] *Dark Night*, bk. ii, ch. iv: vol. i.
[6] I have tried to show this in the essay entitled " A la recherche d'une structure essentielle de la nuit de l'esprit," *Études Carmélitaines*, Oct. 1938, pp. 254–81.
[7] *Living Flame*, stanza iii: vol. iii.
[8] *Dark Night*, bk. ii, chs. xix and xxi.

It means a remoulding of the whole human dynamism. Possibilities change according to the rule and manner and source of any activity. The things of God must be measured not by human but by divine standards, if there is to be any understanding of this powerful dynamism which has all the surety of a divine instinct, and which henceforth lies behind all the manifestations of the life of the soul.

God then possesses the powers of the soul as their " entire master ",[1] because they are transformed into Him, and He orders them about divinely in accordance with His divine Spirit and will. " He who is joined to the Lord is one spirit ".[2] We must beware of being over-sceptical. No doubt it is rare to meet a soul " in all things and at all times " moved by God. But nevertheless " there are yet souls who in their operations are very habitually moved by God ".[3] These are the sons of God, who, according to St. Paul, are moved by the Spirit of God.[4]

As a general rule, instead of having recourse to human prudence and calculated cleverness—even in the light of faith—the soul moves henceforth with the sure instinct of God. It is His child. It has fully regained the rights of its divine adoption. As is only to be expected, its whole activity will henceforth be transformed. "And finally, all the movements and operations which the soul had aforetime, and which belonged to the principle of its natural life, are now in this union changed into movements of God. For the soul, like the true daughter of God that it now is, is moved wholly by the Spirit of God."[5]

With one of those phrases that can illumine a whole life, the saint shows how the soul then feels " in so lofty a way possessed "[6] by God. Could there be a happier way of expressing this possession of the soul by God in living terms—the divine rule and manner, part of the divine movement itself,[7] as described in speculative theology? What power and security in the manifestations of the life of a soul like this! Remember that its very first movements—ordinarily vitiated, since they emanate from a corrupted nature—now fly spontaneously to God. "And it is no marvel that their operations should be divine, since the union of the soul is divine."[8] " Touch not the higher part, even in your first motions."[9] " The soul in this estate has no longer any affections of the will or acts of knowledge of the understanding,

[1] *Ascent*, bk. iii, ch. ii: vol. i, p. 229.
[2] 1 Cor. vi, 17.
[3] *Ascent*, bk. iii, ch. ii: vol. i, p. 233.
[4] Rom. viii, 4.
[5] *Living Flame*, stanza ii: vol. iii, pp. 56–7.
[6] ibid., stanza i: vol. iii, p. 19.
[7] I am in full agreement with the views expressed by R. Dalbiez in *Études Carmélitaines*, April 1933, pp. 248–9.
[8] *Ascent*, bk. iii, ch. ii: vol. i, p. 234.
[9] *Spiritual Canticle*, stanza xxxi: vol. ii, p. 154.

nor any thought or action which is not wholly turned to God, together with its desires."[1]

This whole domain is so entirely consecrated to God that even without the constant surveillance of the soul all the particular parts are, from their very first impulse, ready to act according to God and for God.[2] It is not sufficient to say that the Holy Spirit inspires such a soul; He is *its way*.[3] He is the road it follows. But far from being a straight road laid down in advance, it is a road that is infinitely varied —like the endlessly changing lines traced by birds in the air. There is no end to the kinds of images that could be used to suggest the endless resources of this divine dynamism. The soul is in " the depths of the pure waters of the spirit, where it " has " no support or foothold but" is "engulfed and immersed in God".[4] Finally, there are all the delicate, varied *graces* that symbolize the actual movements of the Holy Spirit in the soul: they would need a whole essay to themselves.

And St. John of the Cross is so moved by love that he cannot refrain from bursting out in praise of " the most glorious Virgin Our Lady, who, being raised to this high estate from the beginning, had never the form of any creature imprinted in her soul, neither was moved by such, but was invariably guided by the Holy Spirit"[5].

II

We should not put false windows in a building for the sake of symmetry, and we must not be determined to make the works of St. John of the Cross fit into a kind of scheme that never entered his head. His point of view was very different from that adopted by a modern psychologist in the development of his theories.

It may well be wondered, then, to what extent the distinction between love and aggressiveness may be traced in the supernatural activity of a soul entirely moved by the Holy Spirit. It must be said that at least some kind of transposition is necessary. And to explain this transposition an analogy may prove helpful.

As far as love is concerned—the faculty involving a tendency, or desire, or joy—the transposition is easy and has often been pointed out.

As regards aggressiveness, its essential features are perhaps to be found in the totality of realization-tendencies manifested by a soul in

[1] *Spiritual Canticle*, stanza xviii: vol. ii, p. 110.
[2] ibid., stanza xix.
Cf. *Novissima Verba*, pp. 125–6: " As my soul is entirely clothed with love, all my actions, even the most indifferent, are marked by that divine seal."
[3] *Living Flame*, stanza iii: vol. iii.
[4] ibid., stanza iii: vol. iii, p. 92.
[5] *Ascent*, bk. iii, ch. ii: vol. i, p. 231.

search of God. The psychological effort involved in achieving a desired good, or in struggling against whatever forms an obstacle to it, is perhaps the best example of a transposition of physical aggressiveness onto the supernatural plane.

It is only necessary to analyze the behaviour of a soul utterly surrendered to the divine will to see these two fundamental impulses at work, and to grasp the order in which they stand related to each other.

A few remarks on the different activities of the soul may help towards a better understanding of the riches of the divine influence and the instinctive intuition that characterises the behaviour of the soul upon which it has seized. The light given by " the Divine Spirit, Who moves and illumines the understanding "[1] is utterly different from that which can be manufactured by our reasoning skill, even with the help of faith. This light is so different from the other that at first it is disconcerting; soon it becomes blinding and hurts. There is absolutely no way of describing it, and nothing to compare it to.[2] But gradually it reveals the things of God in a way beyond all imagining. The soul that has once tasted them is hungry for communications " so lofty and so substantial and so intimate that thou mayest not utter them to the outward senses ".[3]

An examination of the mysteries of Christ in the light of this fact provides the substance of some of the finest pages in the *Canticle* and also a number of most elevated insights into the intimate life of God and the joys of the life beyond. How can such a soul be anything but impatient for the full light to dawn? Despite the calm way in which the longing is expressed at the beginning of the *Living Flame*, it is not difficult to sense that the eyes of the soul, lit by such a luminous faith, are hungry for clear vision.[4]

But it is perhaps the love born of the touches of the Holy Spirit that caused this saint, who was so much in love with love, to linger longest over his descriptions. Who can describe the " touch of the enkindling of love in the will "?[5] When the will is " able to receive, feel and taste that which is Divine and supernatural after a sublime and lofty manner ",[6] what deliverance is experienced, what fulfilment! When the log has stopped " weeping and crying ", what impassioned love inflames the soul, triumphing over every other love: " When this

---

[1] *Ascent,* bk. ii, ch. xxix: vol. i, p. 213.
[2] *Dark Night,* bk. ii, ch. xvii.
[3] *Spiritual Canticle,* stanza xxxii: vol. ii, p. 157.
[4] *Living Flame,* stanza i: vol. iii.
I have insisted elsewhere on the novelty of this knowledge (*Études Carmélitaines,* 1938, pp. 271-2.)
[5] *Dark Night,* bk. ii, ch. xiii: vol. i, p. 440.
[6] ibid., bk. ii, ch. xvi: vol. i, p. 450.

Divine breeze assails the soul, it enkindles it wholly and refreshes it and revives it and awakens the will and upraises the desires which aforetime had fallen and were asleep, to the love of God, in such manner that it may well be said thereof that it awakens the love both of the Spouse and of the Bride ".[1]

It would be necessary to re-read most of the *Canticle* and the *Living Flame* to understand what exactly this love is that is now no longer " reasonable " but divinely impassioned, inspiring in the soul the most beautiful cries of impatience, the most painful exclamations of anguish and the most triumphant outbursts of joy that have probably ever been heard in any literature, religious or secular.

For the soul still ignorant of this divine influence " there has been no act but only dispositions for an act ";[2] it does not really know whether it is succeeding in loving properly. But when a soul's whole power of loving is surrendered entirely to the Spirit of love, " in an instant " the act of love is born, as inevitably as a child will cry out on recognising its father. When the kindling wood is really dry, every spark catches.[3] " Then, with great rapidity, as when one suddenly awakens, the will is enkindled in loving, desiring, praising, giving thanks, doing reverence, esteeming and praying to God with savour of love."[4]

One approaches the summit of this transformation in fear and trembling. For the saint shows the soul drawn into the current of the very life of God, in which it participates, breathing " in God the same breath of love that the Father breathes in the Son and the Son in the Father, which is the same Holy Spirit that They breathe into her in the said transformation . . . which, as I understand, was the meaning of St. Paul when he said: Quoniam autem estis filii Dei, misit Deus Spiritum Filii sui in corda vestra clamanten: Abba, Pater." It is the natural consequence of the divine adoption: " How is it a thing incredible that she should perform her work by understanding, knowledge and love in the Trinity, together with It, like the Trinity Itself, by a mode of participation, which God effects in the soul herself? "[5]

Nevertheless, the possibilities of this divine influence on the soul have still not been exhausted. Naturally St. John of the Cross always remains primarily a Carmelite, a contemplative, even when he speaks as a Doctor of the Church. But the universal value of any doctrine is not impaired by having one of its points emphasised more than the others. For all Christians, as for St. John himself, the most

[1] *Spiritual Canticle*, stanza xxvi: vol. ii, p. 134.
[2] *Living Flame*, stanza i: vol. iii, p. 37.
[3] ibid.
[4] *Spiritual Canticle*, stanza xvi: vol. ii, p. 97.
[5] ibid., stanza xxxviii: vol. ii, p. 176.

important thing is that the *value of being* should be increased in mankind. It is chimerical to put *doing* before *being*. This is worth repeating for the benefit of certain—self-styled—apostles of the faith whom the saint liked to compare to blacksmiths: they love to hear the hollow sound of their hammer on the anvil. The saint's concern for this growth of inner worth shines out in more than one famous passage of his writings, and it was indeed the dominating factor in his vocation as a Discalced Carmelite. The essential problem is to discover how every single one of the souls composing the Church shall arrive at that fullness of supernatural life—in concrete terms, that wealth of love— for which it was created. Compared with this primary concern, the material organization of external works, however necessary it may be, is secondary and entirely subordinate. God knows that when the soul asks the Spirit to blow through Its garden it is certainly not " for the delight and glory which comes to her thereby ".[1] Sharing this breath of love which in God is the Holy Spirit, borne along on the current of God's own life and thus united to Him by love—surely this is to realise the essence of our Lord's wish as He expressed it on the evening of Holy Thursday.[2]

When the soul attains to that unity which our Lord prayed that all who believe in Him might attain, " these acts of love of the soul are most precious, and even one of them is of greater merit and worth than all that the soul may have done in its life apart from this transformation, however much this may be."[3] Who can describe the greatness of this achievement, the heights reached by the blessed soul over whom the Holy Spirit spreads the shadow of the divine attributes themselves?[4] The greatest *service* that can be rendered by a soul that reaches these heights is love.[5]

But it is not the only one. The flame is never still: it is always trying to get higher and consume everything that comes into contact with it.

This symbolizes the external activity of a soul that has been entirely transformed by the Holy Spirit. And this brings us to a point that needs to be emphasised.

The dynamism of a holy soul is essentially alive. Its activity emanates from within—like all life—and spontaneously assimilates everything it meets. Because St. John of the Cross does not deal in the first place with the problem of the Church's external apostolate, this does not mean that he neglects it. In point of fact, this problem hardly arises when a soul has reached its full inner maturity—which de-

[1] *Spiritual Canticle,* stanza xxvi: vol. ii, p. 137.
[2] ibid., stanza xxxviii: vol. ii.
[3] *Living Flame,* stanza i: vol. iii, p. 20.
[4] ibid., stanza iii: vol. iii.
[5] *Spiritual Canticle.* stanza xix: vol. ii.

pends, not on the passage of time, but on the soul's spiritual development—for when this life reaches its fullness it becomes self-pro-
pagating. Such is its law. Well knowing this, St. John of the Cross
makes it his entire aim to nourish the soul of his disciple and thus
enable it to arrive at its full normal growth. The subsequent external
activity is only to be understood as the overflowing of a life that strives
to radiate beyond itself. This is the only true dynamism.

And how powerful this can be when it is the Spirit of God that
causes the activity of such a soul! There is a great contrast between this
activity that comes from within and those lives which seem superficially to show such remarkable energy but which are in reality quite
hollow.

There would be no point in denying the astonishing achievements
that purely human ideals have produced, but one can hardly fail to
notice one striking fact, and that is that any purely human dynamism
ultimately proves powerless to realize its own ideal: it remains essentially
disproportionate to the end it hopes to achieve. If it manages to conceal the insufficiency of its real life-capital, it only does this by making
a show of pseudo-wealth in a way that is usually more reminiscent of
melodrama than of real life.

We must not forget, however, that there is a frightful handicap
weighing on any soul that seeks a supernatural ideal: this is the disproportion between what it possesses so fully by the light of reason,
and what it possesses so imperfectly by the supernatural light. David
will always find Saul's armour difficult to wear, and the children of
men find it hard to forget that they are children of men, and act like
children of God. It is only natural that we should be tempted to
measure all things, even the things of God, by our human standards,
since they are the only standards we really know; the question is, how
can we come to use God's standard correctly?

But this disproportion between things human and divine—which
in good theology is regarded as the fundamental reason why the gifts
of the Holy Spirit are so fitting, if not essential—also determines
the power of radiation in a soul that has succeeded in identifying
itself, as closely as its earthly condition will allow, with the divine,
and has become simply an instrument, a very docile and sensitive
instrument, in the hands of the divine Artist.

The saints' consciousness of their own wretchedness, joined with
their complete conviction that God's infinite power is entirely at their
disposal, forms the basis of their humility and their invincible optimism.
There is a tone of triumph in the appeal that St. John of the Cross
addresses to his fellow-Christians: " O souls created for these grandeurs
and called thereto! What do ye do? Wherein do ye occupy yourselves?

Your desires are meannesses and your possessions miseries. O wretched blindness of the eyes of your souls . . ."[1] So powerful a love ignores all obstacles. One can understand how, to reach this height, one "would rather bear the cross together with pure vinegar and gall, and would count this a great happiness . . . "[2] For once having reached it, " it is a characteristic of the power and vehemence of love that all things seem possible to it."[3] Bergson wrote: " The true mystics simply open themselves to the incoming wave. Completely self-confident, because they feel within themselves the existence of something better than themselves, they turn out to be great men of action, to the surprise of those to whom mysticism means merely visions, transports, ecstasies. The need to pass on to others what they have received is for them an impulse of love."[4]

Since all the powers of such a soul are moved from within with the sureness of instinct, how effectively it is bound to perform all its activity! Having divested themselves of all selfish interests, such apostles " will give their hearts' blood to anyone that serves God, and will help others to serve Him as much as in them lies".[5] There is no trace of egoism in these souls, which " with great generosity . . . give away all that they have, and delight to know that they have it not, for God's sake and for charity to their neighbour, no matter whether these be spiritual things or temporal ".[6]

Earlier, when discussing " more interior spiritual trials ", the saint had noted that such beings " must have rendered Him many services and have had much patience and constancy for His sake, and be very acceptable in their lives in His sight ".[7]

When an apostle is thus " possessed by God ", " the soul considers great works undertaken for the Beloved as small; many things as few; and the long time wherein it serves Him as short, by reason of the fire of love wherein it is now burning . . . Here, for the great love which the soul bears to God, it suffers great pains and afflictions because of the little that it does for God . . . wherefore it considers itself useless in all that it does and thinks itself to be living in vain".[8] The words of such a teacher communicate genuine warmth to souls," for warmth that comes from the living spirit clings ". Otherwise " the spirit . . . goes no farther from its habits than before,

---

[1] *Spiritual Canticle*, stanza xxxviii: vol. ii, p. 178.
[2] *Living Flame*, stanza ii: vol. iii, p. 53.
[3] *Dark Night*, bk. ii, ch. xiii: vol. i, p. 443.
[4] *The Two Sources of Morality and Religion.*
[5] *Dark Night*, bk. i, ch. ii: vol. i, p. 356.
[6] ibid., bk. i, ch. iv: vol. i, p. 358.
[7] *Living Flame*, stanza ii: vol. iii, p. 53.
[8] *Dark Night*, bk. ii, ch. xix: vol. i, p. 465.

since the voice has no virtue to raise one that is dead from his grave".[1]

There is in the concrete lives of the saints a profound connection —that of life itself—between their most sublime moments of participation in the intimate life of God, the spiration of the breath, and their humblest resolves to serve their neighbour. " Refuse not work, even though it appear to thee that thou canst not perform it. Let all find compassion in thee."[2]

Love of the poor grows from this root alone. Dislike of the poor, which is so absolutely opposed to the teaching of Christ, but which is so very obviously felt by some people, can only grow in a sensual soul.[3] There is nothing surprising in the fact that these two things should be interconnected, for the same Spirit not only unites the Father and the Son but also descends into the soul and moves it to love God and its neighbour.

" It is thus the Holy Spirit who, being from all eternity the link between the Father and the Son, then communicating Himself to us by His merciful condescension, joins us in the first place to God in pure love and then by the same love unites us with each other."[4]

This connection between the soul's inner attitude and its external behaviour is brought out clearly in the discussion of graces that are perhaps only rarely found in human life, but are not unknown in the lives of the saints. "And of this good which comes to the soul a part sometimes overflows into the body."[5] Hence the marvellous joy that invades " all the harmony of thy soul and even of thy body."[6]

Along with this there is sometimes a kind of external radiance that suggests the existence in man of something better than man. " They [i.e. these holy souls] bear within them habitually something of greatness and dignity which causes others to stop and respect them by reason of the supernatural effect produced in them through their close and familiar intercourse with God." Thus St. John writes of Moses in Exodus: " They could not look upon his face by reason of the glory and honour which remained upon his person because he had spoken with God face to face."[7]

Here we touch upon the deepest reason for the fruitfulness and also the flexibility of the apostolic work of such souls. For them there are not two separate problems, their personal sanctification and their

---

[1] *Ascent*, bk. iii. ch. xlv: vol. i, p. 333.
[2] *Spiritual Sentences and Maxims:* vol. iii, p. 256.
[3] *Ascent*, bk. iii, ch. xxv.
[4] Bossuet, *Panég. de saint François de Paule.*
[5] *Living Flame*, stanza ii: vol. iii, p. 50.
[6] ibid., stanza iii: vol. ii, p. 64.
[7] *Spiritual Canticle*, stanza xxvi: vol. ii, p. 136.

apostolic work; there is only the one single problem of their inner life, which has grown so full that it cannot help but give itself out to others. This need to give God to others is felt by these souls as a torment, an anguish. They know from experience "the yearning to serve God", the anguish of serving Him, " which is a thing very pleasing to God ".[1] How can such a need to give be regarded, except as the manifestation of the riches of a dynamic life as vital and insistent as an instinct? There is nothing merely theoretic about the activity of such apostles, but a strategic manoeuvring of forces that always attain their object and achieve far more than any merely human activity could ever achieve.

If it was necessary to illustrate the above pages with an example drawn from life we should not have far to seek, for the life of St. John of the Cross provides one of the best possible examples of a soul utterly responsive to the action of the Holy Spirit, a soul in which the necessary synthesis is achieved, so that love impregnates all the saint's movements and inspires him with a strength amply witnessed in his writings. It has been justly observed that there is an oblique way of revealing oneself that can often be more convincing than direct confidences, and St. John of the Cross is one of those who reveal themselves in this oblique way.

There is never anything arch or sentimental about love as St. John of the Cross understands it. His is a love of astonishing power, inspiring an exuberant enthusiasm unequalled by even the most vigorous endeavours of the voluntarists.

Of whom is the saint speaking in this passage? " For the soul immediately perceives in itself a true determination and an effective desire to do naught which it understands to be an offence to God and to omit to do naught that seems to be for His service."[2] It was love, again, that inspired him to write the following lines—the love that is incapable of calculation but is as imperious as a divine instinct: "And with the yearnings and the vehemence of the lioness or the she-bear going to seek her cubs when they have been taken away from her and she finds them not, does this wounded soul go forth to seek its God."[3]

How often the synthesis of love and power is described in his writings; and these are simply a universalized transcription of his own personal experience. Love, with its ardour and impatience, is described in the most moving, affectionate terms—always, moreover, with the

[1] *Dark Night*, bk. i, ch. xiii: vol. i, p. 393.
[2] ibid., bk. ii, ch. xvi: vol. i, p. 455.
[3] ibid., bk. ii, ch. xiii: vol. i, p. 443.

instinctive spontaneity characteristic of a soul in which the divine
initiative no longer finds any resistance. For " it is a characteristic of
the power and vehemence of love that all things seem possible to it ".[1]
He longed so vehemently to possess his God that he could not fail to
be heard: nothing seemed worthy to be compared with this hunger
for God, unless it were Rachel's longing for motherhood: " Give me
children or I die."

At the end of his life, in the light of a cloudless sunset, in the warm
serenity of a radiance that was only just beginning, all anguish had
disappeared from his calmed soul, and the longing to see God had
become a kind of immense river flowing silently but irresistibly towards
the ocean. This longing inspired him to one of his strangest phrases—
a phrase which is so pregnant that it provides the substance of an
entire page of the commentary on the first stanza of the *Living Flame*.
The prose takes on the splendour of an almost unparalleled lyricism.
" Break the web of this sweet encounter." Knowing from this moment
onwards that his longing comes from God, and that he would not be
moved by it if it were not inspired by God; knowing his soul to be
utterly malleable in the hands of God and entirely subject to His
love, he asks only one thing more: that God may break the frail web
of his earthly life. The love that moves him to make this petition still
bears, enclosed within itself, all the strength of a soul that cannot wait
for the web of life to wear out or be cut down slowly: inflict upon it
the slightest pressure, and it will break.

But this last request made by a love as strong as death has only love
for its object; for if the saint asks that the web of his life, which alone
separates him from God, shall be broken at one blow, it is so that he
may love without end, for ever, as his soul desires.

" Break the slender web of this life, and let it not come to pass that
age and years cut it after the natural manner, so that I may be able to
love Thee with the fullness and satisfaction which my soul desires,
without end, for ever."

[1] *Dark Night*, bk. ii, ch. xiii: vol. i, p. 445.

GOD OF WRATH OR GOD OF LOVE?

PÈRE PHILIPPE DE LA TRINITÉ, O.C.D.

THERE is a disconcerting rhythm ebbing and flowing under the whole of reality, a rhythm whose mysterious beat is registered, each in its own way and on its own level, by the natural sciences, physiology and psychology, morals and metaphysics. The attraction and repulsion of molecules; the functions of digestion, growth or reproduction and the functions of libido and aggressiveness; impartial law and brute force; the active and passive powers in Aristotelian metaphysics—in each case these form a kind of double centre to a mysterious ellipse with two focuses. From the relative position of the contrary and complementary elements results order or disorder, power or weakness, war or peace.

Everything is in motion, and this motion does not take place without occasional collision. In fact, whether we like it or not, the world is in a kind of gestation; the animal world is at war, and man, an animal endowed with reason, and also at war, suffers still further because of his mind. The state of conflict is physical and biological before it becomes psychological and moral.

If, as is taught by St. Thomas[1] and the Vatican Council,[2] a revelation is morally necessary to enable all men to attain quickly, certainly and without error to the truths of natural religion, how much more need there will be for this help when it comes to seeking for a solution to the profoundest problem of all, the difficult and painful problem of the existence of evil!

God is always surprising us. His ways are not our ways: " The foolishness of God is wiser than men, and the weakness of God is stronger than men."[3] He has revealed His intentions; it is up to us to understand them properly.

The Gospel message is a message of love, but it is written in letters of blood. Christ Himself said: " I came not to send peace but the sword ";[4] " He that loveth father or mother more than me is not worthy of me."[5] What are we to think of Christ, then? Did He come to add to our trials? Is He a God of wrath or a God of love?

---

[1] *Contra Gentes*, i, 4.   [3] 1 Cor. i. 25.
[2] Denzinger, 1786.   [4] Matt. x. 34.
                    [5] Matt. x. 37.

And what is God—a Father or a Tyrant? And if He is a Father, why does He make so many demands on us, and spread so many horrors around us?[1]

THE ELEMENTARY VITAL IMPULSES

Conflict, like love, is engraved in our deepest being.

Despite the husk of its words, which make it look superficially quite out-of-date, St. Thomas Aquinas's analysis of what he calls in psychology the " irascible " and the "concupiscible" is still valuable to-day, for it goes right to the root of the matter[2]. If this thirteenth-century philosopher's observations are extended by analogy to the whole level of human activity, it will be found that they are not without some resemblance—remote, I agree, but nevertheless quite considerable —with Freud's views on libido and aggression. This similarity between two minds otherwise so different is the sign of a genuine approach to concrete, living reality in its deepest aspects.[3]

[1] The reader may, if he prefers, pass straight on to the more purely religious part of this essay, which is its main purpose (p. 131), without delaying over the next few pages on the Elementary Vital Impulses. These pages make more difficult reading: in them an attempt is made to sketch the psychic life of human nature, so that it may more easily be grasped that human nature is not destroyed, but perfected, by the strong but gentle grace of the love of the Gospels.

[2] I–II, 22, 48, " On the Passions". The passions (or the movements of the sensitive appetite) are for St. Thomas common to both the animals and man, but in man they are to some extent elevated because of the spirituality of the soul. The reader who wishes to embark upon a study of St. Thomas's psychology will find it very useful to read E. Gilson, *St. Thomas d'Aquin*, in the series *Les moralistes chrétiens*, Gabalda, 1925, pp. 109–58. Here I have translated " passions " as " elementary vital impulses". If it is objected that the word " passion ", which implies passivity, is badly translated by the word " impulse ", which implies activity, I should like to point out that although, for the theologian and the metaphysician, animals are, after the vegetable world, and compared with the angels and God, the least active of living things, they are nevertheless not entirely inactive, but just the opposite, despite their very real kind of passivity. According to the Thomist scheme, on the different levels—intellectual (angels)—rational (men)—sensible (animals)—vegetable (plants)—and mineral (matter)—the various beings show a progressive diminution of activity with a parallel increase of passivity; but apart from its various external forms of dependence, is it not true that the sensitive living thing always remains a being able to move itself in an immanent, autonomous way? As regards the creatures of the terrestrial world, animals are the outstanding representatives of activity, and man only " an animal in action " (Lyautey). So true is this that empiricists even claim to be able to reduce the intelligible to the sensible on the plane of the activity of love and knowledge.

[3] It will be understood that I am not trying to compare Freud and St. Thomas Aquinas from the metaphysical point of view, but "There are grounds," writes Roland Dalbiez, "for distinguishing a methodology, a psychology and a philosophy in psycho-analysis " (R. Dalbiez, *Psychoanalytical Method and the Doctrine of Freud*, trans. T. F. Lindsay, Longmans Green & Co., vol. ii, p. v.). Unlike Cartesianism, Thomist hylomorphism has no difficulty in agreeing with

Freud distinguishes between two fundamental impulses, that of love, *libido* (whose meaning is not really sexual but covers every affective movement), and that of aggression, which he studies separately in the last part of his work: on the one hand are the life-instincts and on the other the death-instincts.[1]

Now, St. Thomas distinguishes, amongst the elementary vital impulses, those which spring from the " concupiscible " and those which spring from the " irascible ". These two names are used because concupiscence is typical of the movement that brings us pleasure whereas anger (*ira*) is typical of reaction and resistance to difficulty. In modern terminology, the " concupiscible " equals the movement of libido, and the " irascible ", the aggressive impulse. Here is a table of St. Thomas's eleven elementary vital impulses:

I. Concupiscible: (libido instinct)	+Approach to good	origin: love	1
		movement: desire	2
		end: joy	3
	—Avoidance of evil	origin: hatred	4
		movement: flight	5
		end: sadness	6
II. Irascible: (aggressive instinct)	The struggle against difficulty	Approach towards good: hope	7
		Avoidance of good: despair	8
		Avoidance of evil: fear	9
		Attack upon evil: audacity	10
		Struggle against evil: anger	11

Thus we have: *amor, desiderium, gaudium, odium, fuga, tristitia, spes, desperatio, timor, audacia* and *ira*.

This is not the place for a long dissertation on this subject. I merely wish to emphasise a few of the psychological truths that are to be found on the level of the senses and which, when viewed from the standpoint of libido and aggression, are found ennobled and fulfilled on the spiritual level in the light of revelation. Grace comes to perfect, not to destroy nature, the first gift from the Creator.

---

certain points of view to be found in Freud's writings since, in more than one case, these are also to be found in Thomist psychology. There is no need for surprise in this. On another level—which, it is true, was found scandalous in its day—although St. Thomas's God of Love is not the same thing as Aristotle's impassive divinity, nevertheless his metaphysics was in direct historical continuity with Aristotle's. There is no need to be afraid of this analogy.

[1] See *supra* Dr. Parcheminey's essay on ambivalence.

Libido. On the level of the libido instinct, when we look down the parallel perspectives of love and hatred we find the following facts:

Starting point, attraction or repulsion: impulses 1 and 4, love or hatred.

Movement, pursuit or retreat: impulses 2 and 5, desire or flight.

End, fulfilment or suffering: impulses 3 and 6, joy or sadness.

The love-impulses are positive values, governed, so to speak, by the sign " plus ". The hate-impulses are negative values, opposed to the previous values as contraries, and governed, so to speak, by the sign " minus ".

This record shows, in the normal balanced person, the pre-eminence of love, which finds its fulfilment in joy. In the activity of the senses love necessarily takes the first place.

" There is no . . . passion of the soul that does not presuppose love of some kind. The reason is that every . . . passion of the soul implies either movement towards something, or rest in something. Now every movement towards something, or rest in something, arises from some kinship or aptness to that thing; and in this does love consist."[1]

On the rational level this love becomes correspondingly more complex. Loving means willing good to someone, either oneself or somebody else. The scholastics say that the person loved is loved with the love of friendship, and this is the " oblativity " of modern terminology. The good which one desires for the loved person is loved in a secondary and derivative manner with the love of concupiscence,[2] and this for the moderns is the narcissistic element in love, narcissism itself being the neurotic predominance of the pleasure-loving egoism over oblativity.

Love finds its fulfilment, not in using someone for one's own exclusive benefit, with a view always to self, but in a going-out of self through the gift of self. Love's highest function is oblativity which, by enabling the personality to find its axis in someone other than itself, opens its own potentialities to it, developing and enriching them. This is a law of nature: only if it falls into the earth does a grain of wheat bear fruit.

Harvest-time is a time of joy. Love finds its fulfilment in joy—in man at least; for animals only experience pleasure, i.e. a delectation of the senses devoid of any intellectual character.[3] Pleasure and joy refresh love and help it to grow.

" The chief effect of pleasure is a sort of delectation of the soul,

[1] I-II, 27, 4.
[2] It will be noticed that the love of concupiscence is, for the scholastics, simply the lower element in the love of friendship. It must not be confused with the " concupiscible ", which includes the love of friendship.
[3] I-II, 31, 3.

which grows bigger and wider in order to receive the good upon which it has seized. In this way pleasure leads any act performed by one of the faculties of the soul to its ultimate completion. For the act accomplished by the soul is a good in itself, but pleasure adds another good, the satisfaction of desire by means of the good that has been grasped. And this perfection, moreover, ultimately affects the performance of the act itself, because a thing is done better when it is performed with pleasure, because all the resources of one's attention are brought to it."[1] Love engenders joy, which in its turn facilitates the activity of love.

And this is why St. Thomas quite rightly sees in certain cases of the effects of pain and sorrow an absolute malady which one must make every effort to cure.

For in fact sorrow contracts nature. It harms the body by interfering with its vital functions; it weighs upon the soul; it paralyses all our actions; it weakens the intelligence and the will, sometimes to such a point that it entirely prevents the use of reason and free will, and can thus lead to those states of depression which, in the thirteenth century, were known as melancholia and mania.[2]

One must therefore look after those who are sick at heart. To get them back to a state in which they can again experience pleasure and joy, no remedy is too insignificant. St. Thomas gives concrete suggestions. There is comfort in tears, and so there is no point in being afraid of giving way to them. Sleep, too, is useful, and baths, and all kinds of other remedies—not forgetting either the consolation that can be found in the compassion of friends, or the most powerful remedy of all: the contemplation of the truth.[3]

Health, which is the perfection of the animal body, and holiness, the perfection of the human soul, have the same sign, pleasure or joy in expressing themselves, and, each on its own level, the same profound cause, the flowering of love.

Aggressiveness. We are made for love and happiness: this law is written in our deepest instincts. But as we live in a world of injustice and wickedness (either natural or wilful), this means having to exert a certain force against any obstacle that tries to prevent either the upsurge of our love or the repose of our joy. And this is the function of aggressiveness.

One of the typical mistakes made by students in their examinations[4]

[1] Gilson, *St. Thomas d'Aquin*, pp. 139–40, after I–II, 33, on the effects of delectation.
[2] See I–II, 35, 36 and 37, on the nature, causes and effects of sadness and pain.
[3] After I–II, 38, on the remedies for pain.
[4] They are not without justification: the moderns often seem to use the word " hatred " for " aggressiveness "; but this is a pity.

is to take aggressiveness (*irascibilis*) for hatred (*odium*), whereas the latter is in fact only the negative aspect of libido, whilst the former is itself essentially a positive value, the conquering aspect of love. This is one of the most original and profound of St. Thomas's insights.

It can be difficult to love or hate. This difficulty is a dimension which is to be met with on the level of both love and hatred, and it is precisely this difficulty which forms the characteristic feature of aggressiveness, and engenders conflict.

The good, in so far as it is difficult to achieve, and evil, in so far as it is difficult to avoid, are the objects of aggressiveness.

To tend towards a good that can only be attained with difficulty, but is nevertheless capable of being attained, is to hope (impulse 7).

Despair is opposed to hope " as a movement of retreat is opposed to an advance " (impulse 8). When an endeavour proves to be impossible, it is abandoned.[1]

The object of fear (impulse 9) is the exact opposite of that of hope; it is " an evil with which one is threatened and which is difficult to avoid, which one feels that one will be unable to resist if it arrives, but which one still maintains some hope of escaping ".[2] In this case aggressiveness is repressed, and this gives rise to the phenomenon of anxiety.

At the opposite pole from fear is audacity, in which aggressiveness is triumphant, for it " turns against the danger and attacks it in the full hope of overcoming it " (impulse 10).

In the four cases mentioned above the good or the evil is still remote.[3]

In the case of a present evil, against which one struggles courageously, anger (impulse 11) becomes involved, whose movement is against the thing forming the obstacle on which one wishes to take one's revenge.[4]

If the battle is lost, we have sadness (impulse 6). If it is won, we have joy (impulse 3). True love must know how to be aggressive in time of need.

Libido and Aggressiveness. Hatred and sadness, servile fear and despair, are signs of defeat and weakness; love and pleasure, audacity and confidence, on the other hand, are the impulses that characterise good health. Libido and aggressiveness are functionally interdependent.

---

[1] Gilson, *St. Thomas d'Aquin*, p. 146.
[2] ibid, p. 148.
[3] ibid., p. 152.
[4] The eleventh passion, anger, does not have meekness as its corresponding twelfth passion, since the absence of anger is not in itself a particular attitude: it is simply a privation, the absence of conflict—a kind of conflict, moreover, which only takes place against a present evil. " *Calm is contrary to anger*, by opposition not of contrariety but of negation or privation " (I–II, 23, 3). Meekness and self-control thus have no value except in people who know how to get angry when this is demanded of them. There is no virtue in being lymphatic.

" The irascible is in fact ordered in reference to the concupiscible, of which it is the guardian and defender. It is essential for the animal to be able to overcome its enemies so that the concupiscible power may enjoy in peace the objects pleasing to it. In fact, animals fight always for the sake of securing some pleasure; they fight for the pleasure of love or of food. The movements of the irascible consequently both originate and end in the concupiscible. Anger begins in sadness and ends in the joy of revenge which belongs to the concupiscible; hope is born of desire and completed in joy. Thus the movement of sensuality always proceeds from the concupiscible to the concupiscible by passing through the irascible."[1]

This clearly shows the primacy of love.

However, without in any way repudiating this fundamental fact, St. Thomas Aquinas explains very carefully that though love is in itself superior to hope and anger, nevertheless, on the level of the senses, aggressiveness manifests a certain superiority over libido.

" When the animal tends, by virtue of its concupiscible appetite, to the object yielding it pleasure, it acts simply in a way which is perfectly proportionate to the proper nature of the sensitive soul. But the fact that the animal, under the stress of its irascible appetite, comes to forget its pleasures in order to desire a victory, unattainable except by pain, is the result of an appetitive power extremely close to an order superior to the sensible . . . The irascible obtains results analogous to those of the will. We can therefore place the irascible above the concupiscible, even though its end is to safeguard the act of the latter; we must see in it the noblest instrument with which nature has endowed the animal to maintain its existence and to ensure its own preservation."[2]

It is in fact the property of the human reason to know causally either how to avoid an attractive evil, or to renounce either a present good for a future good, or a lesser good for a greater good, even at the cost of experiencing great hardships. " Both in the matter of knowledge and in the matter of love, certain possibilities are granted by the Creator to the sensitive creature as a direct result of its sensitivity, but there are others that are given to it through a kind of incipient participation in rationality."[3]

[1] *De Veritate*, q. 25, a. 2, following Gilson, *The Philosophy of St. Thomas Aquinas*, trans. E. Bullough, W. Heffer & Sons, 1929, pp. 289–90.
[2] ibid., q. 25, a. 2, in Gilson, *The Philosophy of St. Thomas Aquinas*, p. 291.
[3] ibid. (" modicam participationem ").

This does not mean any reversal of values on the level of love. This relative primacy of aggressiveness at the level of the senses derives from a deep and enlightening insight into the way in which lower values participate in higher ones; hence their evaluation from this point of view, once the proper order has been safeguarded.

The hierarchy of being makes up a harmonious whole. Physical nature is made in the image of intellectual nature, and psychological analysis of the elementary vital impulses opens the way to a better understanding of the functions of the will itself on the truly spiritual level, where we find the movements of love and aggressiveness intimately connected with each other under the banner of reason and freewill.[1] On this level love must know how to control its own aggressiveness, direct it along the right channels, and use it in due measure in order not to degenerate into violence or weakness. Love must have the first word and the last, but in a firm and orderly way.

The relationship between love and aggressiveness is similar to that between law and force. Love without any need for aggressiveness is simply a Utopia, like law without force. Strength is necessary to keep the peace, and this is true whether it is a hero, a saint or a nation that is involved. Aggressiveness without love and force without law are simply brutality.

We long for peace of conscience, peace in the family, peace within the nation and between the nations; the peace which is the tranquillity of order, the primacy and predominance of love over aggressiveness —but a love that is strong, for life is a struggle both biological and moral. This is a simple fact of knowledge and experience.

The question is, can grace help nature to find fulfilment? Does it sow weakness and sadness in fear, or, on the contrary, strength and joy in love?

The wrath of the lion and the meekness of the lamb, the goodness of the mother and the valiance of the warrior, are all to be found in the biblical list of the divine names. God is sometimes presented as the Master, an all-powerful Avenger, and sometimes as a gentle and compassionate Friend. Does the Christian revelation appear under the sign *plus* or *minus*? Does it unfold fundamentally under the banner of wrath or of love? Is religion one of the ways in which God satisfies His need for power, or a way in which He pours out His compassion

[1] From the ontological point of view St. Thomas assigns two distinct faculties, the irascible and the concupiscible, to the functions of libido and aggressiveness on the level of the sensitive appetite, whereas he only assigns one faculty to them on the level of rational appetite, the *will*. This does not by any means mean that aggressiveness is foreign to spiritual love; on the contrary, love and aggressiveness form a still greater unity on the level of spirit than on the level of sense, because on the former level they proceed from one and the same faculty.

upon us? And for us, does it mean crushing servility or, by calling us towards new heights, liberation?

If our sufferings and trials are primarily the effects of a divine rage that knows no bounds; if the cross means the torture of an innocent Victim who was punished on account of the guilty; if merit is in direct ratio to the difficulty met with in performing good works; if the hope of salvation is the result of a jealously-guarded inner tension; if, apart from a few privileged persons, we are all normally expected to arrive at the end of our lives amongst the flames of purgatory, as though destined for them by God Himself (I will not say the flames of hell, for even the ignorant Christian is not quite so rigorous as to imagine that); in short, if God is primarily domineering, aggressive and revengeful, can He still be a good God? The answer is, no: God is a Father, and the key to the mystery of our destiny is to be found in His love.

The Gospels shine with the light of compassion, as has been so well understood, and practised, and sung, by the great Carmelite saints. We need to pierce through to this light; it has been far too frequently clouded over by negative and pessimistic habits of belief.

It would be a mistake to expect in the following pages anything new or original. Their only aim is to help the faithful, those who have goodwill, to establish their religion on authentic doctrine, on the rock of love and confidence. It must be said that in many cases this is, unfortunately, a very necessary thing.

"All too often a religious education fails to build up anything in the soul; it merely stamps it—brands it, so to speak—with the fear of death, the last judgment and hell; impressing upon it a kind of superstitious awe not very far removed from fetichism, whose only effect is to prevent any genuine supernatural activity (i.e., love) completely . . . They do not believe in God, they are afraid of God."[1]

For the last three centuries particularly, the Christian atmosphere has been saturated with rigorist and aggressive ideas deriving from the spirit of Jansenism, and this has led the faithful, first to be discouraged, and then to fall into the indifferentism of a perverse and old-fashioned liberalism.

The Jansenist sect " has done immense harm. The nefarious consequences of their doctrines have been incalculable. In France there are whole dioceses where there has been no practice of religion for over a hundred and fifty years, thanks to a few Jansenist bishops and

[1] Bernanos, *La Grande Peur des Bien-Pensants*, 33rd ed., Grasset, pp. 102-3.

confessors. Many years ago I was told by a very old priest in northern
France that the boundaries of the old Jansenist dioceses could still be
traced by the almost complete neglect of the sacraments".[1]

THE TRINITY

In his first sermon on Providence, Bossuet compares the world
" to those pictures that are like queer optical puzzles;[2] at first sight
they seem to be simply a mass of meaningless lines and colours, but
as soon as anyone who understands them shows you how to look at
them in the proper perspective, or through a cylindrical mirror, the
lines immediately turn into shapes, the confusion sorts itself out, and
you get a beautifully-proportioned picture."[3]

What position does the Christian revelation suggest that we should
take up in our contemplation of the universe?

It suggests that we should consider the flesh as a function of spirit,
and the spirit as a function of God.

Indeed there is no better psychology than to look at the world
from God's point of view—as God is in Himself, in His utter
independence; for the intimate life of God, to which we are called by
reason of our elevation to the spiritual order, is a life formed of the
love of the Father, the Son and the Holy Spirit, a life eternal and
immutable.

This love is perfect and expresses itself in perfect giving. Truly
distinct from each other, the three Persons enjoy an unchanging
equality from the fact of Their common nature. Having an origin
without movement, an order without priorities, a distinction without
differences, it is an exchange of pure wisdom and pure love. There
is nothing to subjugate, for no One is dependent on the Others; nothing
to defend, for no One is threatened. There is no room here for aggressiveness. This love is utterly peaceful and gentle; it is the love of the
infinite and almighty God.

" O Holy Lord, Father almighty, eternal God, who together
with Thy only-begotten Son and the Holy Ghost, art one God
and one Lord: not in a singularity of one Person, but in a Trinity
of one substance. For what we believe of Thy glory as Thou hast
revealed, the same we believe of Thy Son, and of the Holy Ghost,
without any difference or distinction. That in the confession of

---

[1] P. Dehau, O.P., *Le Contemplatif et la Croix*, Editions de l'Abeille, vol. ii,
p. 10.

[2] Bossuet is here thinking of those anamorphoses whose reflection is observed
in a curved or cylindrical or conical mirror. (Editor's note.)

[3] *Oeuvres oratoires de Bossuet*, ed. Lebarq, Desclée de Brouwer, vol. ii, p. 158.

the true and eternal Deity may be adored a distinction in the Persons, a unity in the essence, and an equality in the majesty."[1]

Here, under its covering of abstract metaphysical terms—distinction, unity, equality—is an excellent expression of the psychology of love in its infinite plenitude. To be other whilst remaining oneself, to give oneself without self-loss, to be at the heart of an indivisible unity and a perfect equality, knowing boundless joy—this is pure love indeed. It is the Love of the Father and the Son and the Holy Spirit: " God is charity."[2]

The psychology of this relationship is ultimately the psychology of love. And the metaphysics of the Trinity is the metaphysics of relationship. In the Trinity the divine Person is a subsistent relationship.

" Is the human person an absolute, then? The answer is yes, but on the psychological plane it is relative too. Is this a contradiction? No, it is a mystery . . . The person is essentially in search of the person. Love presupposes knowledge, but it can, in a way, go beyond knowledge; it needs being itself; the person needs the person."[3] And our faith tells us that all the marvels of human love which take place under the sacrament of marriage are simply images, very distant images, of the marvels of the love in God.

" Divinity is found whole and entire in each of the three Persons; it is not less than entire in any One, nor is it increased in the Three. God is not distinct in three Persons but He is in three distinct Persons. This is the triumph of love, of being, of personality."[4]

" Circumincession is a theological term designating the fact that the three Persons of the Trinity mutually dwell one within the other in such a way that there is between them, as it were, a reciprocal circulation."[5] It is an exchange of pure love.

Now God in His mercy wills to enable us to live in His company as adopted children: " I am in the Father and the Father in me . . . And I will ask the Father, and he shall give you another Paraclete, that he may abide with you for ever, the Spirit of Truth . . . The Comforter, the Holy Ghost, whom the Father will send in my name, he will teach you all things . . . Peace I leave with you, my peace I give unto you; not as the world giveth do I give unto you. Let not your heart be troubled, nor let it be afraid . . . In my Father's house there are many mansions . . . I go to prepare a place for you."[6]

[1] Preface of the Trinity.
[2] 1 John iv. 16.
[3] *La Recherche de la Personne, Études Carmélitaines*, April 1936, p. 142.
[4] ibid, p. 144.
[5] M. V. Bernadot, O.P., *From Holy Communion to the Blessed Trinity*, trans. Dom Francis Izard, O.S.B., Sands, 1926, p. 49 n.
[6] John xiv, passim.

As a proof of His infinite goodness, and also to give us every help in the acquisition of supernatural happiness by enabling us to share in the love of the Three Persons, God made man like unto the angels by the addition of the preternatural gifts bestowed on him on the first day of his creation. Having incomparable intellectual enlightenment (through the gift of knowledge), and protected against suffering and death (through the gifts of impassibility and immortality), masters of the flesh, over which they had perfect command (through the gift of integrity), Adam and Eve, if they had remained faithful to the divine command, would have continued to be elevated above their own condition, and been able to make their way more easily during their earthly pilgrimage to the final joy of the beatific vision.[1]

In our first parents the whole of mankind was to have benefited from the overflowing bounty of divine providence. The riches which they had freely received were to have come down to us as our inheritance, from the mere fact of our having been born. Such, seen in the light of faith, was the original nobility of the human race, the inheritor of the divine happiness and love.

ORIGINAL SIN

Inequality, appearing as inferiority, is an essential sign of the relationship of any creature to God. The creature is that which is not, whose existence is not implied in its definition. God alone can name Himself, saying, " I Am That I Am."[2]

But the metaphysical deficiency of the contingent being is not an evil. There is no foolishness in serving the Creator. The heavens sing His glory; the savage lion and the birds of the air, all serve Him in their own way. " Consider the lilies of the field how they grow: they labour not neither do they spin. But I say to you that not even Solomon in all his glory was arrayed as one of these."[3] Everything is cared for in the works of God, down to the minutest detail.

Only a creature endowed with intelligence and will can refuse to be what he should be, and choose not to accept his condition as a faithful servant of his Master and a docile child of his Father. Because he is capable of love he can also rebel.

This is the drama raised by the liberty of a love that is obliged to turn aggressively against any obstacle to its own expression, and which also has the power to turn away from the things it should cherish and, ultimately, against itself. The love-aggression duality exists at the very heart of the creature, as a balance to be maintained and an order to be safeguarded.

[1] *De Malo*, q. 5, a. 1.   [2] Exod. iii. 14.   [3] Matt. vi. 28–9.

" I will not serve" and " I will be like the Most High ".[1] The sins of the angels were pride and jealousy, i.e. a moral revolt against the sovereignty of God, taking the form of a disordered appetite for equality with God; not that the angels absolutely refused to recognise any sort of dependence—they were too enlightened to fail to appreciate their condition as creatures—but, as St. Thomas explains, their refusal of the prospect of supernatural beatitude offered them through grace arose from the fact that they wished to be like God, and to realise their happiness through the instrumentality of their own nature only.[2] This is the sin of the spirit, the sin of those who disobey so that they may be entirely free in their own way, not subject to anybody or anything at all. There is in the heart of the fallen angels, on the one hand, jealousy at the knowledge that God can always perform His own good pleasure without ever sinning (as though the divine good pleasure were not always wisdom!), and on the other hand, running parallel with this malice, there is a determination to have the same dominion over good and evil as God has, without any other criterion except that of their own will!

The sin of the angels was irrevocable because it was fully conscious and entirely wilful.

It is not true, as far too many Catholics still seem to imagine, that the sin committed by Adam and Eve was a sin of sensual weakness; it would have been utterly impossible for the first sin to have been of such a kind, considering the quasi-angelic condition in which God had created them (not subject to death or sickness or ignorance or any rebellion of the senses, because of the gifts which had been super-added to their nature to ennoble and perfect it). But there remained the possibility, open to every reasonable creature, of rebelling against the divine ordinance. "Although the possibility of sinning is not a constituent of free will, nevertheless it is a consequence of freedom in the created nature."[3] "An angel or any other rational creature, considered in its own nature, can sin."[4]

The sin of Adam, like the sin of the angels, was a sin of pride, a revolt, an act of disobedience. The garden of Eden was full of fruit, but Adam was forbidden to touch one of the trees, the tree of the knowledge of Good and Evil. That is why he chose it.[5] The essential

---

[1] Isa. xiv. 14.
[2] I, 63, 3.
[3] *De Veritate*, q. 24, a. 7, ad 4um.
[4] I, 63, 1.
[5] On the subject of the historical character of the first chapters of Genesis, by a decision taken on June 30 1909 (Denzinger, 2125), the Biblical Commission " expressly authorizes whatever liberties may be demanded by reason or have been initiated by the Fathers, to be taken regarding certain expressions in the

TITYUS

Michelangelo: Windsor Castle, Royal Library: by gracious permission of H.M. the Queen

point to realize is that there was a definite wilful revolt against God, instigated by the Father of Lies and proudly aiming to delimit the frontiers of good and evil against the divine law itself. Pascal makes God say: " I created man holy, innocent, perfect. I filled him with light and intelligence. I communicated to him My glory and My wonders. The eye of man saw then the majesty of God. He was not then in the darkness which blinds him, nor subject to mortality and the woes which afflict him. But he has not been able to sustain so great glory without falling into pride. He wanted to make himself his own centre, and independent of My help. He withdrew himself from My rule; and, on his making himself equal to Me by the desire of finding his happiness in himself, I abandoned him to himself."[1]

As a consequence of this, human nature was deprived of those free gifts which prevented it from living in ignorance, from suffering, from dying, and also from knowing any inner conflict between the flesh and the spirit.[2] Love having been weakened, " Free-will has lost its force and acquired a tendency towards evil, without being entirely annulled, however ", as the Council of Trent teaches.[3] Aggressiveness gained the upper hand and began to ravage human nature. Cain killed his brother Abel and the first war broke out. We in our day have known the shameful horror of the tortures prepared in gas-chambers and death-ovens. In the interval between, what mourning and tears, what slavery and bloodshed there have been!

Pope Pius IX reminded rationalists and indifferentists " how cruel and serious the wound inflicted on human nature was, as a result of the sin of our first parents; the mind has been darkened ", he states, " and the will inclined towards evil ".[4]

God had been outraged by a human creature enjoying a quasi-angelic condition of being. The goodness of the Creator and the responsibility of the creature were both more evident in the economy of the earthly paradise than they would have been if human nature had been left to its own proper condition.

It may seem that after the fall of Adam and Eve the divine goodness seems to contradict itself. It is true that in all justice God needs to allow for the difficulties incessantly springing up from a nature as fragile as ours if He is to judge it fairly, but is this an adequate response for a God of Love? If God's forgiveness goes no further than that, is He not still returning evil for evil?

---

account which are improper, metaphorical or anthropomorphic" (art. " Péché originel ", *Dict. de Théol. Cath.*).

[1] *Pensées*, 430.
[2] Denzinger, 788, 789, 793.
[3] ibid., 793.
[4] Denzinger, 1643; the Allocution *Singulari Quadam*, given on Dec. 8, 1854.

To avoid any fantastic kind of explanation, it is necessary to begin by defining clearly the damage caused to us by original sin.

As members of the human race, we suffer the consequences of a sin which, personally, we did not commit. However serious and personal Adam's original sin may have been, it contained no element of subjective guilt for those who came after him—not even to the extent of any venial sin, St. Thomas teaches.[1] And so the theologians speak of a sin of nature, to signify the privation of sanctifying grace and the quasi-angelic gifts which, if Adam had not sinned, would have been granted to us at the moment of our conception.[2]

This idea, of the sin of Adam as becoming for us a sin of nature, is of capital importance. There is a "death of the soul"[3] on the supernatural level, because our nature has been deprived of the life of union with the divine Persons; there is sin " in the true and proper meaning of the term ",[4] because this deprivation is, historically and morally speaking, the result of a culpable revolt by the first man and woman, who justly provoked " the anger and indignation of God "[5]; there is a sin of nature, because it is our nature that has been despoiled; but there is absolutely no personal sin whatsoever, because, clearly, no kind of personal responsibility on our part comes into the question.

Let us try to analyse a little more closely the spoliation of which we are the victims.

As regards the deprivation of sanctifying grace, the divine seed of the beatific vision, St. Thomas says that this is " the least of punishments "—meaning that it is no punishment at all—for anyone who has never sinned personally, and for whom this deprivation does not denote, therefore, any personal punishment—as in the case, for instance, of children who die without being baptised. If there is no suffering in limbo (which is paradise without the beatific vision), this is because, objectively, the possession of the divine essence is, absolutely speaking, something quite beyond the strict requirements of any created nature, and also because, subjectively, all the souls in limbo are personally innocent.[6]

---

[1] *De Malo*, q. 5, a. 1, ad 9um.

[2] By the privilege of her Immaculate Conception, the Blessed Virgin Mary never contracted original sin; she always possessed sanctifying grace in a state of perfect purity from the first moment of her conception. In the seventeenth century the Carmelites of Salamanca, in the course of a long debate, vigorously defended the thesis of the Immaculate Conception, which they felt " very strongly about " (*Cursus Theologicus*, ed. Palmé, 1877, vol. viii, Tractatus xiii, " De vitiis et peccatis", disp. xv, pp. 85–213).

[3] Denzinger, 789.

[4] ibid., 792.

[5] ibid., 788.

[6] *De Malo*, q. 5, a. 1, ad 3um: " mitissima pœnarum ". The Carmelites of Salamanca have interesting theories about limbo (*Cursus Theologicus*, vol. viii,

But in the terrestrial scheme of things, ignorance, concupiscence, suffering and death, which all came into the world through the sin of Adam, are burdens hard to endure. Our condition is tragic, for we are all moving towards death, which is "horrible to human nature".[1]

Does this mean that our nature has been tainted and vitiated, so to speak, as human nature, in its being and operation, by the original sin?

The Augustinians thought so. For them, human nature, in the state demanded philosophically by its own nature, would certainly not have been what it is today; it would have been less evil, it would have been a good deal better. All Augustinians are agreed that the psychic life of fallen man is not only inferior to the psychic life of man as realized in Adam at the moment of his creation, but also inferior to the psychic life of man as our reason can, and must, conceive him to be, when all revelation has been abstracted, in a state of pure nature. The play of our human faculties is no longer quite natural or normal, and the laws of heredity exist to transmit these deficiencies.[2]

What in fact was St. Augustine's opinion on this point? It is difficult to dogmatize about it. The authorities are not agreed as to the judgment they should pass upon him. P. Boyer, the authority on this matter,

---

pp. 442–6). Children who die without being baptised, and others like them (adults without the use of moral reason, who have not been baptised), will find great delight in sharing the natural perfections of God. " They will not miss the original justice destined for them through Adam any more than if it had never been promised them " (p. 444). They are not sad at being without the beatific vision, for they have not been deprived of it: it was never intended for them. And if for any reason they did have the slightest regret, God would owe it to Himself to bring it about that they did not feel any pain—assuming that they have not committed any personal sins (loc. cit.). It will be seen how determined the authors are not to compromise the divine justice and goodness in the slightest degree.

[1] III, 46, 6, c.

[2] Theologians distinguish in man:
   i. the state of *pure* nature (a conception which we know by faith has never been realised in history);
   ii. the state of *integral* nature (which implies a whole series of gifts resulting in the perfect balance of human nature);
   iii. the state of *original justice* (in which Adam was created); this comprises (a) quasi-angelic gifts resulting in a miraculous condition of integrity and (b) sanctifying grace, i.e. elevation to the strictly supernatural level absolutely necessary for the beatific vision;
   iv. the state of *fallen* nature (Adam's state after the loss of the gratuitous gifts);
   v. the state of *redeemed* nature, or state of redemption (ours today); we possess sanctifying grace again without the quasi-angelic gifts, these having been replaced—to our advantage, from the point of view of our growth in love—by the economy of the sacraments, particularly the Eucharist, under the sign of suffering and the Cross.

The Augustinian thesis is thus that our nature, in itself and as actually constituted, is less good than our nature in the pure state would have been, without any preternatural or supernatural gifts (i).

writes: " After examining this question from every point of view it
appears difficult to prove that St. Augustine ever maintained that it is
absolutely impossible to explain the wretchedness of man, as known
to him through his own experience, without having recourse to the
doctrine of original sin."[1]

But Gaudel states that many Augustinians have certainly believed
" that the present wretched condition of mankind cannot be man's
normal and natural state ".[2] In this respect Jansenism, with its extreme
pessimism, is simply a deformed and exaggerated version of Augustinianism: original sin is supposed to have vitiated human nature to such
an extent as to deprive it in practice of free-will. Jansenism was rejected
by the Church in the condemnations of Jansenius, Quesnel and the
Synod of Pistoia.

On the whole the best representatives of the genuine Thomist
tradition make no concessions to the Augustinian principle. For St.
Thomas, the sin of Adam did not vitiate human nature at all, either on its
own philosophical level or in the substances of which it is composed
(soul and body), or in its operative faculties (intelligence, will and
feeling). It has lost everything that was gratuitously super-added to it,
but nothing more. The psychic life of fallen man is natural to man.
St. Thomas often speaks of nature " left to itself ", to denote the
condition of our wretchedness.[3]

In the opinion of the first of the commentators on the *Summa*,
Cardinal Cajetan, the difference between human nature considered in
all its philosophic purity, and human nature after its fall, is the same
as that between someone who has never worn clothes, and one who
has had them taken away from him. Both people are equally naked.
Both natures are equally natural. The corruptibility of the body is the
same for both. But from the standpoint of the reason behind these
things, there is a great difference: pure nature, philosophically considered, is analogous to the person who has never worn clothes, and his
deficiencies are neither faults nor penalties nor wounds, but natural
conditions pure and simple; whereas in fallen nature these missing
assets are historically, as regards their origin, corruptions, wounds,
penalties and faults.[4]

---

[1] " Dieu pouvait-il créer l'homme dans l'état d'ignorance et de difficulté?
Étude de quelques textes augustiniens ", *Gregorianum*, vol. xi, 1. See also
Gaudel, art. " Péché originel ", in *Dictionnaire de Théol. Cath.*, col. 374 et seq.
[2] *Dict. de Théol. Cath.* col. 391 et seq. See particularly some of the Port-
Royal figures and even Bossuet.
[3] See particularly I-II, 82, 83, 86; *De Malo*, q. 4, a. 2.
[4] Here is Cardinal Cajetan's text (Commentary in I-II, 109, 2):
" Differentiam inter naturam in puris naturalibus et naturam lapsam, quae
ut unico verbo dicatur, tanta est quanta est inter personam nudam ab initio et
personam exspoliatum. Et dico secundum rem, secundum rationes vero rerum,

The Carmelites of Salamanca are in entire agreement with Cajetan. For them, too, neither from the metaphysical, nor from the psychological point of view, has original sin had the least effect on human nature as regards anything properly appertaining to it. " As nature it has remained positively unchanged "—neither better nor worse than it would have been in the state of pure nature.[1]

---

multa adveniunt, sicut enim persona nuda et persona exspoliata non distinguuntur in hoc quod una sit magis aut minus nuda, ita natura in puris naturalibus et natura exspoliata gratia et iustitia originali non differunt per hoc quod altera earum sit magis aut minus in naturalibus destituta. Et ratio est quia destitutio sequens exspoliationem gratiae et justitiae originalis non est effectus illius nisi per accidens, ut removentis prohibens; exspoliatio enim abstrulit gratiam et justitiam quae prohibebat vires animae secundum seipsas disponi: ex removente namque prohibens non sequitur maior aut minor effectus naturalis quam ex natura sequatur: non enim magis aut minus movetur lapis remoto prohibente quam a gravitate. Proprie absolute fuisset motus propter quod cum natura ex peccato originali sit sibi ipsi derelicta, tam in anima quam in corpore non maior destitutio est in natura lapsa, quam natura in puris naturalibus, sicut non est magis redditum corruptibile corpus nostrum ex peccato originali sibi derelictum, quam ex natura fuisset simpliciter. Sed quantum ad rationes rerum, magna differentia est quia sicut in persona nuda, nuditas negationis rationem habet, in exspoliata vero habet rationem privationis vestis debitae conservari, ita defectus animae et corporis naturae in puris naturalibus nec culpae, nec vulnerum, etc., rationem habent, sed naturalium conditionum; in natura autem lapsa habent rationem corruptionum, vulnerum, poenae et culpae in parte susceptiva illius."

Gonet and Billuart defend the same thesis. Some Thomists have been the partisans of an attenuated Augustinianism—quite acceptable, however, from the orthodox Catholic point of view—but they are exceptional.

[1] *Cursus Theologicus*, Ed. Palmé, 1877, vol. viii, disp. xvi, dub. iii, §3, p. 244. The Carmelites of Salamanca maintain and defend the Thomist thesis for many pages, clearly and quite emphatically (dub. ii, iii, pp. 229–55).

Thesis. Even in Adam personally human nature was not intrinsically vitiated as nature (pp. 229, 232). Nor is it vitiated in us, either as regards the soul or the body or the operative faculties (p. 230).

I. The argument drawn from the principle of economy, which can be expressed as follows: The simplest explanations should be accepted until they are proved wrong; the exception needs proof and is not to be assumed. (For the principle of economy and the miraculous see the very clear account by R. Dalbiez, " Miracle et Logique ", *Études Carmélitaines*, Oct. 1934.)

A. *On the theological level*. Recalling the old saying, " Spoliatus in gratuitis, vulneratus in naturalibus " (" by original sin man was despoiled of the gratuitous gifts and wounded in his nature "), our authors explain it as follows: " To prove that according to the teaching of the Council of Trent the whole man suffers, body and soul, from original sin, it is sufficient to admit that he has lost original justice in so far as this ennobled his body and soul and ordered his appetite aright " (p. 237). It must not be forgotten that, unlike our sanctifying grace, original justice, which included both sanctifying grace and the preternatural gifts, did in fact improve the psychic life even of nature itself.

B. *On the philosophic level*. " Just as being composed of contrary elements means bearing within oneself the sufficient cause of corruption, if nothing intervenes to prevent this, so being endowed with reason and senses—so long as there is not a perfect subordination of one to the other—means bearing within oneself the sufficient reason for a propensity towards evil and a repugnance against the good, so long as the reason forbids what the senses desire.

Père Monsabré follows exactly the same line of thought when he writes: " Fallen man is neither weaker as regards the good nor more inclined to evil than the purely natural man. Original sin deprives him of what would have been his glory and his strength; it does not add

and the senses oppose what the reason desires. Thus, just as there is no need to have recourse to any positive factor to explain the existence of death in our nature—it is sufficient to abolish what prevented it—in the same way, to explain our propensity towards evil and our repugnance to the good it is sufficient to abolish what held this dual movement of nature in check; nothing needs to be super-added " (p. 236).

Objection: " The weakness of fallen nature is like the fever of an organism attacked by illness or abnormal hunger, like being ' as hungry as a horse '. The reason for this vehemence is the repercussion of Adam's sin onto his own body and consequently onto ours by way of inheritance " (p. 234).

Reply: A comparison is not a reason and this analogy will not do, for " to prove that our nature is ill with its weakness, it is sufficient that it has lost its former disposition of rectitude and integrity, which it possessed as a result of original justice; it was from this that its integrity and health came, and consequently, having lost original justice, it has been rendered, without the intervention of any other positive factor, ill, weak and unstable " (p. 237).

C. *Conclusion.* Theologians and philosophers will agree: " There is no reason allowing one to affirm that in the state of pure nature our physical powers might have been carried towards their objects with less impetuosity and less efficacy than they are today, before, through their own actions, they acquire vicious habits " (p. 235).

II. The metaphysical argument drawn from the ideas of nature and essential or accidental relationship. The intrinsically deforming vice in question is, logically speaking, either essential or accidental.

A. *First hypothesis: The deforming vice as essential.* The natural inclination of the operative powers (which proceed from the substance by dimanation) is no different from the powers themselves, and therefore cannot be added to or taken away from: it is what it is, unchangeable and unvarying (p. 234). Natures are like numbers: if they are impaired intrinsically as natures they make other natures. Thus there cannot possibly be any essential deformation of any nature if it remains the same nature.

Now Adam remained a man before and after he sinned.

Furthermore, God, who is in us the cause of our nature, would, if the opposite were true, become the cause of sin (p. 232).

B. *Second hypothesis: The deforming vice as accidental.*

(*a*) Supposing the impossible—that in Adam the operative faculties had in fact been affected intrinsically, this would have nothing to do with the transmission of original sin, for it would have been quite *accidental* as regards the nature to be transmitted. On any hypothesis (even if there had been an accidental transmission to the children of Adam) this vice would not have been communicable to the whole human race as such (p. 234).

(*b*) Whatever is permanent, always and everywhere fitting to all men, cannot, logically speaking, be accidental, and the infirmities that are to be explained are neither superficial nor secondary. " It is one thing to speak of an infirmity arising simply from a privation of original justice as its occasion, and from nature as its proper cause; it is another thing to speak of an infirmity arising from an accidental disposition " (p. 233).

C. *Conclusion.* The present infirmities of the human race not being able to be super-added to human nature either essentially (for then it would no longer be human nature) or accidentally (for then it would no longer apply to all men), it remains that they must arise substantially from human nature as such, philosophically speaking, unless God Himself intervenes, positively, to suspend their exercise. It will be noticed that this argument does not exclude the possibility any vitiating quality to the constituents of his being . . . His present state is exactly like that of the man whom Gòd could have created without the grace of justice and integrity ".[1] This position is also adopted by Cardinal Billot.

Such are the opposing theses with which we are concerned. Though the Thomist solution is the least pessimistic theologically, since it grants original sin only a hypothetical and subordinate part in the explanation of the present wretchedness of mankind, it is for this very reason all the harder on the philosophic level because, our miseries being what they are, there is, absolutely speaking, no need for any later fall to take place after the super-elevation of our nature to supply an adequate explanation of them: nature is itself sufficient, once it is left to the motion of its own weight.

The fittingness of the preternatural gifts bestowed in the garden of Eden becomes clearer still, if we remember providence on the one hand, and the dignity of the soul on the other, and that is why St. Thomas's conclusion too—like that of certain Augustinians, though it is reached by quite a different process of reasoning—is that the present miseries of the human race are probably real signs—we may say, morally almost certain signs—of an original sin. God owed it to Himself, in a sense, not to throw a reasonable nature as fragile as ours into existence without some kind of compensation, some kind of special help.[2] Let St. Thomas speak for himself.

" We must, in the first place, observe that there are certain probable signs of original sin in the human race. For . . . we can conclude that where there is punishment, there has been sin. Now

---

that God may grant to all men at the moment of their conception preternatural or supernatural gifts, as He would have done in the state of innocence, because these gifts:

    (1) do not vitiate nature;
    (2) respect all its positive natural characteristics;
    (3) ennoble it and elevate it.

[1] *Conférences de Notre-Dame*, 1877, 28th Conference.

[2] If there often seems to be considerable confusion in accounts of these matters it is because insufficient care is taken to distinguish between two different questions: (1) As it exists today, is human nature, by virtue of its very nature, intrinsically vitiated (by an original sin), philosophically speaking? To this the Jansenists reply that it is essentially vitiated; the Augustinians reply that it is accidentally vitiated; the Thomists reply that it is not vitiated at all. (2) Could God have created human nature in the state in which it is today (minus the fact of original sin)? Quite logically the Jansenists say no, and the Church has condemned them (Proposition 55 by Barus: God could not in the beginning have created man as he is born today; rejected by St. Pius V, Denzinger, 1055); the Thomists are bound to say yes, absolutely speaking (including even the divine attributes), but nevertheless St. Thomas considers it much more probable that God would not have acted in this way, as we shall see later. Logically, the Augustinians ought to be on the side of the Jansenists, but for a less compelling reason, since for them the present vice of nature is only accidental.

the whole human race suffers various punishments, both bodily and spiritual. Of bodily punishments the chief is death, to which all others are conducive and subordinate, such as hunger, thirst, and so on. Of spiritual punishments, the principal is weakness of reason, the result being that man encounters difficulty in acquiring knowledge of the truth, and easily falls into error; also that he is unable wholly to overcome his animal propensities, which sometimes even obscure his mental vision. Someone however might reply that these defects, whether of body or of soul, are not penalties but natural defects, and a necessary consequence of the conditions of matter. For the human body, being composed of contrary elements, must needs be corruptible; and the sensitive appetite must needs incline to things in which the senses delight, and which at times are contrary to reason. Again, the possible intellect is in potentiality to all things intelligible, and has none of them actually, but has by its very nature to acquire them through the senses, and therefore with difficulty acquires the knowledge of the truth, and is easily led astray by the imagination.

"Nevertheless, if we look at the matter rightly it will appear sufficiently probable that, divine providence having fitted each perfection to that which is to be perfected, God has united a higher to a lower nature in order that the former might dominate the latter, and, should any obstacle to this dominion arise through a defect of nature, God by a special and supernatural act of kindness would remove it. Wherefore, since the rational soul is of a higher nature than the body, we believe that it was united to the body under such conditions, that there can be nothing in the body to oppose the soul whereby the body lives: and in like manner, if reason in man is united to his sensual appetite and his other sensitive powers, that reason is not hindered by the sensitive powers, but on the contrary, dominates them . . . Accordingly, although these defects seem natural to man absolutely, if we consider his nature from its lower side, nevertheless, if we consider divine providence, and the dignity of the higher part of man's nature, it can be proved with sufficient probability that these defects are penal, and consequently that the human race was originally infected with sin."[1]

Such is the central teaching of the " Summa against the Gentiles." We must not be afraid to conclude that man in his present condition is not properly balanced. Although he is the masterpiece of the material creation, being endowed with reason and therefore ultimately—with the help of grace—capable of the beatific vision, nevertheless he is the

[1] *Contra Gentes*, iv, 52.

poor relation of thinking beings, below the least of the angels. He experiences in his very depths the struggle between the flesh and the spirit, and knows the way the latter can succumb to the former. St. Paul said this, Pascal repeated it in the words of genius, and St. Thomas has analysed the metaphysical reasons for it with perfect lucidity: "Death and corruption are natural to man from the point of view of the demands of matter; but from the point of view of the higher part of man's being it is immortality that is fitting for him; the principles of human nature are not in themselves sufficient to ensure immortality, but because of his soul there is in man *himself*[1] a certain aptitude for immortality."[2]

In short, human nature is, by virtue of its very nature, essentially fragile. This affirmation alone enables one to keep the balance between so many complex problems, which can all too easily be seen from a wrong perspective.

Because human nature is *fragile* the gifts bestowed in the Garden of Eden were eminently fitting to it; and we are driven to deduce that it is highly probable that an original fault was the occasion of our present miseries.

Because human nature is fragile *by virtue of its very nature*, we cannot

[1] As man, soul *and body*. Hence the fittingness of the resurrection of the body.

[2] *De Malo*, q. 5, a. 5. It will be seen what are the immediate metaphysical roots of the love-aggressiveness duality, which plays such an important part in man's behaviour: they are the soul and the body; whereas the deeper metaphysical roots are in men what they are in the angels: nature and personality really distinct from each other and hence distinct in their existence and activity. The divine personality alone is identical with its wisdom and its love (and with an infinite plenitude) because it is identical with its nature as well as its existence.

Either the created personality will accept the fact that it is not its own nature, but has received it and must therefore obey its laws, and then it will maintain its balance—or else it will want to dominate its nature in its own way as if it were its absolute master and then it will be, literally, off its axis. This is the fundamental error of "naturalism". The natural equilibrium must be established between one person and another on the level of nature and according to the laws of nature.

The supernatural order means uniting in love the created person with the uncreated Persons, beyond the limits of the requirements of any created nature as such, but nevertheless not violating the natural laws which become, so to speak, the material conditions of a development that is infinitely superior to them. The supernatural balance should be established between person and Person on the level of infinity. "Whatever you have done unto the least of these you have done it unto Me."

For God, because of the identification of nature and personality, no supernatural is possible.

For creatures endowed with spirit, the supernatural is possible and desirable.

Whatever their density of being all creatures are as such infinitely remote from the divine Persons.

The more deficient the creature endowed with spirit, the more fitting is the supernatural as a means to its ennoblement and the recovery of its balance. The Word, in fact, became flesh, not an angel, and the Queen of the Archangels is a woman, the Blessed Virgin Mary. The " last " have become the " first ".

be metaphysically certain about the original sin, but the chief thing is that the loss of the preternatural gifts does not involve any injustice or arbitrary behaviour towards any of us, even though it is highly fitting that it should summon up divine aid for us in exact proportion to our weakness and misery.

We are not the victims of any injustice: however weak human nature may be, it is still our nature; a man may demand not to be an animal, but he has no right to ask to be an angel. Nor is there any arbitrary measure on God's part in this: solidarity and sociability between man and man is engraved in our deepest being. The personality cannot, in fact, develop, except to the extent that the individuality is part of a whole—a family or a nation, for example—which is as homogeneous as possible. We are obliged to have the same nature, whether we are raised or fallen: such is our human condition. Philosophically we form one single race.

But if there is nothing unjust or arbitrary in God's behaviour towards us, does this necessarily imply that He shows any goodness towards us? According to the extent that one agrees with St. Thomas Aquinas, that it is highly unlikely and most unfitting that man should leave the hands of his Creator in the state of pure nature, the question becomes all the more difficult: why did God permit the Fall, with all its consequences? Human nature exists—inclined to evil, to sin; it exists with all its suffering, tears, blood and death. Were we ennobled only that we might be disinherited? The voice of conscience murmurs that evil cannot be indirectly permitted except with a view to a greater good. Where does the good come in in this case?

" O God, who in creating human nature, didst wonderfully dignify it, and hast still more wonderfully renewed it," replies the liturgy, with resolute optimism.[1]

" Wonderfully dignified ": in the economy of the earthly paradise fatherhood and motherhood would have been a kind of priesthood; we should have received from our parents, after God, by way of inheritance, both the natural life and the supernatural life of the children of adoption.

"Still more marvellously renewed": it is "a general and fundamental idea in patristic theology " to conceive of baptism " as a return to paradise ".[2] We are, in fact, baptised—with the sign of the Cross—in the name of the Father, the Son and the Holy Spirit. The divine seed of the beatific vision is given back to us, but "still more wonderfully ", in a way whose excellence can be judged by the distance that

[1] Offertory of the Mass.
[2] Jean Daniélou, *La vie liturgique dans la primitive Eglise* (unpublished lecture).

separates the Word made flesh, and His Mother, the Virgin Mary, from the first Adam and the first Eve, as they were even before they sinned. This is the mystery of the Incarnation, which is fulfilled in the Redemption: God's answer to man's sin.

THE REDEMPTION

The Word became flesh in our vale of tears, into which He descended to suffer death, the death on the cross. The face of the Child Jesus became the Holy Face, covered with tears, sweat, spit and blood. The Saviour gave up the ghost between two thieves.

Was He a victim of the Father's wrath, an innocent hostage unjustly paying the penalty for the guilty, or was He a " victim of merciful love ",[1] freely giving the ultimate witness of His infinite tenderness, in perfect co-operation with His Father? Is this redemption of sin made under the sign of love or wrath?

The idea of redemption is bound up with that of sin. In sin there are two separate factors to be distinguished: the pleasure inherent in the sin, which would not be committed if it did not please a certain side of our nature, and disobedience to God, this disobedience being in fact implied in the pleasure. Sin is a forbidden fruit. This fruit is not evil because it is a fruit, or because it is pleasant, but because it is forbidden.

As a kind of corollary to this, two elements must normally be expected in any reparation of sin: a pain of affliction, to balance the pleasure, and love and humility, to balance the disobedience. The question therefore arises, which of these two elements was the one that counts for most in the work of the Redemption—the pain, by means of aggressiveness, or love in humility.

Luther's answer was, aggressiveness.

WAS CHRIST CONDEMNED JUSTLY?

Luther writes:

" It will be said that it is utterly absurd and lacking in all respect to call the Son of God a sinner and accursed. I reply: If you deny this you must also deny that He suffered, was crucified and died. For it is no more absurd to say that the Son of God was crucified and suffered the penalties of sin even unto death, than to say that He was a sinner and accursed. If, then, it is not absurd to confess and believe that Christ was crucified between two thieves, it is no

[1] St. Thérèse of Lisieux.

more absurd to say that He was accursed and the greatest of all sinners. By the effect of divine Love sin was planted in Him. The law then intervenes and says: Sin must die. If then, O Christ, You wish to be a warning to sinners, be guilty and bear the penalty of sinners, bear sin and malediction. Not without reason does the Apostle apply to Christ the general law of Moses: Whoever hangs upon the tree is accursed of God. Now Christ was hanged upon the tree. Therefore Christ was accursed of God."[1]

Calvin echoes this:

" It was necessary that Christ should bear all the harshness of God's vengeance in His soul in order to be the object of His wrath and satisfy His need for judgment. Therefore it was required that He should fight against the forces of hell and do battle, as it were hand-to-hand, against the horror of eternal death . . . He was made the principal debtor and as though guilty, in order to suffer all the punishments prepared for us, and thus to annul them."[2]

But Calvin added:

" By this we do not wish to infer, however, that God had ever been His adversary, or been angered against His Christ . . . but we say that He endured the weight of God's vengeance, in that He was struck and afflicted by His hand and experienced all the signs which God visits upon sinners when He grows angry with them and punishes them."[3]

Calvin did not dare to say that God was angered against Christ. Bossuet, however, had no such fear. Speaking of the Saviour, he writes:

" God raises against Him His avenging hand and shatters His criminal soul under the intolerable weight of His vengeance . . . All the other torments, whose extreme harshness we have already described, are no more than a dream and a figment compared with the pains, the oppression, the anguish, suffered by the soul of the divine Jesus under the hand of God . . . Only God has the right to avenge injuries . . . It was therefore necessary, brethren, that He Himself should come against His Son with all His might; and since He had put our sins in Him, He was also obliged to enact His just

---

[1] Luther, *Commentary on the Galatians*, iii, 13, quoted by Rivière, *Le Dogme de la Rédemption*, *Étude théologique*, 4th ed. Gabalda, 1931, p. 388.
[2] Calvin, *Inst. Christ.*, lib. ii, cap. 16, quoted by Rivière, op. cit., p. 392.
[3] *Instit. Christ.*, lib. ii, cap. 16, quoted by Rivière, *Le Dogme de la Rédemption*.

vengeance upon him. This He did, Christians, let us have no doubt about it . . . God looks upon His Son with . . . eyes of rage, He looks down upon Him, not with the look that brings serenity but with that dreadful look that kindles fire before it . . . which rouses fear in men's consciences . . . My God, why must there appear before me that countenance wherewith You strike fear into the hearts of those you reprove . . . All I can see is a God enraged . . . He rejects His Son, and opens His arms to us; He looks angrily upon Him, and upon us He looks with eyes of mercy . . . He vents His anger upon Him, He strikes His innocent Son, struggling under the anger of God. This is what happened on the cross, until the Son of God, seeing in His Father's eyes that He was utterly appeased, realised that at last the time had come for him to leave the world."[1]

Mgr. Gay belongs to the same school as Bossuet. He writes:

" It is not one sin only but the whole immeasurable mass of human iniquity that is suddenly to fall upon Him. He who has an infinite horror of sin, for whom sin is radically impossible—He it is who has to take our sins upon Himself and, so to speak, identify Himself with them . . . This is what He fears. He is afraid too of God's justice . . . He is afraid of the wrath of the Judge who has been righteously angered and whose anger, He can see, has reached the stage of fury. He is afraid of the curse of God; for in truth it is He, Jesus, our infinite living benediction, who, as He has been made a sinner for us all, so is He to be also accursed for us."[2]

But this is not true.

We are here at the antipodes of the thought of St. Thomas Aquinas, who, following St. John Chrysostom, says that it would be wrong to suggest the slightest antagonism between the Son and His Father in the Passion and on the cross.[3]

Catholic tradition has never admitted that Christ ever doubted His Father's love. The mysterious dereliction only refers to the lower rational and physical part of the holy humanity. The Saviour continued to enjoy the beatific vision in the midst of His atrocious sufferings, knowing that He remained the well-beloved Son in whom the Father was well pleased.[4]

Did the Father deliver up His Son to the Passion? St. Thomas's

[1] *Oeuvres oratoires de Bossuet*, ed. Lebarq, Desclée de Brouwer, vol. iii, pp. 369, 384, 385, 387, 389.
[2] *Sermons*, vol. ii, pp. 216–17, quoted by Rivière, *Le Dogme de la Rédemption*, p. 235.
[3] III, 47, 2, 1um, and 3, 2um.
[4] III, 46, 8.

answer to this question is in essence: " God the Father did deliver up
Christ to the Passion. In the first way, because by His eternal will He
pre-ordained Christ's Passion for the deliverance of the human race,
according to the words of Isaias (liii. 6): ' The Lord hath laid on Him
the inquities of us all '; and again (v. 10): ' The Lord was pleased to
bruise Him in infirmity '. Secondly, inasmuch as, by the infusion of
charity, He inspired Him with the will to suffer for us; hence we
read in the same passage: ' He was offered because it was His own will '
(v. 7). Thirdly, by not shielding Him from the Passion but abandoning
Him to His persecutors; thus we read (Matt. xxvii. 46) that Christ,
while hanging upon the cross, cried out: ' My God, my God, why hast
Thou forsaken Me? ' because, to wit, He left Him to the power of
His persecutors, as Augustine says . . . The Father delivered
up Christ, and Christ surrendered Himself from charity, and consequently we give praise to both: but Judas betrayed Christ from greed,
the Jews from envy, and Pilate from worldly fear, for he stood in fear
of Caesar; and these accordingly are held guilty."[1] Such are St.
Thomas's clear and matter-of-fact words.

Mgr. d'Hulst, on the other hand, says bluntly: " Justice had to
be satisfied first. So long as justice demanded its due, mercy was
bound and as though powerless. Therefore God began with justice
. . . Here the shadow of the mystery thickens. A substitution was
decided upon by which the Just One, the Holy One, was to take the
place of the guilty one."[2]

The same note is to be heard from the pulpit of Notre-Dame, from
the lips of Père Monsabré: " God found in His Christ all that He would
have looked for in vain in any other victim—sin, to be punished . . .
God sees before Him as it were living sin . . . and overcome by the
horror which iniquity inspires in His divine sanctity, His holy flesh
becomes accursed, instead of us . . . it was man, universal man, man
substituted for the sinners of all places and all times, the man humanity.
At the sight of Him the divine justice forgets the vulgar rabble of human
beings and has no eyes for anything except this strange and monstrous
phenomenon on which it is to wreak its revenge. Spare Him, Lord, it
is Your own son! No, it is sin; it must be punished . . ."[3] " He is
the accursed one *par excellence*, the curse made man, in the Apostle's
vigorous phrase."[4]

[1] III, 47, 3, c and 3um.
[2] Lenten Retreat of 1891, Good Friday, quoted by Rivière, *Le Dogme de la
Rédemption*, p. 234.
[3] 49th Conference for Lent, 1881, quoted by Rivière, *Le Dogme de la Rédemption*, p. 233.
[4] 47th Conference for Lent, 1880, op. cit., p. 242.

Rivière has rightly become known in our day as the theologian of the Redemption. He has devoted himself to the task of unmasking the falsifications of

Alas, Bossuet himself had said: " The sweetest comfort that a good man can experience in affliction is the thought of his innocence . . . Jesus, the innocent Jesus, did not enjoy this sweetness in His passion;

tradition in modern religious teaching and practice; he quotes many " Catholic " passages which occasionally go one better than even Luther or Calvin.

Here are a few more samples of these quotations. Corne, *Le Mystère de Notre Seigneur Jésus-Christ*: " Jesus appears in His Father's eyes as the Universal Sinner, the Living Sin, a Being accursed . . . God no longer sees in Him His well-beloved Son but the Victim of sin, the Sinner at all times and in all places, upon whom He will unload the whole weight of His justice " (Rivière, p. 232.) " Becoming Universal Sin, in a way He resembles evil, Satan, and all the reprobate; to the just, the angels, the Immaculate Virgin, He is an object of repulsion; God Himself will hurl His anathema at Him: He is to be the Universal Excommunicate, the Accursed. He is horrified at the thought of the terrible blows to which the divine wrath will subject Him so that He shall expiate the crimes of the human race . . ." (Rivière, p. 236). " This is the strange spectacle seen on the cross and nowhere else: God persecuting God, abandoning God, the forsaken God complaining and the God who forsakes proving implacable " (Rivière, p. 238).

Mgr. Gay, *Sermons*: " Here then is Jesus, crushed and annihilated between the iniquity of the whole earth which is so horrible to Him, and the inexorable justice of Heaven which terrifies Him; the divine decree loads the iniquity upon Him so that He shall satisfy justice. He is obliged to absorb both human filth and divine vengeance; He who is the world's sanctuary, the heart of humanity, must become its sewer " (Rivière, p. 236). " To be simply abandoned by God is hell; but for one God to feel Himself abandoned by another God, who can describe it? " (Rivière, p. 239).

Let us add one last specimen chosen by the author as a particularly remarkable example of these doctrinal aberrations. The following extracts are taken from *La Montée du Calvaire* by Père Perroy (Lethielleux, 70th thousand).

" . . . Jesus is above all the Victim who expiates our sins: He knows this, feels it, wills it, and it is as such that His Father primarily sees Him. This is Christ's main rôle, the first reason for His existence: He must satisfy God's justice, repair the outrage done to God, save God's honour; it might almost be said that the salvation of men comes later: in any case, the Father thoroughly intends to satisfy His fearful justice first: Jesus will have to ' pay the whole debt without any remission or mercy ' (Bossuet, *Deuxième sermon sur la Passion*). For more than four thousand years this supreme expiation had been preparing . . . The wrath of God grows from age to age during the life of guilty mankind. Sometimes the arm of God flashes out like lightning and the bold lines it sketches give a suggestion of His rage. He will do things properly later . . ." (pp. 7–8). The author goes on to call up images of the red heifer immolated in front of the temple, the unclean stag hunted through Cedron; Isaac, Job, Jonas . . . " Finally, the time is fulfilled: here is the real expected Victim. Christ is born! With what jealous care God surrounds Him until He mounts the slopes of Calvary! There is a long preparation, like a progressive development of outraged justice " (p. 10). After mentioning the manger, the flight into Egypt, the persecution, Christ's obscurity and manual labour, the exhausting work of preaching, Père Perroy says: " All things have become instruments of vengeance in the hands of God " (p. 10). Now let us read his commentary on the verse " My God, my God, why hast thou forsaken me? ": " It was over. How, over? Was it because God could not hear Him? No. Was it because He did not wish to hear Him? No. Was it because He rejected Him? It was. And rather than stretch out His hand to pull Him out of this sea of horror, He would have leaned over this lost soul in His agony and pushed Him deeper in. O Lord, how cruelly You behaved towards Him! This is what was required in this hour, under the weight of eternal justice . . . ' I could have avoided this

and the consolation that has been given to so many martyrs, the King of
martyrs had to go without . . . He is not allowed to complain, or even
to imagine to Himself that He is being unjustly treated. It is true that
He is innocent in the eyes of men; but what use can the knowledge of
this be to him, when His Father, from whom He hoped for comfort,
regards Him as a criminal? . . . He no longer dares to plead His innocence; He is covered with shame in front of His Father . . . The face
of God which rises up against those who do evil is the face of justice.
It is this face which God shows to His Son . . . In the end He regards
Him as a Sinner, and proceeds against Him with all the apparatus of His
justice . . . The man Jesus Christ was obliged to submit to a rain of
blows showered down upon Him by the divine vengeance ".[1]

We are here again at the opposite extreme from the thought of St.
Thomas Aquinas, who repeats insistently that when the drama is seen

terrible pledge I took it upon Myself to give for the sake of sinners,' cries Jesus
on the Cross: ' I was given the choice, and chose to plunge into this bottomless
sea: and now I cannot get out of it . . . The sins of mankind are nailed to My
flesh as My flesh is nailed to the Cross. I could have escaped the righteous anger
of God; it was I who called it down upon Myself: now I must endure it in its
entirety.' This is what Christ could have said, and as a final consequence He
might have added—as the most bitter sting of His despair—' Not only am
I now beyond all human help, but I do not even deserve the help of God '.
This is the limit: abandoned by men, abandoned by God! . . . There is this
difference between the Agony in the Garden and the Agony on the Cross: in
the first Christ is not without hope . . . But on the Cross there is no longer any
glimmer of hope: not the slightest possibility is left: the Father must be left
to rage, this is the dreadful way in which the pledge must be fulfilled: it was
necessary . . . I had sinned, and it had become necessary for Jesus, ' drenched
with my sins, a Sinner Himself' (Bossuet), to experience the great punishment
reserved for sin—dereliction. This is the terrible punishment of retaliation: an
eye for an eye, a tooth for a tooth, dereliction for dereliction. He had experienced
this, and today He dies for it. But this death is the very thing that saves me,
and it is because of the atrocious abandonment in which, clothed in my iniqui-
ties, *this divine Sinner* [my italics] endures His agony, that I, from now on forgiven and blessed, shall not be forsaken " (pp. 316–21, passim). And our
preacher ends: " If this is the last act of justice, it is also the last act of goodness: in truth He could go no further to expiate my sins and ensure my
salvation " (p. 321). There follows a trusting prayer: " Lord, here I reach the
most masterly example of Your goodness towards me . . ." (p. 321), a prayer
that seems hardly in keeping with what has gone before.
" We in France," writes Père Dehau, " have all too frequently had our minds
and, even more, our imaginations, tainted by Jansenism . . . Too many books
have been written under its influence and been received without sufficient
caution, showing the divine justice fastening upon its Victim in the mystery
of the Redemption. But this is quite wrong; it is love . . . " (*Le Contemplatif et
la Croix*, Éditions de l'Abeille, vol. i, p. 76). "To ascribe to justice what belongs
to love is a diabolic perversion of the truth. Possibly those who go on saying
this do not realize what they are doing, but the evil is no less deep on that
account. Only the devil can deceive to this extent: take the adorable Victim
away from love . . . and turn Him into the victim of justice! . . . Let us avoid
these snares of the devil " (ibid., p. 78.)

[1] *Oeuvres oratoires de Bossuet*, ed. Lebarq, vol. iii, pp. 367, 368, 387, 388.

as a whole, God's justice could in truth do nothing against Christ, because He was innocent. Christ had never committed any sin.[1] Now no penal action can ever be taken against the innocent; therefore Christ could not suffer any punishment by way of justice[2]—neither in His passion[3] nor in His death.[4]

Though St. Paul wrote that Christ was one who " knew no sin ", whom yet " God hath made sin " (" peccatum fecit ")[5] St. Peter, on the other hand, says, "who did no sin" (" peccatum non fecit ").[6] But the two contexts are quite clear. St. Paul is speaking in metaphors: everything happens *as though* Christ had sinned.[7] St. Peter is speaking literally: Christ is innocent.[8] St. Jerome and St. Thomas Aquinas also use an " as if " to interpret the word " cursed " applied by St. Paul to Christ: " Christ is crucified between two guilty people as though He is Himself guilty ". But of course He is not guilty.[9] And when St. Peter says, " the just for the unjust ",[10] he does not say that this is in the name of justice, but the very opposite. Here are his own simple, magnificent words: " For what glory is it if committing sin and being buffeted for it, you endure? But if, doing well, you suffer patiently, this is thankworthy before God. For unto this are you called: because Christ also suffered for us, leaving you an example that you should follow his steps. Who did no sin . . . Who, when he was reviled, did not revile; when he suffered, he threatened not."[11] "And who is he that can hurt you, if you be zealous of good? But if also you suffer anything for justice' sake, blessed are ye . . . For it is better doing well (if such be the will of God) to suffer than doing ill. Because Christ also died once for our sins, the just for the unjust: that he might offer us to God, being put to death indeed in the flesh, but enlivened in the spirit."[12] In order to have compassion on our miseries and to be like unto us, the High Priest experienced all our infirmities—but "without sin".[13]

But let us try to get to the root of the problem. " Very well then,"

[1] III, 22, 4, 1um.
[2] III, 52, 1, 1um.
[3] III, 49, 6.
[4] III, 49, 2 and 3, 35, 6, 1um.
[5] 2 Cor. v. 21.
[6] 1 Pet. ii. 22.
[7] " For Christ, we beseech you, be reconciled to God. Him that knew no sin [qui peccatum non noverat], for us he hath made sin, that we might be made the justice of God in him " (2 Cor. v. 20–21).
[8] " Who did no sin, neither was guile found in his mouth " (1 Pet. ii. 22 etc.) The 11th Council of Toledo of 675 asserted: " Christ was made sin for us, i.e., he was sacrificed for our sins " (Denzinger, 286).
[9] III, 46, 11.
[10] " Justus pro injustis " (1 Pet. iii. 18).
[11] 1 Pet. ii. 20–23.
[12] 1 Pet. iii. 13–14, 17–18.
[13] Heb. iv. 15.

you may say, " it is wicked and cruel to deliver up an innocent person against his will as a substitute for the guilty;[1] this kind of procedure is all right for tyrants, but it could not by any means be applied to the government of God. But that is not the case here: Christ, pure and sinless, freely offers Himself for our salvation. He is not delivered up against His deepest will. ' My Father, if it be possible, let this chalice pass from me. Nevertheless, not as I will, but as thou wilt.' "[2]

And yet to maintain that by offering Himself freely Christ suffered as a matter of justice, as the voluntary victim of His Father's aggressiveness, would in my opinion be an outrage against morality, a real misunderstanding of God's justice and love—logically, in fact, heresy pure and simple. This is a subtle point which needs explaining.

In sin—I repeat—the thing that offends God is not so much the pleasure that may be taken in it as the disobedience it involves, and the essential element in reparation is not punishment so much as love. The metaphysics of love is prior to the metaphysics of suffering and death. The two complete and harmonize each other.

Punishment is fitting: it expiates the guilty pleasure, it makes our regret for sin concrete and helps to strengthen it, it means that the whole man does penance; but ultimately its whole value is to be judged according to the love with which it is accepted and endured. Sufferings embraced with a good will are the sign and instrument of love (and, in the case of those who have sinned, of contrition); the stronger the love, the more capable it is of suffering; but in the last analysis, any difficulty that may be experienced is no more than a sign and opportunity of merit—even when it is properly overcome; the only real cause of merit is love. " We must offer the Lord whatever interior and exterior sacrifice we are able to give Him, and His Majesty will unite it to that which He offered to the Father for us upon the Cross, so that it may have the value won for it by our will, even though our actions may in themselves be trivial," writes St. Teresa of Avila.[3]

" But before all things have a constant mutual charity among yourselves: for charity covereth a multitude of sins."[4]

In any good psychology of education, the more sincere the contrition, the less need is there for any punishment. In any genuine system of justice, the more repentant the love, the less necessary is punishment, and the less fitting it is, even as a matter of punitive justice—whatever may be the case as regards preventive justice in society.

But the love of Christ the Redeemer is absolutely infinite and hence perfectly pure and faultless; therefore neither against Him nor from Him can justice as such claim anything whatsoever.

St. Thomas, with his customary clarity, says: " If, however, we speak of punishment inflicted on account of sin, inasmuch as it is penal, then each one is punished for his own sin only ",[1] and he is punished in the name of justice, but " if we speak of that satisfactory punishment, which one takes upon oneself voluntarily, one may bear another's punishment "[2]; only then, the person who had freely offered himself performs a personal act of charity beyond what is demanded of him. Consider the case of a man who, out of pure generosity, pays a debt incurred by someone who is poverty-stricken: one so generous could not possibly be attacked in justice, could not possibly be reached by the law in any way whatsoever. He would be safeguarding the order of justice, but through love and out of love of the poor person.

However, the case of the Redemption needs to be scrutinized more closely still, for it concerns the very life of the Redeemer. We have been redeemed " not . . . with corruptible things, as gold or silver . . . but with the precious blood of Christ, as of a lamb unspotted and undefiled ".[3]

A person who freely offered to take the place of someone condemned to death would eventually die, in such a case, as a victim of his own charity, and thus would suspend the course of violence against the condemned man whose life he had saved—if a tyrannical decision had been taken against him and he was innocent—or the course of justice, if he was a criminal and it was a reasonable decision that had been made against him.

In the first case it might be opportune, and it would certainly be heroic, for the person to offer himself; but in the second case it would be against all reason for him to substitute himself for the guilty party. In either case, however, it would be quite wrong for any authority to accept the offer and kill an innocent man. It would be an act of murder, not an act of justice.

Now we are guilty, we are sinners; Christ is innocence itself, and He has divine authority, absolute wisdom. Therefore justice is utterly powerless in this case, even in the light of its own rightful claims. If an innocent person is condemned to death, that is objectively a crime. Christ's executioners were minions, not priests performing a sacrifice. They were not acting in the name of God. If Christ is a Victim, he is not a Victim to justice.

It cannot be said, as Luther, Calvin and Mgr. d'Hulst say, that the mystery of the Redemption lies in the fact that the innocent Christ made Himself sin for us, in the fact that, " mercy being bound ",[4]

---

[1] I-II, 87, 8.   [2] ibid.   [3] 1 Pet. i. 18-19.   [4] See above.

He took our place and became the object of God's punishment. Such a penal substitution would not be a mystery; it would be a denial of all morality.

The problem of the Redemption can only be solved by adopting an utterly different standpoint, the standpoint of love, including a justice that is entirely based upon love.

" In this is charity: not as though we had loved God, but because he hath first loved us, and sent his son to be a propitiation for our sins."[1] What does this mean, "a propitiation for our sins "?[2] St. Thérèse of the Child Jesus gives the best explanation of the fullness of this mystery when she describes Jesus as " the Victim of merciful love."[3]

THE VICTIM OF LOVE

The Redemption is a buying back, as the word indicates, and it is the buying back of sin, but it is a buying back done through love. And even from this standpoint the Redemption is only comprehensible as the result of the infinite love of One who disposes of His life in His own way since He is its absolute Master. Because He loved us, the incarnate Word shed all His Blood quite freely. It was a sacrifice of love.

Notice how insistently the Saviour emphasizes the freedom of His love. " I lay down my life for my sheep . . . Therefore doth the Father love me: because I lay down my life . . . No man taketh it away from me, but I lay it down of myself. And I have power to lay it down, and I have power to take it up again. This commandment I have received of my Father."[4] Now, says St. Thomas, " For the same reason Christ suffered out of charity and out of obedience; because He fulfilled even the precepts of charity out of obedience only; and was obedient out of love, to the Father's command."[5] Would not His Father have sent Him twelve legions of angels and more if He had asked Him for them?[6] If He was crucified, it was not because of any lack of ability or power. Children know this from their catechism: the Word was not obliged

[1] I John iv. 10.
[2] By what right does a propitiatory sacrifice render God favourable (propitious) towards us? This in fact is the whole question. It could be *a priori* either because of the demands of justice, or through a free gift of compassionate love. The term " propitiation " is in itself unaffected by this distinction: it simply implies the re-establishment of justice between the guilty and the injured parties. " Now propitiation essentially implies compensation for wrongdoing, atoning for and remitting the guilt and paying the penalty " (Maurice de la Taille, S.J., *The Mystery of Faith*, Sheed and Ward, 1950, bk. ii, p. 223).
[3] See Travert, " La souffrance, son origine et son rôle d'après sainte Thérèse de l'Enfant-Jésus ", in *Études et Documents Thérésiens*, July 1935.
[4] John x. 15–18.
[5] III, 47, 2, 3[um]. St. Thomas emphasizes this point magnificently in *Contra Gentes*, iv, 55, ad 13[um] and ad 16[um].
[6] Matt. xxvi. 53.

to suffer so much to open the gates of heaven to us. " The very least one of Christ's sufferings was sufficient of itself to redeem the human race from all sins."[1] The Word could also have become incarnate without suffering, or might even not have become incarnate at all. St. Thomas says expressly: " But if He had willed to free man from sin without any satisfaction, He would not have acted against justice ", for " God has no one higher than Himself ", and He is not accountable to anyone but Himself. " He is the sovereign and common good of the whole universe."[2] The mere *fiat* of the divine wisdom would in itself have been sufficient to achieve the work of our redemption. In fact it did not take place in that way.

" God (who is rich in mercy), for his exceeding charity wherewith he loved us, even when we were dead in sins, hath quickened us together in Christ . . . that he might shew in the ages to come the abundant riches of his grace, in his bounty towards us in Christ Jesus."[3] Thus Christ was both the High Priest and the Host of His sacrifice.[4] Far from being caused by sin,[5] His death was caused by His love and occasioned by our sins—and that is not the same thing. Dying as God, Christ died through love.

" Christ, indeed, suffered death, but through His own spontaneous desire."[6] "He endured death of His own free will out of charity."[7] " Christ's Passion . . . was the sacrifice of one suffering out of charity."[8] There is no lack of such passages, all pointing to the same meaning. " This voluntary enduring of the Passion was most acceptable to God, as coming from charity."[9]

This gives us the real meaning of the verse from St. Paul which is so often wrongly interpreted and yet whose context is quite clear: " If God be for us, who is against us? He that spared not even his own Son, but delivered him up for us all, how hath he not also with him given us all things?"[10]

Let us now attempt to penetrate a little more deeply into the reason why the Incarnation took place.

Can a greater gift from God be imagined than that which consists

[1] III, 46, 5, 3um.
[2] III, 46, 2, 3um.
[3] Eph. ii. 4–7.
[4] III, 22, 2.
[5] III, 51, 4.
[6] III, 35, 6, 1um.
[7] III, 47, 4; 2um.
[8] III, 48, 3, 3um.
[9] III, 48, 3, c. St. Thomas explains that Christ loved life more than anyone (III, 46, 6, 4um) and that He surrendered His life in the flower of His manhood in order to give us an even more expressive witness of His love for us (III, 46, 9, 4um).
[10] Rom. viii. 31–2.

in one of the divine Persons, the Word, coming to subsist in a created nature, human nature? Our hands have handled the Word of Life, writes St. John the Evangelist.[1] This Man, Christ Jesus, is—in so far as His Person is concerned—the Word of God Himself!

" Jesus Christ . . . being in the form of God, thought it not robbery to be equal with God; but emptied himself, taking the form of a servant, being made in the likeness of men, and in habit found as a man."[2]

The Incarnation is a sort of scandal from the metaphysical point of view. For such self-abasement there needs to be a compensating reason.

On the plane of oblativity the relationships of love exist between person and person, not between nature and person nor between person and nature.[3] Christ's humanity, being a nature subsisting in the Word, is not the origin of a new, personal, independent and autonomous love-relationship. On the person-to-person level the incarnate Word brings no more to His Father, in the unity of the Holy Spirit, than the Word not incarnate. The Incarnation does not bring into existence a new Person capable of a new love. The new thing exists on the level of nature and created nature. The Word, as we say, acquires in His immutability a new, utterly supernaturalized human mode of being, knowing and loving: as Man He has a soul and body full of grace; He has a human consciousness; at the summit of His intellect[4] He enjoys the beatific vision and unites Himself by means of His human will with the spiration of love.[5]

The humanity assumed by the divine Word is thus not an additional personality for Him (how could it be?); it is a second nature. Now every nature is at the service of the personality, as its instrument of action. In the Word made flesh, human nature is thus at the service of the Word. The question is, how?

The " more " has no need to become "less", nor to be interpreted by the " less ". Being the fullness of all perfection, the Word can give; there is nothing He can receive.

What advantage could it be for Infinite Wisdom to enjoy the beatific vision, or to think by means of our multiple and distinct ideas—to

[1] I John i. 1.
[2] Phil. ii. 6–7.
[3] A nature can be defined as a degree of perfection in the hierarchy of being. When you say " a person " you mean " a nature plus a personality ". The personality is the ultimate root of the subject, capable of the gift of self in knowledge and love. In the expression " I have a soul and a body ", the " I ", the personal pronoun, expresses the personality; the soul and the body, human nature.
[4] III, 10.
[5] St. John of the Cross, *Spiritual Canticle*, xxxviii. What St. John of the Cross says in this context about the soul that is in God's grace applies pre-eminently to the soul of Christ.

unite Himself by way of participation with the breath of the Spirit proceeding from Himself and the Father, or to possess a sensitive heart of flesh?

Thus it was not for Himself that the Word was made flesh and dwelt among us, but clearly for us, to unite us to God, in view of our last end. The Incarnation is a manifestation of divinity in the Person of the Word. The Word enables us to grasp God through our senses; He comes down to us so as to incite us to know, love and serve God better. The Incarnation is therefore primarily an example of holiness.

The angels and Adam had sinned, fundamentally, because they had not accepted their condition as creatures. The new Adam freely accepts the human condition with all its consequences. He becomes the incarnation of love, faithful to the duties of His position. Let us follow " his steps ",[1] and feel as He felt.[2] Our greatest study should be to meditate on His life.[3]

If the incarnate Word had been content to be the Adam of an earthly paradise, He would have been able to reveal the wisdom and harmony of the Gospel message, at least by His words and by the example of His life; but would He have succeeded in making Himself understood? If He had been, for instance, the greatest scientist who has ever lived, or the greatest philosopher or poet, living in normal, peaceful conditions —a true bourgeois, in fact—the perfect Wise Man—it is possible that He might have failed to acquaint us with all the fullness of His divinity. In the Incarnation, the Person of the Word gives Himself in a human way. Now God is not man. If God decides to become incarnate so that we may attain to Him, He is still obliged to will to do this as God, for He can lower Himself only in order to raise us up. To do this as God means, finally—as a result of the relationship between man and God—dying on the cross.

There is a certain amount of truth in pessimism, and that is that we live more intensely when we are tested than when we are happy; our pain is more marked than our joy. Why should God, then, if He wishes to reveal to us something of the unplumbed depths of His infinite love, deprive Himself of the means most within our grasp, however hard it may be? " Greater love than this no man hath, that a man lay down his life for his friends."[4] Death is the greatest possible proof of human love. The Word, in fact, had more reason to become incarnate and suffer, than to become incarnate and live and die in peace: on the cross He gives Himself fully, and teaches us to give without counting the cost.

[1] 1 Pet. ii. 21: " Vestigia eius ".
[2] Phil. ii. 5.
[3] *The Imitation of Christ*, i, 1.
[4] John xv. 13.

Thus has Christ Jesus given the most eloquent " testimony to the truth ",[1] both to the truth of His love for His Father—" But that the world may know that I love the Father: and as the Father hath given me commandment so do I "[2]—and to the truth of His love for us. He is the Good Shepherd and " the good shepherd giveth his life for his sheep ".[3] In his turn, anyone who suffers and gives his blood for a noble cause can take as his Model the Son of God, who having freely assumed a passible, mortal nature, willed to bear it unto death, the death of the cross, for love of us.

Is this the full extent of the mystery of the Cross? By no means; there is still more to it. It is one of the insufficiencies of so-called liberal theology that it reduced the passion of Christ to such a level that it became a mere example of heroic courage and a proof of love. Would it have been fitting for Christ to die by shedding His blood if there had been no sins to expiate? No Catholic theologian has ever thought so, as far as I know: it was, in fact, through original sin that death came into the world. Because of this sin, and because of our own personal sins, the passion of the Saviour, which is a true witness to His brotherly and divine love, bears intrinsically the character of a redemption achieved not under the sign of violence and aggressiveness but under the sign of love in the gift of self and reaching the highest level of forgiveness.

" From the beginning of His conception Christ merited our eternal salvation ",[4] because love is the foundation of merit and the love of Christ was infinite from the moment that Mary's *fiat* was realised, and there has been no possibility of any further increase since. But God decided that the effects of our salvation should derive principally from Christ's passion, because this was the work that was essentially fitting for a buying back performed through love.[5] It was at the moment of His death on the cross that the Saviour was fully " a Victim actually offered then,"[6] the Victim of a love stronger than physical death, stronger too than sin, which is a spiritual death; Christ died as a Victim

---

[1] John xviii. 37.
[2] John xiv. 31.
[3] John x. 11.
[4] III, 48, 1, 2um.
[5] III, 48, 1, 3um and 3, 46, 3 and 4. The same teaching is developed in *Quodl.* II, q. 2, a. 2: " The sufferings of Christ other than his death were not in fact designed for the work of our redemption without death " (" absque morte "). The substance of St. Thomas's explanation is that if we want to buy anything we must (1) have as much money as the price that is demanded and (2) use the money for this purpose at a particular moment. By analogy each of Christ's sufferings, being charged with infinite love, could redeem us by itself, but in fact all the Saviour's sufferings have been ordinated as one single suffering to the cross and consummated on the cross, their highest point.
[6] III, 22, 2, 3um.

of *merciful* love. He gave His life *for sinners*. His death reveals love at its highest, in an absolute paroxysm of love. " Love your enemies, do good to those who persecute you." The Master preached by example: it was in that way that He satisfied the demands of perfect justice.

THE VICTIM OF MERCIFUL LOVE

God lowered Himself out of pity to the level of sinful man. This is the triumph of *Agape*, or divine charity.[1]

" For scarce for a just man will one die: yet perhaps for a good man someone would dare to die. But God commendeth his charity towards us: because when as yet we were sinners according to the time, Christ died for us . . . For if, when we were enemies, we

[1] Though I cannot identify myself with the work completely, I should like to refer the reader at this point to the extremely stimulating book by the Protestant Anders Nygren, *Agape and Eros, A Study of the Christian Idea of Love*, trans. A. G. Hebert, M.A., S.P.C.K. Much of this work is in full harmony with the teachings of Catholic theology.

" . . . Jesus must necessarily assail the conception of legal righteousness. Had He been concerned only to claim a place for *love, in the ordinary sense*, in the attitude of God to man, there would have been no need to upset the legal scheme. There would have been no difficulty in finding room there for a Divine love directed to the godly and those who deserve to be loved; such a love would be ' caused ', and readily explicable. But with Jesus it is not a question of this sort of love, but of the ' uncaused ' love which is Agape; and for this there can be no room in an order dominated by Law. Agape is, in fact, the New Wine which bursts the old wine-skins (Matt. ix, 17), and the break with the old legal order becomes inevitable . . ." (pt. i, p. 53). " God's love for the righteous must be just as ' uncaused ' as His love for the sinner. The meaning of Agape can only be rightly grasped when it is seen that human goodness or worthiness is left clean out of the reckoning God's love knows no limits. ' He maketh his sun to rise on the evil and on the good, and sendeth rain on the just and the unjust ' (Matt. v. 45) . . ." (p. 54). " It would however be entirely false to say that we have in His teaching two focal points, the Cross and Agape; the two are viewed together, and are so essentially one that neither of the two can be understood without the other. Apart from the Cross we should never have known God's love and learnt its depths of meaning; and apart from Agape Christ's path would never have led Him to the Cross. As surely as Paul will know nothing else but Jesus Christ and Him crucified, so he will not know of any other love than that which is bound up with Christ's Cross. The central point of Paul's teaching is the Agape of the Cross " (p. 85).

It must not be forgotten, however, that God is the Master of His gifts, and of the way in which He disposes of them. We all live, indeed, under the sign of sin and suffering, but there are exceptional creatures who are granted the beatific vision without ever having suffered (newborn children who die immediately after being baptised) and the holiest of all created beings, the Blessed Virgin Mary, Mother of God, certainly had to bear a heavy cross, but she had never been guilty of the slightest imperfection and never experienced the least movement of nature. The ways of God are not our ways and He remains the sovereign Master.

were reconciled to God by the death of his Son; much more, being reconciled, shall we be saved by his life."[1]

" Because of the exceedingly great love wherewith He loved us when we were yet His enemies, Our Lord Jesus Christ, the well-beloved Son of the Father, has merited our justice by His holy passion on the wood of the cross and has made satisfaction for us unto God the Father."[2] It is perfectly in order that Christ should be merciful towards the weakness of His creatures. He Himself " did not trust himself unto them, for that he knew all men ".[3] He had pity on the multitude, who were like sheep without a shepherd, and He would therefore push the virtue of His mercy quite freely to the point of dying by the shedding of blood for love of us sinners.

Two different dimensions are revealed to us by love when it becomes redemptive: below is the abyss of sin, above the heaven of the divine goodness lit by the sun of mercy. Deep calls to deep: the abyss of darkness calls to the abyss of light. The divine love raises the sinner and makes satisfaction for sin, acting with all the fullness of its powers by way of mercy. Here God is truly God. It is pre-eminently by the occasion of sin, the aggressive revolt against the love of God, that this love can manifest itself in all its fullness.

But by an unexpected reverse, deriving from the mystery at the heart of the Divinity, it is through an act of exceeding love that God, acting in and through Himself, reveals to us something of His justice, which could not in fact appear in the Person of the Son of God in any other guise than that of love; for in God justice is love. This brings us to the very heart of the mystery. St. Thomas, it seems to me, says this in precise terms when he writes: " And this came of more copious mercy than if He had forgiven sins without satisfaction."[4] The work of justice is indeed achieved, but in a superabundance of mercy, and when the Saviour appeared as a Person it could not be otherwise. *Fulget crucis mysterium.*

Mercy manifests itself absolutely when Christ sheds His blood on Calvary for love of us; and at the same time an utterly divine kind of justice is achieved, in a very real way, as though outside and beyond what could in justice be expected of justice.

As though outside: for though justice had some claim against the guilty, it had no claim against the innocent. We could be justly punished, but not Christ.

As though beyond, since justice is satisfied by the Innocent One, by love and in love, in a world beyond justice—so true is it that in God

[1] Rom. v. 7–10.
[2] Council of Trent, Denzinger, 799.
[3] John ii. 24–5.
[4] III, 46, 1, 3um.

love is everything and that " God is love ". Is not this, in fact, the very definition of love given by St. John?[1]

But the divine justice has thus been very truly exercised, for love *is* everything in God, even justice; this is in fact the whole object of the mystery of the Redemption. It is a justice entirely composed of love and mercy.

God reveals Himself to us in His unutterable transcendence. But though it can and must be confessed that the flesh of Christ on the cross manifests the divine justice because it is indeed the Flesh of a Victim and because an expiatory sacrifice[2] is genuinely involved, it is essential to realize that the Word in His holy flesh could only be a victim of His own merciful love. The expiation was made through love. Mercy, and mercy alone, foresaw in all its detail the sacrifice made on Calvary and decided to enact it. Indeed this was impossible except in and through mercy. Thus, for those who can read aright the Redemption is the tangible expression, written in blood, of the primacy of divine love in the order of justice, as these two things, mercy and love, mysteriously meet in God. Justice, far from being separable from love in God, is in Him kindled entirely by love. It is primarily love and it is identical with love.[3]

---

[1] I John iv. 16.

[2] Rom. iii. 24–6: " . . . Christ Jesus, whom God hath proposed to be a propitiation, through faith in his blood, to the shewing of his justice, for the shewing of his justice in this time: that he himself may be just, and the justifier of him who is of the faith of Jesus Christ."

[3] The fact is that analogy can be extended to infinity when we are speaking of the divine attributes.

From the logical and technical point of view we have the following picture: the work of love in the Passion is formally described as a work of justice with respect to our human justice:

(1) *equivocally*, by liberal theology. (This means the exclusion of justice.)

(2) *univocally*, by the theology deriving from Luther and Calvin. (This gives rise to systems of punishment, expiation or penal substitution.)

(3) *analogically*, in the proper meaning of the term, by orthodox Catholic theology. (This involves vicarious satisfaction and moral reparation.)

I am in full agreement with the names and definitions of the analogical terms and perfections used by Père Le Rohellec, *Problèmes Philosophiques*, Editions Téqui, 1933, pp. 97–132.

A perfection is realized in two subjects in a genuinely analogical way, when it is found intrinsically in both in a way which is essentially both the same and different, as seen from two distinct but inseparable standpoints.

Now we only know God analogically, and the divine attributes are not mutually exclusive. " The multiplicity of viewpoints we take of that Reality is demanded, necessitated, justified by the ineffable plenitude of the divine simplicity " and " each of the divine perfections, though infinite, finds itself further engulfed by the content of all the others. No single perfection can possibly encompass the indivisible ocean of the divine simplicity, which, properly speaking, therefore remains unnamed, unsignified, uncircumscribed " (Journet, *The Dark Knowledge of God*, trans. James F. Anderson, Sheed and Ward, 1948, pp. 26–7, on the distinction and reciprocal implication of the divine attributes.) But we know by philosophy as well as by faith that the very thing

Looking at the matter from this metaphysical point of view, can we perhaps enter a little into the intimate psychological sufferings of our Redeemer in His agony? We may say—with proper circumspection before the psychological aspect of the mystery, which is no less mysterious than the other aspects—that in His human consciousness—not only in His feelings but deep down in His actual intellectual powers, which at their highest point were in full enjoyment of the beatific vision—Christ Jesus experienced voluntarily the pain of a profound sorrow, devoid of the least trace of personal guilt or contrition but nevertheless perfectly pure and, so to speak, infinite in extent, as a result of His very wisdom and love. The suffering is engendered by merciful love seeing itself wilfully rejected by all sinners, and this to the full extent of their own personal responsibility; a suffering, not of damnation, but of desolation at the thought of those who by their own fault remain in a state of everlasting revolt; a compassionate suffering for the contrite sinners who confess their ingratitude. His soul is " sorrowful even unto death ".[1]

This mercy transcends justice, without however ceasing to contain justice, and for this reason it is one of the loveliest expressions of the love of the Trinity, a perfect gift of pure love.

Properly speaking, at the very heart of the divine life justice disappears, for there is so perfect an equality between the three Persons that it reaches the identity of a common nature. There is only one God. No single One of the divine Persons is anterior to the Others (there is no temporal succession in eternity), no single One of them is dependent on the Others (there is no kind of causation in God, He is His own *raison d'être*, which means that He is infinitely more than anything that can be caused), no single One is under any sort of obligation to either of the Others. In that indivisible unity, that ineffable simplicity, there is a procession of wisdom from Father to Son, which lies at the root of the procession of love from the Father and the Son to the Holy Spirit, the love of the Father and the Son, the crowning point of the eternal Trinity. The concept of relationship here becomes infinitely purified. Wisdom is love and love is light, and there is a mysterious relationship between all three. Though by reason of their absolute nature, which is identical in all Three and common to all Three, all are equally both providence and justice, nevertheless the divine Persons are really distinct from Each Other, on the relative plane of Their mysterious communication of wisdom

---

that we are unable to name is the *wisdom of love*, and that the divine justice is, *in the first place*, love, although this love is in itself always just. This is, so to speak, the metaphysical root of the mystery of the Redemption.

[1] Mark xiv. 34. See III, 46, 6–8.

and love, in a world beyond all justice.[1] The Incarnation reveals to us the divine riches; becoming Redemption, it attains the fullness of its own *raison d'être*, proportionate to the unfathomable abyss of our misery as human creatures. Everything that can be said about both sides is manifest in the love of Christ on the cross. The divine love enlightens us not by the wisdom of the Greeks, not by extraordinary signs such as the Jews demanded, but by the" foolishness of the cross ".[2]

---

[1] Although there is in God no precedence as between one Person and the Others, no exchange of justice, there is nevertheless a harmonious ordering by which, in a purely relative sense, wisdom is pre-eminent over love. Love proceeds from Light. *Verbum spirans Amorem*, says St. Thomas Aquinas.

For the way in which, in my opinion, the Word is our life through the sanctifying grace which is inherent in the soul, see *Recherche de la Personne, Études Carmélitaines*, April 1936, p. 155. This last point of view enters analogically into the category of a formal cause, the Word Himself, however, not exercising any formal causality since He remains sovereignly independent, although the soul lives in Him through grace.

[2] I Cor. i. 23. *A Note on Thomism and Scotism*.

The question arises, whether the Incarnation would have taken place if there had been no sin and therefore no redemption to be achieved.

To this theological question the Thomists answer, no, on the grounds of probability, and the Scotists answer yes, as a matter of absolute certainty.

The reason for this divergence of opinion does not seem to me to derive from the moral order, nor even from Scripture, but rather from the speculative order, each position being derived logically from the metaphysical position adopted towards the human element that is assumed in the hypostatic union.

For the Scotists the humanity of Christ is that of a perfect Man and lacks none of the ontological elements that make us men in concrete actuality (*homo assumptus*). " God," says Scotus, " wishes to be loved by Someone who can love Him as much as He is worthy of love and who is exterior to Himself (a creature) . . . He foresees His union with this Being who will love Him as He should be loved even if no one had ever sinned." (This passage appears in these words and is specially emphasised by the Very Rev. Fr. Bello, General of the Friars Minor, in his Encyclical Letters of the 29th October 1933.)

How can the Man who is assumed remain as Someone capable of love, " someone who can love God ", without being as a result of this a human personality (any affirmation of personality would be heretical)? I do not see how this can be so; but once it is admitted, the Redemption can no longer be regarded as the determining reason for the Incarnation. The reason is as follows. In our hierarchy of values love is pre-eminent over suffering and suffering is at the service of love. The contrary is not true. Consequently, as, on the Scotist hypothesis, the Incarnation brings to God the new love of a new Individual, the *homo assumptus*, it could not possibly be determined by the Redemption in any way whatsoever, even though it is in fact redemptive. This conclusion seems logically inevitable.

But for the Thomists it is not Christ Jesus, it is His Mother, the Virgin Mary, who gives to God a new love, autonomously, on the level of created nature. The holy humanity of Christ is, on the level of nature, God's masterpiece. On the level of persons, God's masterpiece is the Blessed Virgin Mary, the Mother of the Incarnate Word. Morally, these two masterpieces are one.

What the Scotists say metaphysically about the *homo assumptus*, we assert of the Blessed Virgin Mary, full of grace; only we go on to confess (logically, as it seems to us) that this creature is a human person. What we say about her Son is something infinitely higher: He *is*, as a matter of the strictest identity, the

" Per crucem ad lucem." The Cross leads to the light, the only light that can fully satisfy us in utter truth and justice, the light of merciful love. It enlightens every man who comes into this world, but only in the measure that he becomes conscious of the darkness of his misery and sinfulness.

On the cross everything happens materially as though a condemned man were paying the penalty of his own crimes. Blood is shed. When we contemplate Christ on the cross we are led on to meditate upon the " divine severity " which willed (in fact) not to remit sin until satisfaction had been made for it.[1] Thus everything happens as though the Flesh of Christ were the flesh of a sinner: " Who his own self bore our sins in his body upon the tree; that we, being dead to sins, should live to justice."[2] God " in Christ Jesus hath delivered [us] from the law of sin and death . . . sending his own Son, in the *likeness* of sinful flesh and of sin, hath condemned sin in the flesh: that the justification of the law might be fulfilled in us who walk not according to the flesh, but according to the spirit ".[3] This is a striking image of how God's justice might have been enacted upon us, although the Saviour was not one of the condemned.[4] The torture endured on Calvary is a most effective warning against the aberrations of sin; for offending God means crucifying anew the Flesh of Christ.

This Passion and Death are the fundamental origin and the historical

---

actual Personality of the Word of God, on the level of the relationships that exist in the Trinity.

For Thomists Christ's humanity is a nature perfect as human nature but minus its ontological personality, and it can thus become the instrument, the psychological, physiological and physical instrument of the Word which is incarnated in it. It can in any case be assumed without any contradiction in the economy of our earthly happiness, but, as has been seen, its rôle is infinitely more startling in the economy of our redemption. The probability remains that if there had been no Redemption to be effected there would have been no Incarnation.

It is to be noted—and it is in any case obvious on the face of it—that in spite of the risk of going, wrongly (despite themselves), from the level of nature to the level of persons, the Franciscans often seem to have analysed Christ's human feelings more perspicuously than the Thomists. They are more concerned with the Saviour's human consciousness. We believe that the psychology of the one side merely needs to be accommodated to the metaphysics of the other—and vice versa. This would not mean any eclecticism, the two points of view being really distinct from each other. It would then be possible to unite these two great currents of spiritual thought and so gain a deeper conception of our Christ.

In any case, both sides acknowledge that the best world is morally possible and exists in fact: the world of the Cross on which a Man, the Son of God, died for love of sinners.

[1] III, 47, 3, 1um.
[2] 1 Pet. ii. 24.
[3] Rom. viii. 2-4.
[4] It is a case of metaphorical analogy as regards its material causality. Cf. III, 46, 3.

source of our justification; in Jesus Christ " we have redemption through his blood, the remission of sins."[1] It was because He foresaw the death of His Son that God the Father granted all grace even before the Crucified One gave up the ghost, and it is through the application of the merits of this Death that all grace has been given ever since.[2]

It is by our love that we shall be justified. It is the Cross that moves us and calls out to us. The Cross is our lodestone. It is the way of truth and life. This Flesh, being delivered up for our redemption, is an image of what we can achieve—proportionately to our stature— in our endeavours to share in the superabundant merits of the Saviour on the cross—as a matter of pure justice, to expiate our own sins, but above all as a matter of love, working gratuitously as co-redeemers with Christ for the salvation of poor sinners. It leads us to love, and it tells us how to get there.[3]

The Cross is the incarnation of love, which is the ultimate end of all our supernatural activity and the fullness of all perfection.

TOWARD A GREATER LOVE

By revealing to man God Himself in His infinite mercy, the divine Crucified One reveals man to himself in his own infinite misery. " If we say that we have not sinned, we make him a liar and his word is not in us."[4]

" Jesus Christ is then the true God of men . . . Not only do we know God by Jesus Christ alone, but we know ourselves only by Jesus Christ."[5]

". . . That the truly spiritual man may understand the mystery of the gate and of the way of Christ, in order to be united with God, and may know that, the more completely he is annihilated for God's sake, according to these two parts, the sensual and the spiritual, the more completely is he united to God and the greater is the work which he accomplishes. And when he comes to be reduced to nothing, which will be the greatest extreme of humility, spiritual union will be wrought between the soul and God, which in this life is the greatest and the highest state attainable."[6]

[1] Col. i. 14.
[2] Justice takes its value in this respect from the Cross by attributive analogy as an efficient instrumental cause. Cf. III, 48, 6, 3um.
[3] Justice takes its value in this respect from the Cross by attributive analogy as a final cause. Cf. S. Th. 3, 48, 6, 3m. This is the last aspect of the analogy which remained to be considered in the Redemption from the standpoint of justice and love.
[4] I John i. 10.
[5] Pascal, Pensées, nos. 547–8.
[6] The Complete Works of St. John of the Cross, trans. and ed. E. Allison Peers, Burns, Oates and Washbourne, vol. i, pp. 92–3.

Truly, absolute humility is our highest state.

" Some considering nature as incorrupt, others as incurable, they could not escape either pride or sloth, the two sources of all vice . . . The Christian religion alone has been able to cure these two vices . . . For it teaches the righteous that it raises them even to a participation in divinity itself; that in this lofty state they still carry the source of all corruption, which renders them during all their life subject to error, misery, death and sin; and it proclaims to the most ungodly that they are capable of the grace of their Redeemer."[1]

In the angelic conditions of the Garden of Eden, at the foot of the tree of the knowledge of good and evil, the wickedness of man was revealed in all its fullness. There, mysteriously, two different freedoms met. God in His omnipotence has given us freedom of a psychological kind. This gift He respects to such an extent that He permits an evil which He cannot will, and He remains for ever full of mercy towards the sinner; in this way He manifests His infinite power and goodness, since He can and will always draw a greater good from evil, even for the guilty one himself—on condition that the latter will truly consent to it by a movement of contrition.[2]

The incidence of sin does not make us any worse than we are: it simply shows us what we really are.[3] All the helps granted to Adam

---

[1] Pascal, *Pensées*, no. 435.

[2] In the paradoxical mystery of the divine Power and our freedom it must not be forgotten that our freedom is a real power and that the divine creative power is a real freedom.

There are four terms involved: God and ourselves, good and evil.

(1) God is the cause of good (Denzinger, 816).
(2) We are the cause of evil (ibid., 200).
(3) God permits evil (ibid., 816).
(4) We are the cause of the good we do freely (ibid., 814) but through God, with His grace (ibid., 812, 813).

Christ died for *all* men (323, 795); and if the sinner is condemned, he is condemned " because of his own iniquity " (321, 322); he has no one to blame but himself, there is no kind of fatality involved, for " he could have behaved differently " (ibid.). As regards the just, they must recognise the initiative and gratuitous prevenience of the divine mercy: " We are not the ones who initiate good works, and it is the divine mercy that helps us to go on pursuing them " (200).

This is the equilibrium which it is essential to maintain in this field, following the teachings of the Church.

The Church, without whose existence it may be questioned whether the idea of spiritual freedom would still exist in the world, has good reason to be acquainted with the actual deficiencies of this freedom, which is so often sinful in character; and that is why it regards our creaturely freedom simply as a means and not as any kind of end in itself—a means, moreover, which is worth only as much as the workman brings to it. By a curious reversal, those who, in the name of a materialistic determinism, refuse to allow man any real freedom, clamour for freedom for man and for society with a frenzy that frequently amounts to folly: it is in them and not in us that the contradiction lies.

[3] *The Imitation of Christ*, i, 16.

THE RISEN CHRIST
Michelangelo: British Museum

and Eve in the Garden of Eden are there to help us to avoid useless regrets and vain illusions: properly speaking, we have only one kind of greatness, and that is our weakness. Our weakness is part of our nature; and from the moment that we are endowed with sanctifying grace, the gift above all other gifts, the divine seed of the beatific vision, it is better for us to know the shame of our nakedness. Why is this?

The Council of Trent " knows and confesses ",[1] " that a source of concupiscence remains in those who have been baptised ", " the concupiscence of the flesh, and the concupiscence of the eyes, and the pride of life ".[2] It teaches that though St. Paul sometimes calls sin concupiscence, this is not, properly speaking, because concupiscence has any pre-eminence over sin in souls who have been baptised,[3] but only because, historically, it derives from the original sin and because for us it is an occasion of sin. But " as this concupiscence exists to incite us to combat, it is unable to harm those who refuse to give it any guilty consent, and fight against it in manly fashion through the grace of Jesus Christ. Furthermore, he who fights against it lawfully will be crowned (2 Tim. ii. 5) ".[4] Ignorance, suffering— whether coming from outside or within—even death itself, are all thus subject on the level of aggressiveness to a love growing ever stronger and more virile, ever more humble and generous, either by the way of innocence or the way of contrition. Trials and humiliations, harsh and austere climate though they may be, ensure that we shall be granted the divine indulgence and are, positively, much more favourable to the growth of love than the state of innocence.

Ultimately the thing that counts is the gift of self, in a love growing ever more pure and strong, and that is why the economy of the Redemption is in the end superior to that of the Garden of Eden. Baptism, Confirmation and the Eucharist—the sacramental triptych of Christian initiation—give access to a spiritual garden far superior to that in which Adam and Eve were born, even as seen with the eye of love. The reason for this is that we must lose our souls to find them. "A minus times a minus gives a plus ", as we say in algebra. Therein lies the whole philosophical mathematics of spirituality. To renounce created things for love of God is a positive act, and it is by far the best use that we can make of them.

According to the teaching of St. John of the Cross, the demands made by the "Ascent of Mount Carmel " and the " Dark Night " lead to the " Living Flame of Love ".

[1] Denzinger, 792.
[2] I John ii. 16.
[3] In those who are not baptised either by desire or sacramentally, concupiscence remains stained by original sin.
[4] Council of Trent, Denzinger, 792.

" How are we to initiate, and accept in all its fullness, the transformation of our being and our entire human activity, impure and infirm as it is, under the influence of the Spirit of God, who is all-powerful and infinitely pure? The best image that the Saint found to express this intuition of his was the log of wood set burning by fire."[1] The log turns black, crackles and smokes, becomes much uglier to look at than it was in the first place. A bad smell comes from it. All the grosser elements that oppose the action of the fire have to be eliminated from it. Then gradually the wood becomes fire. Growing hot, it gives out heat. Growing bright, it gives out light.

Life has no meaning unless it is set alight by the fire of love. And everything in life is good enough to be burned in the fire of love.

" A shepherd lad was mourning his distress
Far from all comfort, friendless and forlorn.
He fixed his thought upon his shepherdess
Because his breast by love was sorely torn.
It grieved him more that he had been forgot . . .

Only to think that he had been forgotten
By his sweet shepherdess, with travail sore,
He let his foes (in foreign lands begotten)
Gash the poor breast that love had gashed before.

Then, after a long time, a tree he scaled,
Opened his strong arms bravely wide apart,
And clung upon that tree till death prevailed,
So sorely was he wounded in his heart."[2]

Let us respond freely with our love to the love of Christ on the cross.

Pius XI, in his Encyclical Letter of the 11th Dec. 1925, recalled the whole world to the kingship of Christ, reminding it that " up to this day no one has ever been loved as much as Christ Jesus is loved and that in the future likewise no one will ever be loved as much as He is loved ".

His kingdom is an interior one entirely, it is within us.[3] It is " a kingdom of truth and life, a kingdom of holiness and grace, a kingdom of justice, love and peace ".[4] It depends on us whether we enter it or not: we have been invited.

[1] Père Lucien-Marie de St.-Joseph, Les oeuvres spirituelles du Bienheureux Père Jean de la Croix, pp. xxxii-xxxiii.
[2] Poems of St. John of the Cross, trans. Roy Campbell, The Harvill Press, p. 43.
[3] Luke xvii. 21.
[4] Preface for the Feast of Christ the King.

LOVE AND CONFIDENCE

The mystery of the redemptive Incarnation—the highest expression on both the physical and the metaphysical planes of the mystery of love in the Trinity—should inspire our whole Christian spirituality with a vigorous optimism.

God is infinitely greater and more generous and more beautiful than the world is shabby, sordid and ugly. Love—the love that is gentle and strong, that can be violent when necessary, but always remains love—is more powerful than aggressiveness. " O Death, where is thy victory? O Death, where is thy sting? . . . Thanks be to God, who has given us the victory through our Lord Jesus Christ."[1] Since Christ died for us it depends entirely on us whether He is to be our justice and our love. We can and should share the infinite merits of His passion by exercising the virtues, and the gifts of the Holy Spirit, and by partaking of the sacraments, which in the state of redemption correspond to the preternatural gifts in the state of innocence; but above all we should surrender ourselves more completely, under the sign of the Cross, to the ardours of love.

Although a lot could be said about the dignity of the Christian priesthood and Christian marriage and the surpassing greatness of the mystery of the Eucharist—in short, concerning the marvellous testimonies of love in our seven sacraments—and also about the way in which these have been distorted, both in their nature and their effect, under the influence of Jansenism—I shall confine myself, in the following pages, to a discussion of one single point, centring round the fact that the theological virtues of faith, hope and charity do not exist in an atmosphere of aggressiveness. We have not received a spirit of servitude, to be still in a state of fear, but a spirit of adoption whereby we cry, Father, and which itself " giveth testimony to our spirit, that we are the sons of God".[2]

PRELIMINARIES

Modern atheism often accuses us of being the victims of a facile illusion because we believe in a life to come and thus have a less pure, less noble idea of duty and the gift of self than the unbeliever or the sceptic. This old charge of a kind of spiritual Benthamism—it was brought against Christianity by Jouffroy—arises as a result of the divorce that has been effected between duty and love, notably by Kant. The categorical imperative is, in a way, " irascible " and cold. It gives its orders and leads into battle without deigning to say a word

---

[1] I Cor. xv. 55, 57. [2] Rom. viii. 16.

of explanation. And in this, we are told, lies real austerity, real renunciation.

But—looking at the matter merely from the psychological point of view—has the sincere believer therefore more of a " proprietary interest " than the unbeliever (assuming the latter to be equally sincere)? I think not. During his life on earth the unbeliever will certainly struggle against himself less than the practising believer, and will suffer less on this account. Christian morality demands real sacrifices. True, the atheist who gives his life for a noble cause expects to relapse into nothingness, and has no vision of any happiness beyond the grave. But he has no judgment to fear either.

What about the lax, lukewarm Christian? He often longs to believe that God does not exist, for he can only see the negative side of Christian dogma and morals, which hamper his self-expression.

What about those who believe whole-heartedly? For them there is the anguish of the dark night, or there are temptations against the faith; and these crosses of an intellectual kind are amongst the hardest that have to be endured.

Who suffers more, the believer or the unbeliever? This is one aspect of the problem of atheism. It is not in my opinion the fundamental one.

Before there can be any question of embarking upon any philosophical or religious investigation, the first thing, surely, is to have a sincere desire for the truth, whatever this may prove to be: " If it is so, it is so; if not, not." It cannot be assumed *a priori* that the most desirable or the most difficult solution is the one that must be true. If a thing is, it is true; if it is not, it is false.

In any case, believers and unbelievers alike have each to carry their own cross; what they will be judged by is their own conscience, the integrity of their search for truth in love and love in truth. Even if it were true that the first and most important thing is suffering and struggle, it would still be necessary to love, for love alone is the soul of life. But the first thing, for everybody, surely, is " to do the truth in charity ",[1] whatever it may cost. There is no greater truth than love and there is no greater love than the love of truth, which must never be betrayed, not even by a hair's breadth.

For us Catholics, problems like those concerning the metaphysical proofs of the existence of God, or the historical evidence for the divinity of Christ, or the apostolicity of the Roman and Catholic Church, are not matters of sentiment but of reason. " In order not to be deceived in a matter of such importance the human reason must carefully enquire into the fact of divine revelation, so that it may recognize it

[1] Eph. iv. 15.

with certainty."[1] " Right reason demonstrates the foundations of faith."[2]

Christian philosophy and church history, dogma and morality, are what they are. In them, as in anything else involving a categorical assertion, there is a certain doctrinal intransigence that needs to be balanced by a profound sense of human brotherhood. If we can radiate goodness we shall be manifesting the highest aspect of the truth. To draw souls to the doctrine of life there is no need to be sectarian or aggressive. Christian apologetics, whether they are on the attack or on the defence, should always be bathed in an atmosphere of love.

People can be gifted and cultured and have a good will, and yet, through no fault of their own, as a result of their upbringing, be unable to perceive the grounds for the motives of belief. We must not assume our opponents to be in bad faith.

" No salvation outside the Church " means that one must belong to the Church of Christ to be saved, but this may be by implicit desire. This baptism by desire can take on many different forms.

As St. Paul wrote in his Epistle to the Romans:

" God . . . will render to every man according to his works. To them indeed, who, according to patience in good work, seek glory and honour and incorruption, eternal life; but to them that are contentious, and who obey not the truth, but give credit to iniquity, wrath and indignation. Tribulation and anguish upon every soul of man that worketh evil, of the Jew first and also of the Greek: but glory and honour and peace to every one that worketh good, to the Jew first and also to the Greek. For there is no respect of persons with God.

" For whosoever have sinned without the law, shall perish without the law: and whosoever have sinned in the law shall be judged by the law. For not the hearers of the law are just before God; but the doers of the law shall be justified. For when the Gentiles who have not the law, do by nature those things that are of the law; these, having not the law, are a law to themselves: who shew the work of the law written in their hearts, their conscience bearing witness to them, and their thoughts between themselves accusing, or also defending one another, in the day when God shall judge the secrets of men by Jesus Christ, according to my gospel."[3]

St. Thérèse of the Child Jesus includes all who live unwittingly in ignorance of the faith. " For a long time I had wondered why God

---

[1] Pius IX, *Qui Pluribus*, Denzinger, 1637.
[2] Vatican Council, Denzinger, 1799.
[3] Rom. ii. 6–16.

had preferences, why so many poor savages died without even hearing
Our Lord's name . . . I saw . . . that Our Lord's love shines out
just as much through a little soul who yields completely to his grace
as it does through the greatest . . . God has created the child who
knows nothing and can only make feeble cries and the poor savage
with only the natural law to guide him, and it is to hearts such as these
that he stoops."[1]

It remains for us in our day not to cast into outer darkness, *a priori*,

[1] *The Story of a Soul*, trans. Michael Day, Cong. Orat., Burns, Oates and
Washbourne, 1951, pp. 5–7. Unfortunately, as the historical essay *Le Problème du
salut des infidèles* (Toulouse, Grand Séminaire, 1934) by Louis Capéran shows,
French religious life in the seventeenth and eighteenth centuries was in this
respect, as in many others, infected by Jansenism. We of today suffer the consequences of this conflict between Jansenism and orthodoxy—which is still far
from being satisfactorily explained in the eyes of a great many people, who therefore remain in all good faith misguided and bewildered. "It is only a follower of
Pelagius who could doubt that all Americans were damned before they were
enlightened by the light of the Gospel ": these words are to be found in the
posthumous work of the great Arnauld on the salvation of pagans, published in
1701 (op. cit., p. 327). Alas, Arnauld's spirit had hovered over the seventeenth
century and was to go on darkening the eighteenth. "In France strict opinions
became fashionable from the second half of the seventeenth century onwards
. . . Under the influence of the natural tendency of his age—a tendency which
he helped to strengthen—even Bossuet was too ready to assume the quasi-
universal damnation of all the unfortunates who lived without the light of faith,
plunged in the darkness of idolatry " (op. cit., pp. 381–2).

Voltaire and Rousseau had a fine time exploiting this situation. Here is
Voltaire for instance (*Le Pour et le Contre*, quoted in op. cit., p. 394):

"Quoi! Dieu voulut mourir pour le salut de tous,
Et son trépas est inutile! . . .
Ce Dieu poursuit encore, aveugle en sa colère,
Sur ses derniers enfants l'erreur d'un premier père;
Il en demande compte à cent peuples divers,
Assis dans la nuit du mensonge,
Il punit au fond des enfers
L'ignorance invincible, où lui-même il les plonge,
Lui qui veut éclairer et sauver l'univers! . . ."

[What! God willed to die for the salvation of all men
And His death was useless! . . .
Blind with rage, He still visits
The sin of the first father on his latest children;
Exacting retribution from a hundred different races
Lost in the night of untruth;
Consigning to the depths of hell
The invincible ignorance in which He Himself plunges them,
This God who wills to enlighten and save the universe! . . .]

And Rousseau's "Vicaire Savoyard " says: "If there were on earth a religion
outside which there was only eternal torment, and if, somewhere on earth, there
was a single person of good faith who had not been convinced of its truth, the
God of that religion would be the most cruel and iniquitous of tyrants" (quoted
in op. cit., p. 391). This would be true if there was no baptism by desire, which
may be implicit even in a misguided conscience; but it is not in fact the teaching
of the Church.

all those contemporaries of ours who say they doubt the existence of God or are unable to believe in Him in any personal way.

" The speculative refusal of God as a final end and as the supreme rule of human life does not necessarily imply, for a mind so blinded, a practical refusal to order one's life with regard to that same God, whose name is no longer known . . . Under many names, names which are not that of God, in ways only known to God, the interior act of a soul's thought can be directed towards a reality which in fact truly may be God. For, as a result of our spiritual weakness, there can easily be a discordance between what in reality we believe and the ideas in which we express to ourselves what we believe, and take cognisance of our beliefs."[1]

It is true, then, that every reasonable adult of genuine goodwill will be saved and ultimately enjoy the beatific vision, but the will is not genuinely good unless it is rectified with regard to the true as well as to the good. Baptism by desire can be accompanied by sanctifying grace even without the knowledge of the recipient.[2]

We, the baptized members of the visible Church, have thus no absolute monopoly of sincerity. But since the deposit of revealed truth is in our possession, and since it is the Catholic Church which provides the world with the most examples of the highest sanctity and those of the greatest perfection, let us remember that our exalted rank carries with it obligations. Let us increasingly manifest the truth in love. " Woe," says Bossuet, " to the knowledge that turns not to love." Those who have received more are obliged to give more.

We must therefore spread the knowledge of the truth, which alone

---

[1] Jacques Maritain, *True Humanism*, trans. M. R. Adamson, Geoffrey Bles, 1938, p. 56. For further study of this delicate problem I refer the reader to this book and also to the remarkable essay by Mouroux, "Structure personnelle de la foi," which appeared in *Recherches de Science religieuse*, Jan.-Feb. 1939. True faith is necessary for salvation (a belief at least in a God who rewards merit), but the whole theological problem lies in showing how this principle may still operate accidentally in the psychology of certain atheists. I am substantially in agreement with Mouroux, whose essay appears to me to be particularly searching: it makes use of some excellent passages from St. Thomas Aquinas.

[2] A convert preparing to receive the sacrament of Baptism is already in a state of grace, and he knows it. A pious Mahomedan will also be in possession of grace through Christ, but without knowing it. For this reason some people say that " No salvation outside the Church " means " No salvation outside the invisible Church ", but this may tend to give a false impression that there are two Churches, one visible (the Roman) and the other invisible (the souls of the just), whereas in reality all the just, whether they know it or not, are just by reason of the Redemption and the holy sacrifice of the Mass, offered unceasingly throughout the whole earth in the one Church of Christ. It is better to say " No salvation outside the Church ", and mean that people can belong to the Church implicitly, even without knowing it. There are not two Churches. Cf. C. Journet, *L'Église du Verbe incarné*, Desclée, vol. i, pp. 45-6: " The just outside the Church are *invisibly* part of the visible Church."

redeems the human heart; remembering that embodying the dogma is the best kind of apologetic. A fortress's first defences are within. To enlighten any spirit seeking the truth, it is much more efficacious to reveal all the inner wealth and harmony of the truth than to attempt to analyse the distress of the enquiring spirit, which really needs to be consoled. There is a profound truth in Aristotle's observation that before human wisdom can be acquired there has to be complete trust in the master. Any knowledge, to be certain, must be stronger than doubt; for to doubt anything seriously it must first be known, i.e. have been assimilated with the utmost seriousness. This is self-evident: how can one appreciate a cathedral if one refuses to go round it, both outside and within?

God of injustice or God of love?—this is how many of our contemporaries see the problem of God. Let them know our answer, then: God is a God of love.

Let them know that the precious pearl of the Gospels, which in our eyes is worth every possible sacrifice that can be made by human beings in their wretchedness, is love, a living personal relationship between our souls and the Word of God and His Father and His Spirit, maintained by sanctifying grace and the theological virtues. The least glimpse—such as Plato had in the *Symposium*—of the supreme beauty of the beatific vision to which we are effectively ordained, is infinitely superior to the most luminous and spiritual ideas of the highest angel; and from this possession of God, from this spark of God Himself, will burst a flash of love which will make the fire burning in the purest and most passionate of hearts seem no more than a shadow of nothingness.

" Christianity is strange: it tells man to recognize that he is a base, in fact an abominable, creature; and it also tells him to try to be like God. If it were not for this balance," Pascal goes on, " either his elevation would make him horribly vain, or his abasement would make him horribly abject."[1]

If the world is not absurd, it can only be, in Bergson's words, " a machine for the making of gods ".[2]

LOVE AND DIFFICULTY

The relationship between merit and difficulty is intimately connected with the relationship between love and aggressiveness. " O sweetest love of God that art so little known! He that has found the veins of this mine has found rest."[3]

[1] *Pensées*, art. iv, 5.
[2] *The Two Sources of Morality and Religion*, Macmillan, 1935, chap. iv, p. 275.
[3] St. John of the Cross, *Spiritual Sentences and Maxims*, in *Complete Works*, ed. and trans. E. Allison Peers, Burns, Oates and Washbourne, vol. iii, p. 242.

Let us get this matter of merit and difficulty clear once and for all. In hell there is suffering without merit and without love: in purgatory there is suffering without merit but not without love: in heaven there is no suffering and no merit but only love. And on earth there is room for love, merit and suffering all at once, but the supernatural merit is a result of the love, not of the suffering or the aggressiveness. The main thing, the essential thing, is to love greatly, not necessarily to suffer or to struggle greatly.

It is not the difficulty that causes the merit. Far too many souls fail to realize this and thus create endless difficulties for themselves— difficulties which are usually useless and very often harmful.

Loving God means, essentially, conforming one's will to His in order to please Him. " He that hath my commandments, and keepeth them; he it is that loveth me."[1] It is not the person who promises to do something and then fails to do it, but rather the one who does a thing without having promised to do it, who is the loving son.[2]

" The more perfectly a person practises it [i.e. conformity with the will of God] the more he will receive of the Lord and the greater the progress he will make on this road; do not think we have to use strange jargon or dabble in things of which we have no knowledge or understanding; our entire welfare is to be found in what I have described "— such is the teaching of St. Teresa of Avila.[3] "Always try to obey," she says again, " however much it may hurt you to do so, for that is the greatest possible perfection."[4] " What profit is it that thou give one thing to God if He asks of thee another? Consider that which will please God and do it," writes St. John of the Cross.[5]

There is a noticeable, indeed a striking contrast between the moral healthiness of the great mystics, who ask human beings to transcend their humanity, and the semi-neurotic condition of so many human beings who have lost the courage and the taste for taking risks. As Dr. Parcheminey aptly puts it, the neurotic is " absolutely incapable of oblativity ",[6] " in a state of inner revolt against his destiny".[7] In order to love God a creature must accept his condition, must indeed love it as being God's will for him.

Now man's natural condition—as seen from the philosophical point of view—and his supernatural condition (as regards the actual facts) involve struggle, suffering and death. A man cannot evade the demand

[1] John xiv. 21.
[2] Matt. xxi. 28–31.
[3] *Interior Castle*, II: *Complete Works of St. Teresa of Jesus*, ed. and trans. E. Allison Peers, Sheed and Ward, vol. ii, p. 217.
[4] *The Way of Perfection*, xxxix: op. cit., p. 170.
[5] *Spiritual Sentences and Maxims: Complete Works*, vol. iii, p. 248.
[6] p. 92, *supra*.
[7] p. 97, *supra*.

to bear lovingly with many struggles and sufferings during his earthly life. That is his fate. Usually the person who is called upon to love greatly is called upon to suffer greatly too.

Psychologically, suffering is a proof of love. Suffering is not freely and voluntarily accepted out of indifference: and the greatest proof of love is to give one's blood.

Suffering is also instrumental to love. It helps love to know itself better, and to grow strong. No heart that has not bled really knows what love is. A child may have a perfectly genuine affection for its mother but it will not realize her full worth until it loses her or lives in fear of losing her. Labour and hardship increase love by rousing it out of its sleepy routine and forcing it to develop and give itself. The economy of the Redemption is more fruitful in love than that of the Garden of Eden, and for this reason it is superior to it.

" Love consists not in feeling great things, but in having great attachment and suffering for the Beloved."[1]

" Would you be perfect? Go and sell your will, give it to the spiritually poor, come to Christ in meekness and humility, then walk in His footsteps to Calvary and the sepulchre."[2]

This interconnection between suffering and love, between struggle and merit, has a metaphysical reason deriving from man's very nature as a composite of soul and body, and a historical cause, the sin of Adam; but we must never forget that the amount of difficulty that is experienced is not in itself any index either of the purity of the love, or of the quality of the merit. This is a golden rule in the spiritual life. The more real progress a soul makes in virtue, the easier virtue becomes for it because it loves more.

It is necessary to love, then; that is the essential thing; if love turns out to be costing, this may be fruitful, but it remains secondary. St. John of the Cross is never tired of repeating that perceptible consolations are not in themselves proof of the divine favour, nor aridity or dryness signs that God is less present in the soul. " Truly a man has conquered all things if the pleasure that they bring him move him not to joy and the insipidity which they leave behind causes not sorrow."[3] " See that thou carest nothing for anything."[4]

The purpose of prayer is not to conform the will of God to our will but on the contrary to conform our will to the will of God.[5] Our Father, Thy will be done on earth as it is in heaven—Thy will, not mine. This is the perfection of love.

---

[1] St. John of the Cross, *Points of Love: Complete Works*, vol. iii, p. 253.
[2] ibid.
[3] id., *Spiritual Sentences and Maxims: Complete Works*, vol. iii, p. 246.
[4] ibid., p. 248.
[5] II–II, 83, 2.

LOVE AND WORKS

In the Church of God there will always be actives and contemplatives, since both are necessary. The spiritual temperament of the first category tends to be aggressive; that of the second, loving. " Love tends to receive its object, for it desires one thing only: to be united to that which gives it pleasure. The irascible, on the other hand, is orientated towards action, since it tends to struggle to master whatever threatens it."[1]

Nevertheless, though action means struggle against the exterior obstacles arising from people and things, the solitary life also takes the form of struggle, in a grim attempt at self-mastery with the aim of attaining to divine contemplation. "At the beginning of the *Institutions* . . . Cassian portrays the monk as a soldier armed for battle; a little further on, he compares the novice who submits himself to his elders for the purposes of his education to a youth who longs to take part in the Olympic games. It is always combat that is involved; the comparisons being taken either from the military life or from athletics . . . It was from the language of athletics that our word for spiritual labour, ' asceticism ', was derived."[2] It would therefore be wrong to attempt to erect any fundamental opposition between actives and contemplatives. The contrary is true: love needs to be strong in both cases, both for doing and for contemplating, and the aggressiveness that is based on love has no supernatural value except according to the amount of love that is involved. That is why the contemplative life is eminently apostolic and superior to the life of action;[3] it is also the reason why the mixed life that comprises both action and contemplation is ultimately the best and the most harmonious of all. " It is better to give to others the fruits of one's contemplation than merely to contemplate."[4]

It would be quite ridiculous, in choosing one's vocation, to go against one's aptitudes and desires; this would simply be asceticism turned inside out. Grace does not destroy nature. The variety of the states and conditions of existence corresponds to the diversities of temperament and character. God is quite capable of raising His own

---

[1] *De Veritate*, q. 25, a. 2. St. Thomas is here speaking of the irascible and concupiscible, but body and soul form a unity, the libidinous and aggressive functions also exist on the spiritual level of the will and, moreover, grace does not destroy nature. The Kingdom of Heaven is taken by force.

[2] Jean Brémond, *Les Pères du désert*, Gabalda, 1927, i, pp. 31–2. " A religious, being the soldier of Jesus Christ and always ready for battle, must always have his loins girded. The Scriptures show those who laid the foundations of this sacred profession in the Old Testament—Elias and Eliseus, for instance—as wearing a belt " (Cassian, *Institutions*, i. 1., quoted in op. cit., p. 36.)

[3] II–II, 182, 3.

[4] II–II, 188, 6.

obstacles in the way of those He chooses: it is sufficient to let Him act upon us.[1]

In any case, close scrutiny will show that there is no kind of existence from which all works can be entirely absent. Every existence necessarily implies, in some form or other, works arising from the duties of one's station in life and from brotherly love.

The entire spirituality of St. John of the Cross is based on the proper performance of the duties of one's station, which are to be fulfilled lovingly. Before he gives his nine spiritual " cautions "—three against the world, three against the devil and three against the flesh— he expresses himself quite simply as follows:

" With habitual care and with no further labour or other kind of exercise, failing not of his own part to do that which his state enjoins on him, he will progress very quickly to great perfection, gaining all the virtues together and attaining to holy peace."[2]

But if a living faith always produces works (whether these are insignificant or important from the human point of view makes no difference in the eyes of God), they are only valuable in proportion to the love that informs them. " Faith . . . worketh by charity."[3] " The Lord does not look so much at the magnitude of anything we do as at the love with which we do it," as St. Teresa of Avila succinctly puts it.[4]

And St. John of the Cross adds: " More does God desire of thee the least degree of purity of conscience than all the works that thou canst perform."[5]

This is why St. Thérèse of the Child Jesus can even say, " God has no need of our works but only of our love." But this is an intentional paradox: her example proved that a genuine love of God includes works of brotherly love. In this she was a true daughter of Teresa of Avila, whose words have the genuine spirit of the Gospels: " When I see people very diligently trying to discover what kind of prayer they are experiencing and so completely wrapped up in their prayers that they seem afraid to stir, or to indulge in a moment's thought, lest they should lose the slightest degree of the tenderness and devotion they have been feeling, I realize how little they understand of the road to the attainment of union. They think that the

---

[1] There is the well-known quip attributed by the Bollandists to St. Teresa of Avila. " O, Lord," she exclaims, in her delightfully familiar way, " when will you stop spreading difficulties under our feet like this? " " Don't complain, daughter," replies the divine Master, " that's the way I always treat my friends." " Yes, Lord," replies Teresa, " and that's why you have so few! " (Bollandist *Histoire de Sainte Thérèse*, Paris, Retaux-Bray, 1888, vol. ii, p. 362.)

[2] *Cautions: Complete Works*, vol. iii, p. 220.

[3] Gal. v. 6.

[4] *Interior Castle*, vii: *Complete Works*, p. 350.

[5] *Spiritual Sentences and Maxims: Complete Works*, vol. iii, p. 242.

whole thing consists in this. But no, sisters, no; what the Lord desires is works. If you see a sick woman to whom you can give some help, never be affected by the fear that your devotion will suffer, but take pity on her: if she is in pain, you should feel pain too; if necessary, fast so that she may have your food, not so much for her sake as because you know it to be your Lord's will. That is true union with His will . . . I have said a great deal about this elsewhere, sisters, because I know that if we were to fail here we should be lost."[1] " If we have attained great perfection here [in our love for our neighbour], we have done everything."[2] The theological virtue of charity governs the two precepts of the love of God and the love of one's neighbour, and whatsoever we do unto the least of our brothers we do unto Christ.

" If I speak with the tongues of men, and of angels, and have not charity, I am become as sounding brass or a tinkling cymbal."[3] Faith, knowledge, prophecy, are nothing without charity. And philanthropy without charity is nothing either. But what exactly is love? " Charity is patient, is kind . . . Charity . . . rejoiceth with the truth; beareth all things, believeth all things, hopeth all things, endureth all things . . . Charity never falleth away."[4] Patience, says St. Francis de Sales, best ensures our perfection. " The soul enkindled with love is a soul that is gentle, meek, humble and patient."[5] This love—with its works— is the only kind of love with which the heart of God is concerned. " We do so much good when we give ourselves and all that we have."[6]

LOVE AND PENANCE

In practice the duties of one's station involve a whole complex of compulsions and privations that enter quite naturally into line with renunciation, with the will of God, and hence with love. But this is not enough.

People who do no more than this do less than they should. We must now turn to the aggressiveness of asceticism—not as it concerns others (this is the tactic of false piety), but as it concerns ourselves. Anyone with any character must lay certain works of supererogation upon himself. But the question arises, how to be guided to discern aright, since not every inner prompting necessarily comes from the Holy Spirit. St. John of the Cross gives two criteria: reason and faith:

" Enter into account with thy reason to do that which it counsels

[1] *Interior Castle*, v: *Complete Works*, pp. 262–3.
[2] ibid., pp. 261–2.
[3] I Cor. xiii. 1.
[4] ibid., 4–8.
[5] St. John of the Cross, *Spiritual Sentences and Maxims: Complete Works*, vol. iii, p. 244.
[6] Père Jacques de Jésus.

thee on the road to God, and it will be of greater worth to thee with respect to thy God than all the works that thou doest without this counsel and than all the spiritual delights that thou seekest."[1] What then, in this matter of asceticism, is the criterion of reason, whereby one may discern the real value of an inspiration or a decision? St. Thomas answers with his usual clarity. " Can one sin by fasting excessively or going without too much sleep? " he asks.[2] Here is his reply:

"According to Aristotle [*Pol.*, I], advice should vary according to whether it is the end or the means with which we are concerned. The end should be sought without qualification; the means should be employed according to the end: medicine improves health as much as it possibly can because health is its end, but it uses remedies only to the extent that they are beneficial to health.

" In the spiritual life the love of God should be regarded as the end; fasting, denying oneself sleep and performing other bodily penances—these are not sought as ends, because, as St. Paul says in the Epistle to the Romans [xiv. 17], ' The Kingdom of God is not meat and drink'; these penances are used as means necessary for a certain end—to overcome the lusts of the flesh, according to the Apostle's words to the Corinthians [1 ix. 27]: ' I chastise my body and bring it into subjection '. They should therefore be used to a reasonable extent—for example, as a remedy against concupiscence —but without exhausting nature, in conformity with the words of the Epistle to the Romans [xii. 1]: ' Present your bodies a living sacrifice, holy, pleasing unto God, your reasonable service '.

" But if, by fasting, and depriving oneself of sleep, and other practices of a like kind, the natural powers are weakened to such an extent that the actions required by duty are unable to be per- formed—as, preaching by the preacher, teaching by the teacher, singing by the singer—then there is no doubt that sin has been committed. Similarly, too, sin would be committed by anyone who was prevented by his voluntary privations from fulfilling his duties as a husband to his wife. Hence, Saint Jerome's sayings: 'Anyone who burdens his body immoderately with fasts and excessive watch- ings offers the sacrifice of a criminal, the holocaust of a robber ', and again: 'Anyone who considers fasting more important than charity, going without sleep more important than the proper exercise of his bodily faculties, forfeits his dignity as a reasonable human being '."

[1] *Spiritual Sentences and Maxims: Complete Works*, vol. iii, p. 246.
[2] *Quodlibet* v, a. 18.

One is reminded of St. Francis de Sales' saying: I am a man above all things. How careful St. Thomas is here, as always, not to asphyxiate poor human nature by strangling love under aggressiveness. This is not Port Royal! But there can be special cases. Discussing the extreme forms of penance adopted by St. Margaret of Cortona, François Mauriac observes very justly: "A contemplative lacking in physical charm and untouched by carnal love cannot know this appetite for destruction, nor these audacities of a holy vengeance. In the case of a woman who is bent on a direct mortification of the flesh, the plough of penance must sink to the level of her former sensual satisfactions. The more delicious these have been, the deeper must the plough cut through. But apart from penance, mere prudence should oblige a sanctified soul to mortify the body that has been pampered for so many years."[1]

There are other calls made by Christ on the cross. There are saints like the Curé d'Ars who never knew the sins of the flesh and yet have left us frightening examples of penance, inspired as they were to unite themselves in this way through love to the redemptive sufferings of our Lord Jesus Christ.

But no one is a good judge of his own case. " He that desires to be alone, without the support of a master and guide, will be like the tree that is alone in the field and has no owner. However much fruit it bears, passers-by will pluck it all, and it will not mature."[2] " This is what happens when we perform excessive penances in order to make ourselves believe that, because of what we are doing, we are more penitent than others. If we conceal our penances from our confessor or superior, or if we are told to give them up and do not obey, that is a clear case of temptation."[3]

Studying the Gospels, weighing the circumstances, asking advice as to what best suits the love of God and the love of the neighbour— which together form one perfection, one and the same love—these are what is needed: the theological virtue of charity, in fact, the fullness of all perfection, embodied in the two great commandments, the second of which is like unto the first: Thou shalt love the Lord thy God with all thy strength, and thy neighbour as thyself for the love of God.

Let us learn from St. John of the Cross, then, how to distinguish renunciation from penance.

" Renunciation is love ": self-renunciation means doing the will of God and being ready for any eventuality—without excluding in advance any divine invitation. Not loving father or mother, son or daughter,

[1] *Margaret of Cortona*, trans. Barbara Wall, Burns, Oates and Washbourne, p. 51.
[2] *Spiritual Sentences and Maxims: Complete Works*, vol. iii, p. 241.
[3] St. Teresa of Jesus, *The Way of Perfection*, ch. xxxix: *Complete Works*, vol. ii, p. 170.

more than God, means being willing to say, if the necessity arises, " The Lord gave and the Lord hath taken away; blessed be the Name of the Lord." When St. John of the Cross counsels the harder, the more costing thing, in preference to the easier and more delightful one, he obviously means only in so far as the will of God demands it— only to that extent, but to the full extent of God's demand. We must love with all our might: this will mean more for some than for others, but however much or however little it may be, it is always the absolute that is demanded of us. " Thou shalt love . . . with all thy heart and with all thy mind."

Mortification is, in itself, a punishment, a privation that hurts. It belongs to the sphere of aggressiveness. It is simply a means, and as such its value must be carefully estimated. There is no virtue in any compulsion unless the resulting obedience comes from love. " One of the criteria of health, of moral and physiological equilibrium, lies in the quantitative connection between these two antagonistic impulses (love and aggressiveness)."[1] A tree is only pruned so that it will give more fruit—in this case the fruit of love.

A contemplative monk is obliged to mortify himself more than the father of a family, obviously, but at the end of their lives both will be judged by love. We all have to learn how to love greatly. Only a love that is pure and disinterested will enable us to persevere to the end.

PATHOLOGICAL CASES

Unfortunately it is only too true that circumstances can arise in which the natural equilibrium of the soul is upset, or even destroyed. In certain cases an individual may find himself, through no fault of his own, subject to disorders of such a nature that they are beyond his control. This does not mean that he will lose merit in the eyes of Him who sounds the reins and the heart.

" The practice of psycho-analysis gives one the impression of human illogicality," writes Roland Dalbiez. " It is an impression which is too often lacking in jurists and moralists. We certainly do not dream of denying the specific and irreducible value of law and of morality, but we cannot refrain from regretting how completely most of their exponents neglect the study of the findings of psycho-pathology. The result of this procedure is that the judgments they deliver often exhibit a shockingly unreal quality."[2]

[1] See *supra*, p. 95.
[2] *Psychoanalytical Method and the Doctrine of Freud*, trans. T. F. Lindsay, Longmans, Green and Co., vol. ii, p. 302. Spiritual directors will also find much useful information in *Les Deux Sources, consciente et inconsciente, de la vie morale*, by Dr. Charles Odier, Neuchâtel, éditions de la Baconnière, 1943.

A person who has lost his mental balance may be driven irresistibly to perform actions which in other cases would be reprehensible (one has only to think of certain cases of suicide or attempted suicide, morbid habits of blasphemy, some kinds of impurity). If such a person's mind was lucid, would he go on hating God? Not necessarily. He may be the victim of some kind of mechanism over which he has no control. The disorder may be unable to stop him from wanting God. As has been very justly observed: " It may happen in rarer and more difficult cases, in which purely material sins are involved, that the director is obliged to tell his penitents not to bother about these sins, advising them not to go to confession and even in some cases refusing to allow them to go. In these cases, confession would only plunge them more deeply into despair.[1] For here one is faced with Christians who, burdened with the very heavy Cross of an unavoidable obsession, no longer dare to look God in the face. They drag their way through life without ever experiencing a moment's joy, either natural or supernatural, because they do not properly understand their condition, because they imagine that the physical depression following upon certain acts is a sign of reprobation, and finally because they believe that they are under an unavoidable compulsion to commit sin. No one is tempted beyond his strength; if the contrary seems to be true, there needs to be an enquiry into whether the ' fall ' is really a fall in the moral sense."[2] This last remark is particularly relevant. It is a mistake to be so much " under the influence of a purely objective morality " that one forgets " the possibility of subjective non-imputability ". The director should not neglect the " purely pathological territory "; " by reconciling himself to its existence ", he " will prepare more happy souls for eternal life ",[3] at the same time doing all he can to estimate the extent to which the particular sick or unbalanced person in question may be made responsible for his condition through his own inner behaviour.

Such people, as the author rightly insists, may by no means be without a longing for perfection or the gift of mystical prayer. This seems to be the opinion of the best theologians on the subject—for instance, Père de Guibert, Père Garrigou-Lagrange, Père de Tonquedec.[4]

---

[1] Dr. Parcheminey observes very pertinently that a neurotic condition can be aggravated by too strict an attitude on the part of the director: " If the patient, faced with a growing feeling of guilt, has no other resource except one that accentuates his neurosis, he may be tempted to reject all constraint, and then his aggressiveness breaks through his defences with an iconoclastic rage that knows no bounds " (supra, p. 103).

[2] Canon Dr. Adalbert Brenninkmeyer, " Défaitisme moral et victoire chrétienne", in Le Risque Chrétien, Études Carmélitaines, April 1939, pp. 170-1.

[3] ibid.

[4] Nuit Mystique, Études Carmélitaines, Oct. 1938, p. 188.

" There is nothing to prevent some unfortunate soul who is subject to fits of madness from rising during his lucid intervals to a very high level of love and sanctity, despite all the acts he may commit without being responsible for them; if he is conscious of these acts, they may be a rare source of humility and merit for him."[1] It is a mistake to think that " real sanctity " must always be " the kind of sanctity that can be proved in a court of law and then set up for the faithful to venerate ".[2] The Sacred Congregation of Rites is in any case an essentially prudent body of men. However difficult discernment may be in such cases, it is all the more necessary for the spiritual director to be capable of it " when in the soul of some abnormal person an efflorescence of mysticism mingles with the artificial flowers of psychosis ".[3]

" The world is so full of melancholy," wrote St. Teresa in the sixteenth century (instead of " melancholy " we should say today " depressive states "), " that confessors have very good cause to be afraid of it and to watch for it very carefully."[4]

The director can sin by excess or defect in his estimate, by being either too rigorous or too lax, and this is made all the easier for him by the fact that there is no mathematical frontier between neurosis and normality. " If the neurotic represents the typical schema of the dualism between conscious and unconscious activities, the difference is frequently only one of degree between the neurotic, the 'nervous' person in the ordinary meaning of the word, and the genuine normal type."[5] "The same laws of psychic life apply throughout the whole of psychology."[6]

Between the madman who has lost the use of his reason and the healthy, vigorous, balanced personality, there is a chromatic scale comprising an infinite number of cases.[7]

The philosopher and the theologian should aim to be psychologists too, and keep on the look-out not only for cases that are explicitly pathological but for any case that shows the slightest sign of neurosis. In serious cases " the joint action of psycho-therapist, doctor and priest "[8] is eminently desirable. It is demanded by the virtue of prudence. Spiritual directors " should not be semi-educated and afraid of everything ", like the ones who cost St. Teresa " so much ". She describes the torture experienced by the soul who " comes to a con-

[1] Père de Guibert, " Le cas du P. Surin ", ibid., p. 187.
[2] ibid.
[3] T.-L. Pénido, " Grâce et Folie ", in *Études Carmélitaines*, April 1939.
[4] *Interior Castle*, Sixth Mansion: *Complete Works*, vol. iii, p. 272.
[5] *supra*, p. 90.
[6] *supra*, p. 97.
[7] " We are all mad, but we don't all manage to bring it off ", as an excellent teacher at the Catholic Institute in Lille used to say jokingly.
[8] *supra*, p. 103.

fessor so careful and inexperienced that he thinks nothing is certain ";
" he is afraid of everything, he doubts everything ", she says[1]—and he
is unbearable!

Some acquaintance with psycho-analytical knowledge is therefore
highly desirable; more important still, however, is a receptive attitude
towards the gifts of the Holy Spirit, so that the smoking flax may not
be quenched, the bruised reed not broken. We must not be sons of
thunder; on the contrary, we must be kindly disposed towards all who
endure their share of human misery, whether this be physical, psychological or moral.

It is undoubtedly true that moral lapses have repercussions in the
domain of faith, but it should also be realized that in this field too a
loss of psychological balance may have a pernicious influence for
which the individual is not necessarily, *a priori,* responsible. The
physical nervous system can indirectly be the source of intellectual
crisis—I say the source, since sense-impressions are only an incidental
factor in the play of ideas, an image is an instrumental cause and the
imagination is the mistress of error. Thus organic balance is necessary
for a normal intellectual life.

"An intellect operating on the basis of elements that are subject to
perturbations of a pathological kind will inevitably come to wrong
conclusions, and as a result of this the will, in its turn, will be diverted
into abnormal channels . . . Anyone who is deficient in his natural
faculties will have more difficulty, not perhaps in meriting, but in
turning himself into a perfect example of morality, even of the supernatural kind."[2]

Conscience is our immediate and universal rule of action. A thing
that is objectively good—such as abstaining from fornication and
believing in Christ—St. Thomas teaches, becomes evil for anyone
who considers it evil.[3] Hence the need to distinguish between the
outer act and the inner motive when judging the morality of any act.

When the Vatican Council teaches that " those who have received
the faith under the direction of the magisterium of the Church can
never have any *just* cause for modifying this same faith or for putting
it in doubt ",[4] it is taking its stand on a historical, philosophical and
dogmatic objectivity, but it does not for all that mean to exclude the
possibility of subjective non-imputability of a total or partial kind.[5]

[1] *Interior Castle, Fifth Mansion.*
[2] A. Gardeil, O.P., " A propos de la Madeleine de Pierre Janet ", *Études Carmélitaines,* Oct. 1931, pp. 129, 131.
[3] I-II, 19, 5.
[4] Denzinger, 1794.
[5] See L. de Grandmaison, *La Crise de la Foi chez les Jeunes,* 5th ed., Paris, Beauchesne, 1932, esp. pp. 92–102: Gardeil, *La Crédibilité et l'apologétique,* Paris, Gabalda, 1928, p. 299.

Objective truth is not involved here, but only the accidental psychology of the individual. So true is this that the Sovereign Pontiff himself, despite his ability to pass infallible judgment on any case of heresy, leaves to God alone the decision as to whether the heretic is guilty of mortal sin. So true is it, again, that between the instructed and well-balanced believer, on the one hand, who consciously preserves and strengthens his faith, and the imbecile who goes mad and loses all control of his mind, there is a whole scale of variations that includes the believer by logic and habit; the conscious believer who is illogical about some particular point of his faith; all the neurotics who have doubts and hesitations and are more to be pitied than blamed—victims, too often (in varying degrees of responsibility) of " an intellectual intoxication followed by vertigo, which—though these things are not in themselves able to cause the absolute destruction of the infused virtue of faith—nevertheless give those who experience them the impression that their belief is crumbling ";[1] before we come down to the absolute renegades, the genuinely guilty.

Not every kind of moral or intellectual disorder, of course, is mere sickness, or entirely sickness; and that brings us to the question of sin.

CONFIDENCE AND SIN

The way of spiritual childhood is not the prerogative of a privileged sect: it is open to all who have a genuine desire to keep, or discover, the soul of a child.

Far from being an insurmountable obstacle, sin can providentially, by way of permission, become a means to our soul's greater good. " To them that love God all things work together unto good ", says St. Paul;[2] even sin, *etiam peccata*, adds St. Augustine.

The great principle of love dominating the mystery of the Redemption is announced by St. Paul in the Epistle to the Romans: " Where sin abounded, grace did more abound."[3] It is easy to see how this applies in the economy that governs the Fall and Redemption of mankind. The liturgy for Holy Saturday says, " Happy fault, that won so holy and so high a Redeemer! " It is not so often realized that this scheme of merciful love is, by this very fact, valid for each one of us in particular, from the moment that we learn to have confidence and to be of goodwill. " There is no doctrine more appropriate to man," says Pascal, " than this, which teaches him his double capacity of receiving and of losing grace, because of the double peril to which he is exposed, of despair or of pride."[4]

---

[1] Grandmaison, *La Crise de la Foi chez les Jeunes*, p. 98. [3] Rom. v. 20.
[2] Rom. vii. 28. [4] *Pensées*, 523.

The worst sin for any soul to commit is that which was committed by the angels and by Adam; or, again, the sin of despair, which is simply another form of their sin of pride.

The thing that is objectively intolerable is for a soul to admire itself and feel self-satisfied, as though its perfection or happiness came from itself alone. Cardinal de Bérulle said of the Blessed Virgin Mary: " In her the Sun of God has no shadow." Every soul should surrender itself to the divine light; its first beneficial effect will be to bring out the ugliness of its faults.

The proper function of falls and imperfections is, precisely, to reveal our own weakness to us. Sin is the surest sign of our wretchedness, and in the scheme of our sanctification its purpose is, quite simply, to humiliate us. In a sense sin is its own remedy. When a soul far advanced in virtue falls from grace, God permits this so that it may have a chance of extricating itself from the sticky webs of its own self-satisfaction.

And therefore, as St. Thérèse of the Child Jesus explains, when we have sinned, a kind of dual reaction should take place in us, so that in the first place we are sorry for the pain we have caused Almighty God (this being the negative aspect of our reaction) and then—on the positive side—we should go on to rejoice (yes, rejoice!) over our weakness rather than be annoyed by it. For annoyance would be a sign of pride and self-love; whereas joy means humility.

Like so many holy souls, St. Thérèse of the Child Jesus is profoundly convinced of her own weakness and misery. "All our acts of justice," she says, " are faulty in the eyes of God." " The greatest thing the Almighty ever did in me was to show me my own paltriness, my utter inability to do good." " To me too come many weaknesses, but they never surprise me." " O God, it is true, I rejoice to feel how small and weak I am in your presence: it brings peace to my heart."

To rejoice in one's own wretchedness is the key to the " Little Way ". " For when I am weak, then am I powerful ",[1] for I am strong with the strength of God in the abasement of my own nothingness.

When we have sinned—even though we have sinned mortally, and again and again—it always depends on our free consent to God's grace whether or not our sins turn to our greater good and thus cause in us a greater abundance of grace. For God is mercy. Our Lord tells us in the Gospels not to return evil for evil, and He exemplifies His teaching by forgiving us again and again after dying for us on the cross. In the Gospels there is an immense compassion for all forms of suffering and an infinite mercy towards sin.

" True love is shown in self-abasement, and if everyone were like

[1] 2 Cor. xii. 10.

the saintly doctors who adorn the Church, it would seem that God had not far enough to stoop when he came to them."[1] And so He had pity on thieves and publicans and died for them—for each and every one of us.

" It is not only because I have been preserved from mortal sin that I fly to Jesus with such confidence and love; even if I had all the crimes possible on my conscience, I am sure I should lose none of my confidence. Heartbroken with repentance, I would simply throw myself into my Saviour's arms, for I know how much he loves the prodigal son. I have heard what he said to Mary Magdalene, to the woman taken in adultery, and to the Samaritan woman. No one can make me frightened any more, because I know what to believe about his mercy and his love; I know that in the twinkling of an eye all those thousands of sins would be consumed as a drop of water cast into a blazing fire."[2]

A person who truly repents of his sins—even mortal sins repeated again and again—and rejoices in all sincerity at the realization of his own wretchedness (even to seventy times seven) will always receive far more in return—through being humiliated and forgiven—than he ever loses by thus falling from grace.

Is this quietism? or laxity?

" Shall we continue in sin that grace may abound? " asks St. Paul, voicing this objection. " God forbid. For we that are dead to sin, how shall we live any longer therein? Know ye not that all we, who are baptized in Christ, are baptized in his death? "[3] No; for, whilst we accept our weakness joyfully, we have no desire to offend voluntarily One who died for us, and who thus gave proof of the greatest possible love. Love cannot wish to cause pain to the One it loves. Furthermore, nothing is more exacting or more devoted than love. It is always wanting to do more. If we are docile and persevering and generous-hearted, and abandon ourselves to the inspirations sent to us by God, we shall ultimately reach the haven of our sanctification.

What prevents us from ascending to God is not sin—even though it be mortal, and repeated again and again—if we are sincerely sorry each time we sin, and have a firm purpose of amendment, but a conscious, habitual determination not to break a certain binding link—it may be as light as a feather—that God wants us to break.[4] According

---

[1] St. Thérèse of Lisieux, Story of a Soul, p. 6.
[2] ibid., p. 181.
[3] Rom. vi. 1–3.
[4] " Any one of these imperfections, if the soul has become attached and habituated to it, is of as great harm to its growth and progress in virtue as though it were to fall daily into many other imperfections and casual venial sins which proceed not from a common indulgence in any common and harmful attachment, and will not hinder it so much as when it has attachment to any-

to the virile teaching of St. John of the Cross, therefore, these habitual, voluntary attachments must be broken, even though they only involve slight imperfections. If the soul is attached to some imperfection against God's will, it has still not succeeded in uniting its will with His. If, consciously and obstinately, we hold on to a thing, or a function, or a person, that is against or outside the will of God, we are behaving like a bird that is unable to fly because it is caught in lime or held back by a thread, and it makes no difference how fine the thread is.[1]

When we go to confession or examine our consciences, therefore, the essential thing is not to be able to foresee with absolute certainty that we shall never again indulge in any repetition of our sin, but to wish with all our heart that this will be the case, and to ask God that it may prove to be so. At the moment of wishing, at least, our attachment to the sin is broken, no matter what weakness we may show afterwards; if it recurs, it must be broken again.

If we cannot manage to be sorry, if we cannot wish to amend, if, in fact, we are certain that we shall persist in an attachment that needs to be broken, then, faced with the difficulty of making the break, we must go on hoping against hope that we may discover a holy aggressiveness, and ask God, tell Him, that we must be delivered from it; then we are sure to be heard. " My God, I cannot do this thing, but You will do it." And indeed He will effect the renunciation, the liberation, for you. " God does not demand the impossible, but He tells us to do what we can and to ask for what we cannot do, then He helps us to be able."[2]

One thing we are sure to obtain by confident, persevering prayer— no matter what our failings and deficiencies may be—and that is our sanctification.

Any prayer of petition for our own personal perfection is bound to be absolutely in line with the will of God, and it will unfailingly be heard if it is made with faith and perseverance. There is no need to enunciate here the conditions that must inevitably accompany any petition for temporal objects (success, health, business, etc.); they can all be reduced to one: " If it be Thy will, O Lord "—for it is indubitably the will of God that we shall ascend to Him through love,

thing " (St. John of the Cross, *The Ascent of Mount Carmel*, bk. i, ch. xi: *Complete Works*, vol. i, p. 53).

[1] " Even if it be slender, the bird will be as well held as though it were stout, for so long as it breaks it not and flies not away. It is true that the slender one is the easier to break; still, easy though it be, the bird will not fly away if it be not broken " (ibid., p. 53). See Père François de Ste. Marie, *Initiation à Saint Jean de la Croix*, ed. du Seuil, pp. 83 et seq. " There is attachment when we take *pleasure*, knowingly, voluntarily and habitually, in the very things that God wants us to sacrifice."

[2] Council of Trent, Denzinger, 804.

rising higher and higher every day and being entirely freed from our slightest attachments. " Lead us not into temptation, but deliver us from evil."

Thus the theological virtue of hope is based on the mercy and omnipotence of an infinitely loving God. It is in no way dependent on the virtues, or the moral progress, or the spiritual effort, or the merits, of the petitioner, but it depends from first to last on the infinite love of God, which, as St. Thérèse of the Child Jesus says, is revealed just as clearly in the soul of a savage or a tiny child as in the soul of a man of learning or one who can work miracles. Ascending the way of perfection does not mean struggling, it means resting on God; it is not so much a case of acquiring things for oneself as of losing oneself: God is the One who gives. The motive of hope has to be divested of all human self-interest and directed towards God alone, until we become strong with the strength of God and powerful with His power. When they find themselves faced with this power, all our attachments will give way, because God is stronger than they are.

Undoubtedly there is a need for aggressiveness in the service of God: the Kingdom of Heaven is not taken by the lukewarm but by the violent. Only, the aggressiveness is not the fundamental thing, for it does not lead to love: love must come first in us as it comes first in God. Religion is not a " business "; it is not, in the first place, a " struggle "; it is the activity of the one true love.

To what extent may we have confidence in God, as regards our ultimate end?

Every Christian knows that he can and must avoid hell, but far too many Christians fail to realize that they can and should avoid purgatory too, however grave their sins may be and however great or small may be the degree of glory to which God has predestined them in His infinite wisdom—that wisdom which is a composite of independence and love.

THE MYSTERY OF INIQUITY[1]

" The concrete facts of the problem that each individual has to solve for himself . . . can vary a great deal. It is required by justice, not that all the problems should be the same, but only that each problem should be soluble; in other words, that each person's particular difficulties should be taken into account, and that he should not be expected to do more than is reasonable. What counts towards retribution is precisely the way in which each person solves the entirely personal problem that has been set him. Divine justice does not mean that every soul shall be set the same problem, but that each person shall be

[1] 2 Thess. ii. 7: " For the mystery of iniquity already worketh."

set a problem proportionate to his character. And it means taking full account of the way in which each person solves this problem, considering the means at his disposal . . . ' Let no temptation take hold of you, but such as is human. And God is faithful, who will not suffer you to be tempted above that which you are able, but will make also with temptation, issue, that ye may be able to bear it ' (1 Cor. x. 13). We know that this must be proportionately true for every human life, and that at the last day none of the damned will be able to rise up and accuse God of injustice."[1]

Every damned soul, having refused God's grace, will witness to its own responsibility for the evil it has done and to the implacable hatred which it has freely assumed against the love that opposed its dastardly schemes. This witness will be given by the damned before One who shed His blood on the cross to purchase their redemption, One who had compassion on the poor, the sick and the sinful, who told the high priests and the elders that the publicans and sinners would go before them into the Kingdom of Heaven,[2] One who condemned in the most violent terms the selfishness of the Pharisees, the proud, the avaricious, the hypocrites. Under the eyes of a just Judge who is at the same time merciful towards all forms of human weakness, sordid covetousness and conscious, intentional infidelity will be unmasked and revealed in all their nakedness, whilst genuine sincerity and purity of intention will appear in all their splendour, no matter what dark labyrinths of pathology, objective error and moral evil they may have been involved in against their will on earth. Those who refused to sacrifice to love— in so far as they could perceive it—will then persist in their refusal no less freely than they did during their last moments on earth, and they will receive from Christ the well-merited reply: Since this is the way you wish it to be, and will always wish it to be—" Depart from me, you cursed, into everlasting fire which was prepared for the devil and his angels. For I was hungry and you gave me not to eat: I was thirsty, and you gave me not to drink. I was a stranger, and you took me not in: naked, and you covered me not: sick and in prison, and you did not visit me. Then they also shall answer him, saying: Lord, when did we see thee hungry or thirsty, or a stranger, or naked, or sick, or in prison, and did not minister to thee? Then he shall answer them, saying: Amen I say to you, as long as you did it not to one of these least, neither did you do it to me. And these shall go into everlasting punishment: but the just, into life everlasting."[3] We are dogged by our actions.

[1] Charles Journet, " De l'inégale égalité des créatures ", *Études Carmélitaines*, October 1939, pp. 200–2, *passim*.
[2] Matt. xxi. 31.
[3] ibid., xxv. 41, et seq.

All the evil and privation that exist in hell have been created by angels and men who have misused their liberty in full consciousness of what they were doing; for hell is the creation of their own sinfulness—and sinfulness, from its very nature, cannot be the work of God. " The wicked do not perish because they are unable to be good, but because they do not want to be good."[1] " If anyone says that it is not within man's power to turn from his evil ways, and that evil works, like good works, come from God, meaning not only by way of permission but properly and essentially, so that the treachery of Judas is no less God's own work than the calling of St. Paul: let him be anathema."[2]

" Little by little, by the exercise of our free will, we construct our freedom "[3] and even in the beyond this freedom remains. Freely anchored in evil, the damned have not only sinned in the past, they go on sinning for ever. They are essentially in everlasting rebellion, incessantly repeating their refusal to love love, continually setting themselves up voluntarily against the love from which they separated themselves before they departed from this earth. The mystery is, that having always been free and perfectly lucid in mind, the damned will not repent; for this is something that they will never do. By their own free act they are immobilized in evil.[4] The violence and aggressiveness are not on God's side—for God is by definition love—but on the side of hell, where hatred has always reigned and will reign for ever.

" The sin lasts for all eternity and the punishment should not come to an end so long as the sin lasts."[5] " It would be unjust if . . . punishment continued after . . . [the] will is good ",[6] but " the devils are obstinate in their wickedness "[7] and it will be given them to see " how justly "[8] they are damned.

Hell is not inhabited by beings who have repented, who are sorry for their sins and would like to lead a better life but have come to this conclusion too late. This would be a caricature of hell and an insult to the wisdom and goodness of God.

" In all ages writers on criminal law have asserted that the aim of lawful punishment is not revenge but that its severity is designed to prevent any recurrence of the crime that has been committed; and

[1] Third Council of Valence, Denzinger, 321.
[2] Council of Trent, Denzinger, 816.
[3] Rondet, S. J., " Les Peines de l'enfer ", in Nouvelle Revue théologique, April–May, 1940, p. 423.
[4] Denzinger, 3028: " Iniquos autem arbitrio voluntatis propriae vasa irae apta in interitum permanentes "—" the wicked, remaining vessels of wrath fit for perdition and remaining such by the free motion of their own will ".
[5] St. Thomas, In IV. Sent., dist. 46, q. i, a. 3, c.
[6] Contra Gentes, iv, 93.
[7] In IV. Sent., dist. 46, q. 2, a. 3, sol. i, ad 1m.
[8] III, 54, 4, " quam juste damnentur ".

with this the Christian spirit is in entire agreement. If this is the
Christian spirit on earth, why should there be a different spirit in
heaven, giving rise to eternal torments which can only be the signs of
an eternal vengeance? "[1]

Thus wrote Alfred de Vigny, but he assumed, quite wrongly, that
there is no evil in hell; whereas evil persists there. Nicolas Berdyaev's
words will meet with general approval: " There is something hideous
and morally revolting in the idea of eternal torments as a just retribution for the crimes and sins of a short moment of life",[2] but in reality it
is not a moment's crime that is involved but an everlasting crime, willed
in complete freedom for all eternity; and that is quite a different thing.[3]

Love of the creature easily changes into aggressiveness. We can
put into the hearts of the damned when they stand face to face with
God the feeling aroused in Dostoievsky's hero by the sight of the
woman who made him suffer such torments: " I looked at her . . .
with fearful hatred—that hate which is only a hair's-breadth from love,
from the maddest love! "[4]—this hair's-breadth symbolising the free-

[1] Alfred de Vigny, *Journal d'un poète*.
[2] *The Destiny of Man*, Geoffrey Bles, 1937, p. 354.
[3] This point is worth insisting on, as it is not sufficiently well known. " ' I
could have avoided this dreadful misfortune,' they cry in despair, ' and now I
can no longer get out ': such will be the worm that dieth not of the damned "
(Père Perroy, *La Montée du Calvaire*, p. 319). This is not so. " I *can* no longer
get out," is not what the damned cry; that is not the way their psychology
works. They do not want, they never will want, to get out, i.e. repent. That
is their everlasting vice. " It is thus not necessary to accept literally the naïve
idea of the saintly Curé d'Ars " (is it really his? I have not verified it) " who
used to say that if confessionals were placed at the gates of hell the damned
would rush towards them to be forgiven and granted their freedom. With such
an idea of hell and of the spiritual condition of the damned, how can one
possibly not accuse God of cruelty and cruelty of an appalling kind? " (Lahitton,
Theologiae dogmaticae theses, Beauchesne, vol. iii, p. 464). This is obviously
true.

The following passages from St. Thomas, concerning the psychology and the
immorality of the damned, leave no doubt about his opinion on this point.
" Since the demon has a perverse and obstinate will, he is not sorry for the
evil of sin " (I, 64, 3, 3m).
" The devil's first sin still remains in him according to desire; although not
as to his believing that he can obtain what he desired. Even so, if a man were
to believe that he can commit murder, and wills to commit it, and afterwards
the power is taken from him; nevertheless, the will to murder can stay with
him, so that he would he had done it, or still would do it if he could " (I, 64,
2, 3m). " The minds of the damned are so firmly established in evil that every
movement of their free will is disordered and is a sin . . ." (*De Ver.*, q. 24, a. 11,
c.). " Just as the devil turned away from God voluntarily, so he is voluntarily
fixed there, having made his choice: he goes on doing evil voluntarily but un-
changeably " (*De Malo*, q. xvi, a. 5, ad 8m). " Diabolus habet libertatem
servandi rectitudinem si eam haberet " (ibid., ad 19m); i.e., " The devil is
free to remain good, but there is no goodness in him." " And this is in fact for
St. Thomas the ultimate explanation of the existence of hell; hell is eternal . . .
because sin is eternal " (Michel, art. " Enfer ", *Dict. Théol. Cath.*, col. 97).
[4] See above, p. 61.

dom of the damned. Thus " the pains of hell are not a punishment inflicted from outside but an ineluctable consequence of sin, the revelation of the sinner's conscience ",[1] torn in pieces, so to speak, between love and aggressiveness.[2]

The love that is rejected appears in the first place as justice towards those who voluntarily reject it—because it remains love, worthy of its name, a love which is not weakness, the only love worth loving, and worth loving infinitely since it is the supreme Good.

On the moral and psychological level, it is for us to choose between a proud rebelliousness and humble docility in our personal response to love's invitation. It is up to us, whether we transform our weakness into a means to our salvation or not.

We can reject love: such is the depth of our wretchedness. God died to save all men: such is the extent of His mercy. Let us get this firmly into our heads: we are not involved in a game of chance, in which we have no say.[3] He who created us without our assistance will not save us without our co-operation. If we work and struggle *as though* prayer were useless and—and this is even more important—pray *as though* our efforts were useless, we shall keep the necessary balance as we walk through the darkness of this mystery.

[1] Rondet, " Les Peines de l'enfer ", *Nouvelle Revue théologique*, April–May, 1940, p. 401. This suffering is proportionate to the individual's wickedness. But St. Thomas tells us that it remains less than would be demanded by justice untempered by mercy (I, 21, 4, 1m).

[2] Corresponding to aversion to God is the pain of damnation; to the unlawful pleasure found in sin, the pain of sense or the fire of hell—on the nature of which the Church has made no pronouncement.

[3] It is of course an insoluble mystery because—amongst other things— two of the ideas that are vitally involved in it—the idea of power and the idea of freedom—are ultimately one (for a being is free to the extent that it can govern itself and its circumstances); but the idea of power is more accessible on the metaphysical level (active power means action), whereas the idea of freedom is more accessible on the psychological level (it can be described more easily than it can be evaluated from the ontological point of view). As these two aspects of the mystery are not equally clear to us, we shall never understand it absolutely.

Calvinism effects a unilateral systematization from the standpoint of the divine power—which means the end of any human freedom or any psychology of a God of Love.

Pelagianism effects a unilateral systematisation from the standpoint of human freedom—which means the end of God's omnipotence or any influx of grace on human freedom.

I am not unacquainted with the learned controversies on these great questions. It will be sufficient to say here that I am neither on Bannez' side nor on Molina's.

I have considered it sufficient to emphasise in the text the personal responsibility of each damned soul and its eternal guilt, on the moral and psychological level. No system of thought has the least right to question these dogmatic assertions, for God is justice as well as love and wisdom and it would lead to frightful misunderstandings if St. Thomas's *metaphysical* assertions regarding the eternal immutability of heaven and hell were transposed on to the *psychological* level.

To the question, are many souls saved? no definite answer can be given. Christ and the Church have told us nothing about this question —and when all is said and done, that is surely something we can see the wisdom of.

St. Thomas Aquinas was pessimistic about the human race, most of whom he thought would be damned,[1] and optimistic about the angels, most of whom he thought had been saved.[2] There is no need to go into the reasons here for the difference between these two estimates,[3] but it is worth noting that in St. Thomas's view the number of the angels is incomparably higher than that of all the creatures in the universe put together, including not only the different species but all the individuals within the species;[4] altogether, therefore, even in the eyes of the "Angelic" Doctor, there are far more of the elect than of the damned, his rigorism applying only to human beings, and these being ultimately only a small proportion of the creatures endowed with intelligence and freedom.

This rigorism is itself generally rejected today,[5] and is certainly not in the spirit of the opening pages of such a book as *The Story of a Soul*, in which St. Thérèse of the Child Jesus speaks with such compassion of the infidels and pagans.

But " one dies alone, others have nothing to do with it ".

" There was once a man who was very anxious, and wavered between fear and hope. One day, overcome with sadness, he lay prostrate in prayer before the altar in church, and pondering these matters in his mind, said, ' Oh, if only I knew that I should always persevere !' Then he heard within his heart an answer from God: ' If you knew this, what would you do? Do now what you would then, and all will be well.' "[6]

When Judas (not Iscariot) presented Christ with the problem of predestination in these words: " Lord, how is it, that thou wilt manifest thyself to us, and not to the world? " Jesus simply said in reply, " If anyone love me, he will keep my word, and my Father will love him, and we will come to him, and make our abode with him. He that loveth me not keepeth not my words. And the word which you have heard is not mine; but the Father's who sent me ".[7]

---

[1] I, 23, 7, 3m.
[2] I, 63, 9.
[3] ibid.
[4] I, 50, 3.
[5] See Capéran, *Le Problème du salut des infidèles*, Toulouse, Grand Séminaire, 1934, vol. i, p. 507. " Nothing would be easier than to draw from sermons, lectures, mystical treatises, even pastoral letters, expressions of tremendous hope for the millions of infidels who to all appearance have been left forsaken."
[6] *Imitation of Christ*, bk. i, ch. 25.
[7] 1 John xiv. 22–4.

" If anyone love me, my Father will love him." The essential thing is, therefore, to love greatly. But to what extent can we and should we love?

Confidence and Purgatory

" Love can only be paid back by love," says St. John of the Cross. Deeply wretched as we are, how near perfection will our response be to the love of God?

" That we may have confidence in the day of judgment," writes St. John the Evangelist, and goes on: " Fear is not in charity: but perfect charity casteth out fear, because fear hath pain. And he that feareth is not perfected in charity. Let us therefore love God: because God first hath loved us."[1]

St. Thérèse of the Child Jesus, who saw into the depths of this verse of Scripture, makes use of it to reveal one of the most audacious aspects of her " Little Way ", gently insisting that whatever degree of the beatific vision God intends us for, He certainly does not will that any of us should endure the flames of purgatory. On the contrary, God wants to see us leaving this earth absolutely pure and purified, as abandoned to His will as the prodigal, repentant little child, who, having simply fallen asleep in her Father's arms, wakes up immediately in the light of heaven and thus throws herself without delay into the eternal embrace of the merciful love, and this immediately, and without delay.[2]

As regards this delicate point, here, from St. Thérèse's own pen, are a few statements made with all her amazing theological precision:

" You have not enough trust," she said to a timid sister, " you are far too afraid of the good God. I assure you that this hurts Him. You should not be afraid of purgatory because of the punishment there: you should try to aim not to go there and thus please the good God, who hates having to impose such a form of expiation. As soon

---

[1] John iv. 17–19.

[2] The magisterium of the Church explicitly envisages the case of souls who do not need to pass through purgatory. According to the Council of Florence (Denzinger 693), these are souls who either did not commit any sins after baptism or purified themselves from their sins during their life on earth (" in suis corporibus . . . purgatae "). There is no more interesting, more readable and more concentrated piece of writing than St. Catherine of Genoa's little *Treatise on Purgatory*. It is a book that every Catholic should read. See particularly Chapter XII on the joy and suffering of souls in purgatory: " It is true that love for God, which fills the soul to overflowing, gives it, so I see it, a happiness beyond what can be told, but this happiness takes not one pang from the pain of the souls in Purgatory. Rather the love of these souls, finding itself hindered, causes their pain; and the more perfect is the love of which God has made them capable, the greater is their pain." It is precisely this love which, in the divine scheme, should not be delayed (*Treatise on Purgatory*, trans. Charlotte Balfour and H. D. Irving, Sheed and Ward, 1946).

as you begin to try and please Him in everything you do, if you have
an absolutely unshakeable trust that you are being purified every
moment in His love and that He will not let the slightest trace of sin
remain in you, you may be perfectly certain that you will not go to
purgatory."[1]

Not to go to purgatory " to please the good God ", what a pearl of
wisdom this is! " I would not pick up a straw to avoid going to purgatory. All that I have done, I have done to give God pleasure and to
save souls."[2]

" I also know," she says elsewhere, " that the Fire of Love is far
more sanctifying than the fires there " (i.e. in purgatory).[3]

" It seems to me that there will not be any Judgment for the victims
of love."[4]

" In spite of your little failings you can hope to go straight to
heaven . . . the good God wants this more than you do."[5]

And St. Thérèse is not afraid to assert as a consequence of this that
the sufferings of purgatory are " useless ".[6] What exactly does she
mean by this? The theologians are unanimous in teaching the same
thing: in purgatory one cannot merit any further, one cannot mount
any higher in love; the sufferings endured there are therefore useless
from the only point of view that ultimately counts towards the increase
of our life of glory—growth in the love of Christ. We are judged on
our love, and the judgment takes place at the end of this life.

By enduring their suffering, which God permits " as though turning
a blind eye to it ",[7] the souls in purgatory expiate their sins—justly,
since they did not do this, as they should have done, on earth; and,
still more, mercifully, since in this way, despite their past half-hearted-
ness, they are prepared to enjoy God face to face, and God brooks no
impurity.[8]

St. Thérèse is quite precise about this: " Purgatory is only for souls

[1] Extract from a circular from the Carmel at Lisieux signed by the Rev.
Mother Agnes and dated 17 Feb. 1924.

[2] *Novissima Verba*, Burns, Oates and Washbourne, 1929, p. 93.

[3] *Story of a Soul*, trans. Michael Day, Burns, Oates and Washbourne, 1951,
p. 132.

[4] *Conseils et Souvenirs*, p. 281.

[5] *À l'École de sainte Thérèse de l'Enfant Jésus*, 5th ed., p. 37.

[6] *Story of a Soul*, p. 132.

[7] *L'esprit de sainte Thérèse de l'Enfant-Jésus*, p. 106. " It is great pain to
Him thus to fill our cup with sorrows " (*Collected Letters of St. Thérèse of Lisieux*,
ed. Combes, trans. F. J. Sheed, Sheed and Ward, 1949, p. 49).

[8] Do the souls in purgatory suffer and pray for us? The theologians are not
agreed on this point, but one thing is certain in the opinion of St. Thérèse
of the Child Jesus: if they do suffer and pray for us, it is not, ideally, according
to the divine scheme that they should do so. They should have accepted their
Cross of redemption more generously beforehand, on earth (and on earth the
Cross is not so hard to endure as the sufferings of purgatory); immediately, as

who have disdained the merciful Love or had doubts about its purifying power."[1] Doubt is here an insult to God's goodness.

How does God use the flames of purgatory to purify souls consumed with divine love?

In the divine scheme purgatory, like hell, is not intended for anyone.[2] In God there is not the slightest trace of indifference or injustice or aggressiveness towards anyone. God is Justice and Mercy in a love that respects each person's freedom. It is always love that forms the hidden motive of His intention.

God, whose joy is infinite, whose peace surpasses all human imagining, whose power is unbounded, has absolute control over His creatures. Nevertheless, we are free to refuse the gift of love whenever we feel like it. Let us accept it with all our hearts. Let us trust in God, despite all appearances, like little children, and we shall not be disappointed. " The soul obtains from Him as much as it hopes for from Him ",[3] and " God is well pleased with those who hope in His mercy ".[4]

Are there many souls who in fact do not pass through purgatory at all? The general opinion is that there are very few. St. John of the Cross says in the Dark Night that only a tiny number of souls go straight to heaven as soon as they die.[5]

St. Thérèse of the Child Jesus is no less precise on this point, but it is worth noting that it is " a multitude of little souls ", " a legion of little victims ",[6] that she wants to draw after her in the shining wake of her spiritual childhood. Popes Benedict XV, Pius XI and Pius XII have done everything they could to emphasize the universality of her teaching and the demands it makes upon each one of us. " The ' Little Way ' is the secret of holiness for all the faithful throughout the world."[7]

---

soon as they die, the incense of their prayers should ascend into the glory of heaven.

[1] À l'École de sainte Thérèse de l'Enfant Jésus, 5th ed., p. 36.

[2] It is not always realized—and this ignorance is much to be regretted—that the main purpose of Extreme Unction is to help us to arrive directly and immediately at the beatific vision, as soon as we die. St. Thomas says: " In Extreme Unction man is prepared for the immediate attainment of glory " (III, 65, 1, 4m). This doctrinal point is developed in Vie Spirituelle, Jan.–Feb. 1945: " Even after a long and sinful life, the Christian who receives the last sacraments with the requisite dispositions goes immediately to paradise without passing through purgatory" (Père Philipon, pp. 16–17).

[3] St. John of the Cross, Dark Night of the Soul, bk. ii, ch. xxi: Complete Works, vol. i, p. 273.

[4] Psalm xxxii. 18 (author's rendering).

[5] Bk. ii, ch. xx.

[6] Story of a Soul, trans. Michael Day, Burns, Oates and Washbourne, 1951, p. 196.

[7] Benedict XV, Allocution of Aug. 4, 1921.

CHRIST ON THE CROSS
Michelangelo: British Museum

Let each of us remember in practice the words of St. John of the Cross that were so dear to St. Thérèse: " The soul obtains from Him just as much as it hopes for from Him. " To ask for heaven " the moment we die " is not asking for the moon; it only means asking God " that His will be done on earth as it is in heaven, and that His Kingdom may come "[1] at the moment He desires.

" To live in an *act of perfect love*, I OFFER MYSELF AS A BURNT OFFERING TO YOUR MERCIFUL LOVE, calling upon You to consume me at every instant, while You let the floods of *infinite tenderness* pent up within You flow into my soul, that so I may become a *Martyr* to Your *Love*, O my God . . .

" When that *martyrdom* has prepared me to appear before You, may it cause me to die, and may my soul hurl itself in that instant into the eternal embrace of *Your Merciful Love* . . ."[2]

THE HEAVENLY MANSIONS

Heaven is for everyone without exception, though in differing degrees.[3]

" For a long time I had wondered why God had preferences, why He did not give the same degree of grace to everyone, " writes St.

---

[1] This petition, made with humility, confidence and perseverance, is bound to be answered.

[2] From the " Act of Offering " drawn up by St. Thérèse of the Child Jesus (*Collected Letters*, ed. Combes, trans. F. J. Sheed, Sheed and Ward, 1949, pp. 330–1). The same thought is to be found in the venerable Abbot Blosius: " He who is about to die . . . should offer himself to the greater glory of God, to the Lord Himself, as a living victim, to bear patiently according to His most acceptable will, with true love, all pain and languor and death itself, in one word whatever the Lord may will to send in time or in eternity. If he can really do this, if from pure love, with perfect resignation of himself, he can offer himself with a will ready to bear every pain in honour of the justice of God, he will go neither to hell nor even to purgatory, though he himself had committed all the sins of the whole world. No exercise then can be more useful at death than to resign oneself absolutely to the divine Will, humbly, lovingly and fully trusting in the mercy and goodness of God.

" This is certain, that anyone who, in a spirit of true and perfect resignation and holy confidence in God, goes forth from this world, will fly immediately to the Kingdom of Heaven. For just as no pain, no touch of the fire of purgatory, could possibly affect God, so also would it be powerless to affect a man perfectly united to God in entire and loving conformity of will.

" In this spirit did that repenting thief dying on a cross become a righteous man. He asked not from the Lord the healing of his body, nor did he pray to be delivered from purgatory, but willing to die for his sins and for the glory of God he resigned himself wholly to the will of God, and offered himself entirely to Christ that He might do with him whatsoever would be pleasing to Him. He asked for nothing except mercy and grace, saying ' Lord, remember me when Thou shalt come into Thy kingdom ' " (*Comfort for the Fainthearted*, trans. B. Wilberforce, Art and Book Co., 1908, pp. 98–9).

[3] Denzinger, 693.

Thérèse.[1] Jesus instructed her in this mystery. " If every little
flower wished to be a rose, nature would lose her Spring adornments,
and the fields would be no longer enamelled with their varied flowers.
So it is in the world of souls, the living garden of the Lord."[2]

The flowers are for the Master. We are Christ's joy. Our perfection
is simply one spot of colour bringing its own tiny contribution to the
total composition of an immense flower bed. " The happier they
[the flowers] are to be as He wills, the more perfect they are."[3]

" God is said to have equally care of all, not because by His care He
deals out equal good to all, but because He administers all things with
like wisdom and goodness ",[4] in an act of love that is infinite, unique,
simple and always consistent with itself.[5]

Two complementary truths are involved here and it is essential
that they should be properly grasped.

God distributes unequal gifts both in the order of grace and in the
order of nature. He shares them out as in the parable of the talents;
one receives more, another less. No one would be better if God had
willed to load him with more gifts; in this sense no one would be
better if he was loved more by God.

But in the eyes of anyone looking at the loving wisdom that orders
these gifts, God loves us all equally—and equally with the Blessed
Virgin Mary herself.

Love means willing good to someone. And the way in which a thing
is given is more important than the thing itself, so that the divine way
of giving anything is to give whatever is given, great or small, with a
love that is literally infinite.

This love is our hope and our strength. The best response that we
can make to it is to have the confidence to abandon ourselves utterly
to it. Loving God means allowing oneself to be loved by Him as He
wills, in His own divine way.

Let us prepare ourselves for the contemplation of the Father and the
Word in their ineffable light, according to the extent that we are personally called; whatever this may be, it is the only one that is possible
for us, and it is the best—as it is the best for the splendour of the total
Christ.

Having faith, let us from this moment onwards love the Father and
the Son with the love with which they love each other. This love is
the Holy Spirit, who also has been given to us. To live in the company

---

[1] *Story of a Soul*, trans. Michael Day, Burns, Oates and Washbourne,
1951, p. 5.
[2] ibid., p. 6.
[3] ibid.
[4] I, 20, 3.
[5] ibid.

of the divine Persons is the hidden treasure, the precious pearl of the Gospels, worth more than all the gold of the world and all the sacrifices put together.

"O souls created for these grandeurs and called thereto! What do ye do? Wherein do ye occupy yourselves? Your desires are meannesses, and your possessions miseries. O wretched blindness of the eyes of your souls, which are blind to so great a light and deaf to so clear a voice, seeing not that for so long as ye seek grandeurs and glories ye remain miserable and deprived of so many blessings, and have become ignorant and unworthy!"[1]

It is time we came out of the mists of Jansenism and rigorism and sailed in the full sunshine above a sea of clouds as white and shining in the light of God as they were grey and opaque down below, seen from the earth. "For that which is at present momentary and light of our tribulation, worketh for us above measure exceedingly an eternal weight of glory."[2]

Let us have a good will and we shall be saved: this is the Gospel message, the good news. "Peace on earth to men of goodwill."

God is not a God of wrath: He is a God of love. "Where sin did abound, grace does more abound."

In our hours of trial let us love repeating at the foot of the Cross the Magnificat of pain, and Our Lady, Mother of God, will pray for us sinners at the hour of our death:

"My soul doth magnify the Lord:
And my spirit hath rejoiced in God my Saviour.
Because he hath regarded the humility of his handmaid:
For behold from henceforth all generations shall call me blessed.
Because he that is mighty hath done great things to me:
And holy is his name.
And his mercy is from generation unto generations,
To them that fear him.
He hath shewed might in his arm:
He hath scattered the proud in the conceit of their heart.
He hath put down the mighty from their seat,
And hath exalted the humble.
He hath filled the hungry with good things:
And the rich he hath sent empty away.
He hath received Israel his servant, being mindful of his mercy,
As he spoke to our fathers: to Abraham and to his seed for ever."

[1] St. John of the Cross, *Spiritual Canticle*, stanza xxxviii: *Complete Works*, vol. ii, p. 178.
[2] 2 Cor. iv. 17.

The Christian religion, says Pascal, " making those tremble whom it justifies, and consoling those whom it condemns, so justly tempers fear with hope through that double capacity of grace and of sin, common to all, that it humbles infinitely more than reason alone can do, but without despair, and it exalts infinitely more than natural pride, but without inflating; thus making it evident that alone being exempt from error and vice, it alone fulfils the duty of instructing and correcting men ".[1]

[1] *Pensées*, 435.

LOVE AND VIOLENCE IN THE GOSPELS

John Baptist Reeves, O.P.

From beginning to end the Bible reveals God as both just and merciful: He punishes sin with wrath and forgives it with loving-kindness. The emphasis fluctuates, but over all there is a steady transition from the stressing of anger in the Old Testament to the stressing of love in the New.

Even in the New Testament, the full revelation of God's love comes gradually. There are abundant proofs of it in Matthew, Mark and Luke; but until we have read St. John and St. Paul it is hard to reconcile some of our Lord's words and actions in the Synoptic Gospels with His declaration there that He is " meek and humble of heart ". As we work our way through the New Testament, forgetting what has still to come and remembering only what has gone before, our breath is taken away by the explosive novelty of St. John's " God so loved the world as to give his only-begotten Son, that whoever believes in him may not perish but may have life everlasting ". Later we find that St. Paul had preceded him by many years in this boldness of speech: " The charity of God is poured forth in our hearts by the Holy Ghost who is given to us. For why did Christ die for the ungodly? Scarce for a just man would one die, though perhaps for a good one someone would dare to. But God commendeth his charity towards us: because when as yet we were sinners Christ died for us."

Statements as full and clear as these had to wait until the doctrine of the Holy Ghost and the Trinity of Persons in God had been revealed. This revelation was begun by Gabriel to Mary, but its final unfolding came only when our Lord, after the Last Supper, opened His whole mind and heart to His Disciples as far as they could bear it. The full manifestation followed when the Holy Ghost Himself descended upon them at Pentecost. The Synoptic Gospels were written after that, but, being graphic narrative, they describe events as they were seen and heard by contemporaries. The writings of St. John and St. Paul are meditated sermons; their aim is less to give information in narrative form, than to enlighten by explanation the understanding of those who are already informed about matters of fact. When St. John wrote his Gospel he had lived, probably for many years, with Mary, the Mother of Jesus, who had pondered the mystery of God's love since before either Jesus or John was born. If we wish to solve the problems of the Gospels without going beyond them to the Epistles it is to John that we must go for the key. Indeed he clarifies much that St. Paul's more disjointed writings leave obscure. The Fourth Gospel is in many senses the last word of revealed Christian doctrine: it is the last word of the last of the Apostles, and its most important part consists entirely of our Lord's last words before His agony.

The angry God of the old Testament reappears in the angry Christ of the New, but with one important difference. In the Old Testament God corrects the sins of men with temporal punishments. Christ refuses even to judge them. Under the Old Law God's wrath is roused by every sort of sin; Christ's anger is reserved for those who sin against the light, against the truth, against faith. His most violent words are provoked by those who say " We see " and will not see. What is common to the old wrath of God and the new wrath of Christ is that both are inflamed most of all by idolatry; but whereas the old sin that provoked God was His being misrepresented in graven images, the new sin that provokes Christ is misrepresentation of His Father and Himself in the minds of men. In the Old Testament God is always angry when He has to assert Himself for what He is against ignorance and misunderstanding; in the New Testament God's Son is angry only when He has to assert His identity of nature with His Father against those who will not see or believe it. Men cannot serve a God they do not love, and cannot love a God they do not know. Christ limits His ministry to making God known; He leaves it to another Paraclete to give them, through His means, the grace to love and serve Him. Christ Himself is " full of grace and truth ", but in His personal mission to us He is the word of truth, the light, the revelation that must precede grace. He reveals God not only by what He says, but by what He does and what He is. His anger only comes out against those who reject His words as lies, His works as diabolic, Himself as merely one of themselves, and amongst themselves as one of no account. As against His meekness and humility His wrath is all the more para-doxical because it is self-assertive.

All this is urged by St. John in his Gospel as its one and only theme. " These things are written so that you may know that Christ is the Son of God, and believing may have life in his name." First, know-ledge; then faith grounded on knowledge; then, given to us in His name, life abounding in good works until it is consummated everlastingly. " In the beginning was the Word . . . and the Word was God . . . In him was life, and the life was the light of men. And the light shineth in darkness and the darkness did not comprehend it . . . That was the true light which enlighteneth every man that cometh into the world. He was in the world and the world was made by him, and the world knew him not. He came unto his own and his own received him not. But to as many as received him he gave the power to be made sons of God: to them that believe in his name. And the Word was made flesh and dwelt amongst us full of grace and truth."

St. John develops this theme in orderly' stages. His Gospel is not a constructed literary work like St. Luke's. It bears every sign of having been dictated to another in the white heat of inspiration, and recalls the psalm: " My heart hath poured out a good word; I speak my works to the king. My tongue is like the pen of a scribe writing swiftly." More like a sermon than a composition, it hastens headlong to its conclusion, sometimes perplexing us by inversions of order, but never leaving us in any doubt about the Evangelist's main purpose.

As in the other Gospels, John the Baptist introduces Christ, and the continuity of their joint mission is shown by Christ's attracting as His first Disciples some who had hitherto followed John. Then in the first stage of his argument[1] St. John illustrates in terms of life what St. Matthew, in the Sermon on the Mount, has illustrated in terms of law. In the Sermon our Lord insisted that He was not come to dissolve the Law or the prophets but to bring them to their fulfilment. He then proceeds to treat of the Commandments of the Decalogue showing, in a preliminary exposition which His later teaching and example will complete, that they imply more than they express, and are in their inner meaning a rule of perfection. The Decalogue, though supernaturally revealed, is in content the natural law instinct in man's conscience since his creation. St. John takes the first four vital institutions of nature—marriage, birth, drink and food—in their natural sequence, and shows, for the most part in Christ's words, that, far from being abolished, these are to be retained as the bodily means to everlasting life. It is in this section that St. John bursts upon us with the declaration that the Incarnation manifests God's great love for the world. The story of Cana—the marriage with its pendant, the cure of the ruler's son—of Nicodemus, of the Samaritan woman, and of the loaves and fishes, are all instances of our Lord's loving-kindness. But there is a note of aggression in the conversation with Nicodemus, and, much more strongly, in the discourse to the crowd after the multiplication of the bread. And immediately following the marriage at Cana, St. John has inserted the fiercest example of our Lord's wrath in all the New Testament: the expulsion of buyers and sellers from the Temple.

[1] Chapters ii, iii, iv and vi. If chapters v and vi are read in the order in which they stand, our Lord's movements, the temporal sequence of events, and the logical development of doctrine are all difficult to follow; if the order of these two chapters is inverted everything falls into place.

The incidents of Nicodemus, of the Samaritan woman, and of the loaves, are all followed by, or interspersed with, verbal doctrine. But the story of the marriage has no such commentary; instead, the violent scene in the Temple is interposed to round off its meaning. There are two plain indications that these incidents are to be taken together as the introduction to the doctrine of the revelation of God in our flesh: first, the other three Evangelists, as narrators, place the Temple incident immediately after Christ's triumphal entry into Jerusalem on Palm Sunday, whereas John, more concerned with meditated doctrine than chronology, has placed it here at the very beginning of the ministry; second, all these early incidents and discourses refer to matters vital to the life of man in the flesh, and St. John concludes his account of the scene in the Temple by stepping forward in his own person to explain that this had a reference to the destiny of our Lord's own Body.

At Cana Christ and His Mother are guests at a wedding. The feast begins merrily, as weddings commonly do. But the first joy of married life from which Christ is absent does not commonly mature; it tends rather to break down and turn to misery. Here, through a failure of cheering wine, joy threatens to break down during the actual feast. The first to notice the failure of the service is the " Handmaid of the Lord ". She calls her Son's attention to what has happened, not suggesting what He should do, or even that He should do anything: she leaves all to His own initiative. He objects that His hour has not yet come. A moment later His hour has come, and He works His first " sign " of His divinity. The wedding ends more merrily than it began.

What happened in that brief interval to bring Him from a time when He might not do such a thing to a time when He might? Nothing except that Mary had said to the servants: " Whatever he shall say to you, do it."

We know from St. Luke, who evidently had it from Mary herself, that once before this, when He was twelve years old, Jesus acted on His own initiative without His parents' authority. His explanation of His conduct then was that He was in His Father's house, or about His Father's business. His Mother's account of Him after this is that He then returned with her and His foster-father to Nazareth, where He remained subject to them as He grew to man's estate, became wiser, and merited increasingly the favour of God and men. The story of Cana follows so closely on St. Luke's narrative, Mary is so conspicuous in both, and her influence with both Evangelists is so far beyond doubt, that we cannot resist supposing Him to be still under His Mother's authority at Cana. He is just back from His baptism by John; His

Father in Heaven has acknowledged Him and the Holy Ghost has come down upon Him; the Baptist has testified publicly to this and proclaimed Him the Lamb of God: and yet His hour to begin His ministry has not yet come. His Mother commands the servants to obey Him, and it has come. Clearly He has taken this 'as implying her command to Him to command them. One is reminded of a young priest who has received the power of priesthood in the sacrament of Holy Order, yet may not exercise his faculty until his immediate human superior commits to him a definite flock to be ministered to. Christ has now received from the superior God has placed over him His mission to exercise His divine power. The faculty granted to Him is to act entirely on His own initiative; a faculty so large that He now has no human superior. His Mother attempts no jurisdiction over His future work. He takes her away from the wedding, not to Nazareth to support her there, still less to be subject to her there, but to Capharnaum where she, as homeless as he henceforth, must depend on others for comfort and sustenance. " Who is my Mother? " He will ask more than once.

But He is still His Father's Son. His own initiative restored to Him, straightway, as eighteen years ago, we find him in His Father's house acting with all the extravagant authority of a son whose parent has charged him with the cleaning up of the home. His whip is a new broom.

Marriage is the foundation of a home. Society is in a sorry pass when a young man must rise from his wedding feast and take his bride back to the home in which he or she was a child. Cana was not a modern Christian city where Christ has been and gone. The bridegroom, a man much of an age with Christ or younger, has surely gone to a home of his own, where he will be lord and master, subject to none. But Christ has gone back to His Father's house. His manhood's work is to renew the life of mankind, but not by the natural joyous way of the flesh in wedlock, which is His right as much as any man's, though love may oblige Him to sacrifice it that others may live and marry. Even in nature there can be such an obligation. No household is naturally complete without servants, and no servants are fit for their privileged place and maintenance there unless they serve lovingly. Christ was sent by His Father into the world with a vocation to minister, not to be ministered to. His Mother, herself a Handmaid, has trained Him to service and commanded Him to command servants, Himself subject to none.

In the business He found going on in the Temple there were no doubt abuses, but it was not inexcusable. Beasts and birds had to be bought and sold for sacrifice, and the coinage of Rome and other heathen lands had to be changed into Temple currency bearing no man's image and superscription. And the traffic was not in the enclosures sacred to Jewish worship, but in the Court of the Gentiles, a recognised market-place. It cannot have been because they were sinners that Jesus attacked the traders and money-changers, for He attacked the innocent beasts also and ordered even the doves out; just as later he blighted the fig tree and let the swine be rushed to their ruin. He was simply asserting Himself, acting like the lord of creation, intending the world to know that that is just what He was. True, He himself cried out that the business (according to Matthew, Mark and Luke, dishonest business) was desecrating His Father's House, but John and others were reminded of the psalm: " The zeal of thy house hath eaten me up." A consuming zeal indeed! The new broom! When pressed to say by what authority He acted so, He made it plain that the Temple, no matter how clean it might be swept, as swept to the ground it would be, could never be clean enough for His Father to dwell in or be worshipped in. The only fit place for that was His own Body, and His Body it should be. He will soon be hinting the same thing to the Samaritan woman. To her, however, while defending the Temple, He will explain how He can better it. God will be found and worshipped in Him " in spirit and in truth ".

The natural consequence of marriage is birth. Nicodemus, being a Jew, was well-born; no race on earth is better born, and he was a prince of his people. But he needed to be better born still, or he would not go far. What begins in the flesh goes the way of all flesh. What begins in time ends in time. Nicodemus, good man and fair, is roughly told that he does not know what life is, where it comes from or where it goes to. But he is talking to One who does know: knows all about it from beginning to end, and by experience. For birth to be a good start in life it must be ante-dated, and start where the Speaker started, at the source of life itself, from all eternity.

How can a late starter do that? By believing in the Speaker, who will be lifted up like the brazen serpent, so that all may draw life from Him.

After birth the first natural need is the breast, drink. Lack of it means thirst, the herald of death. Even the water from Jacob's well cannot stave off thirsty death. But Christ assures the Samaritan woman that He has a cure for it. He can plant a thirst-quenching fountain where He plants life itself. When she asks for this labour-saving draught He lets her see He knows how very thirsty she is, not merely for drink but for life itself. This is Christ's earliest recorded encounter with a sinner. He is very gentle with her, as with all of her sort.

He was kindness itself the day he multiplied the loaves and fishes; and that night too when He walked the sea to rescue His Disciples in a storm. It is St. Mark (that is, St. Peter) who tells us they had not yet seen the point of the miracle of the loaves. What St. John enlarges on is Christ's different manner with everybody next morning. The miracle was a ruse. Here they come again, hungry again. The bread they had yesterday is no good to them today. The bread they labour to provide for themselves perishes in their stomach, and they with it. The bread their forefathers ate without labour in the desert did not keep them alive though it came from heaven: they are all dead. Happily, better bread than that has come down from heaven. It is He Himself, Christ. He is meat and drink. If they eat His Flesh and drink His Blood they shall live; unless they do so they shall die. To ears not over-familiar with it, that is a horrible thing to be told. Few can stand it, so most go away, and for good. The few that remain are rudely challenged: Are you not going too? But no, not they. They are simple fellows who can stand anything He may say. None of them wants to die, and He is the only one they have heard promise an everlasting life. Whatever He may say, they cling to the hope that He will be as good as His word. How, does not matter. That is all He wants. That is exactly what He wants, for that is exactly what He is. " I am the way, the truth and the life."

St. John has already assured us that all this is the manifestation of God's great love for men. And He is showing us that the Son God gave us is one with Him, in love of us as in everything else. But is not John making Him out to be a very forward lover? He pushes Himself at us, whether we like Him or not. And He is forever talking to us about Himself, and in His own praise. He knows everything. He can do everything. And we must believe everything He says about Himself simply because He says it, or " even if you do not want to believe me, believe what I do, so that you may both know and believe that the Father is in me and I am in the Father " (John x. 38). Nor may we complain that His unsupported word has no witnesses to confirm it. He needs no witnesses, though in fact He has one—John the Baptist. But He will not cite John to those who have not believed Him either. So we must take Him on His word alone or leave Him.

Pushful, self-assertive, violent He most certainly is. But does any-one expect God to be otherwise? To hang back shyly and wait for us to meet Him half-way? Is that what He did when He created us?

The second section of the Gospel (chapters v, vii, viii and ix), is a treatise on sin. It contains very much that Jesus said, but very little that He did. Three of the incidents however are outstanding: the cure at the pool of Bethesda; the dismissal of the adulteress; and the cure of the man born blind. The whole subject-matter is the quarrel between Christ and the religious leaders of the Jewish people. The

terms in which He denounces them sound less vigorous than in the
other Gospels, but their sense is more searing. Throughout the controversy He is the aggressor; it is His violence that provokes violence
on the other side. Like all the miracles noticed by St. John, the
two cures He works here are "signs" unsolicited by anyone and
wrought on His own initiative in His own way.[1] Knowing well that this
would incense the Pharisees and others, He chose the Sabbath day and
a public place for both cures. When they taxed Him with breaking the
Law He retorted: "My Father worketh until now, and I work," and
went on to accuse them of not knowing what the Law was all about.

Though they had recently been inquiring into His origin and
schooling, and found that He was the son of an unlettered carpenter,
they took Him to mean by His Father, not Joseph who built country
carts and other wooden structures, but God who built the world. It
was for this blasphemy, as they called it, that they first decided to kill
Him. What He was attacking was their false notion of the Sabbath,
and the false idea of God that it implied. If they knew God they would
know Him, the Son of God, and if they saw Him as He was, with
minds cleansed of their own unclean inventions, they would see God.
His saying this scandalized them. His way of saying it exasperated
them.

For them the Sabbath was the day on which they imitated God's
rest. On other days they worked as God worked six days building
the world. They considered their work the necessary complement
to God's. Christ knew that God never labours and that what we call
His work never disturbs His rest. The building of the world was but
the work of a moment. There remained the work of keeping it going,
which never ceases for a moment while creation lasts. Our work is
important, not because of its external results—which can be as valuable
when they fail as when they succeed—but for the perfection to which
it can bring us, the workers. It is God's work, not ours, that keeps the
world going. The Sabbath is the day on which we rest from our work
to remember its purpose for our souls, and to thank God for constantly
preserving and energizing us and the world of which He has appointed
us masters while still His children, just as He has appointed His Son
Master and Provider in His household. This work, which God has
hitherto done from heaven, His Son is now taking upon His human
shoulders on earth. To the priests, Scribes and Pharisees, who are

[1] At Cana His Mother did not ask for a miracle, still less specify one. Martha
and Mary asked that their brother should not die, not that he should be raised
from the dead. When Martha suggests this later, she does not ask for it openly,
but says she knows that whatever Jesus asks His Father will be granted. When
He sets about the miracle in His own way she is horrified and protests, but in
vain.

persuaded that God needs them to manage His affairs on earth, and satisfied that they are serving Him well in His need, this is not only a criticism of their understanding of their own business; it is also a threat to replace them in it.

Our Lord presses both the criticism and the threat. With all their learning, they have never heard the Father's voice or seen His face. Their minds have not rightly conceived what He has taught them about Himself; this is proved by their not believing Him whom the Father has sent. " You search the Scriptures, because you believe that in them you have eternal life. But it is of me that they speak. Yet you will not come to me that you may have life . . . I have come in my Father's name, yet you will not accept me; if another man come in his own name you accept him." Their own credentials, He adds, they accept from one another, but they will have none of One whose credentials are from God. They are not to suppose that He is going to accuse them of this to His Father: there is already one who will accuse them—Moses in whom they trust. " He will accuse you, because if you really believed him you would believe me; for it was of me that he wrote. But if you will not believe what he wrote how can you believe what I say? "

When He next went up to Jerusalem He found everybody looking for Him and talking about Him, some for and some against. But even on those who are coming to believe in Him He rounds quite fiercely. He has said that if they continue to believe in Him the truth of His teaching will set them free. But what need, they ask, have they to be set free? Are they slaves? Are they not the children of Abraham? " I know that you are the children of Abraham; but you seek to kill me, for my teaching has not a firm hold on you. If you are the children of Abraham, do as your father did. What you do shows who your father is." God, they say, is their only Father. " If God were your Father you would forsooth love me, for I have come here from him. Nor have I come of myself: He sent me. The father from whom you come is the devil, and you want to do what your father wants done. Whoever comes from God hears the words of God; you do not hear because you are not from God." They tell Him He is a Samaritan and possessed by a devil. " I am not: but I honour my Father and you have dishonoured me. If anyone does what I say he will never see death." They are contemptuous: Abraham and the prophets are dead, and he has something to say that will save all from dying! Is he greater than Abraham and the prophets? "Abraham your father rejoiced to see my day; he saw it and was glad." They object: " You are not yet fifty and you have seen Abraham! " "Amen, amen, I say to you, before Abraham was, I am." They took up stones to hurl

at Him. It was He who had picked this quarrel. They were prepared
to believe that He was the Messiah, but ready to kill Him for claiming
to be the Son of God. He had provoked them into betraying themselves.

The man born blind made a very explicit act of faith in Jesus. It
had been agreed among the Jewish leaders that whoever confessed
Him should be expelled from the synagogue. They sent for the man
who had been blind and said to him: " Give glory to God; we know
that this man is a sinner." He answered: " Whether he is a sinner I
do not know. One thing I do know: though I was blind I now see."
" How did he open your eyes? " " I have told you once, and you
heard me. Why do you want to hear again? You have not become
his disciples, have you? " They cursed him and said: " You are his
disciple; we are disciples of Moses. We do not know where this man
comes from." The man who had been cured said: " It is strange
that you do not know where he comes from and yet he has opened
my eyes. We know that God does not answer the prayers of sinners;
but he hears whoever worships him and does his will. That anyone
opened the eyes of one born blind is a thing unheard of since time
began. If this man were not from God he could not do anything."
They said: " You were wholly born in sin," and threw him out. Jesus
heard that they had expelled him, and when He found him said:
" Do you believe in the Son of God? " " Who is he, Master? " He
wants to know so that he may believe (St. John's theme). " You have
both seen him and heard him talking to you now." The man said:
" I believe, Lord " and falling down he adored Him. Jesus said: "I
came into the world as a judgment, so that those who do not see
might see, and those who see may become blind."

Some Pharisees, who were near, heard and said: " But we are not
blind, are we? " Our Lord's answer refines on what He has just said.
" If you were blind you would not have any sin. But you say ' We
see '. Your sin remaineth." And with those words, more terrible
than any in the Gospel, He has finished with them. They return to the
attack, but He turns it aside with what sounds like their own casuistry
(John x. 34–6). All that Christ has said against the Scribes and Pharisees
in the first three Gospels has been here reduced to one single central
charge: they are teachers who can only teach. They cannot learn, even
from God. They know it all already, and whoever differs from them
is wrong. Christ never accuses them of any fault that does not spring
from this root. By the simple method of contrast He has exposed them
—to " some who trusted in themselves and despised others "—in the
neatest of His parables (Luke xviii. 9–14). As far as any eye but God's
can see, the Pharisee there is an exemplary religious man. He is at
home with God. He prays not merely with his lips but from his heart.

He is all that he says, and thanks God for it, not himself. He is sincere, at least in the sense that he has no suspicion of being wanting in anything. What is wanting is pointed out by contrast with the Publican. This man is a sinner and knows it; he consequently fears God for His justice, but at the same time appeals to Him for His mercy. God's mercy does not interest the Pharisee, for he is not conscious of any need of it. The God he worships is simply just, yet, conscious of his merits, he does not fear Him. How can he indeed, since his God is a creature of his own mind, made in his own image and likeness. The last thing the Pharisee wants is that God should reveal Himself as He is. Yet God so loves the Pharisee as to send him His only-begotten Son, that in Him He may be seen as He really is: tender as well as terrible. But, almost inevitably, with one voice, contentious though they are amongst themselves, all the Pharisees, saving only such as Nicodemus, band themselves together to repudiate the Son of God as most ungodly. They know God well, and this is not He. Though each has his own god, they have a common idol, the image of their tribe, and they have given him a tribal name: the God of Abraham, now a name to them only, but still to Christ the true God, His Father. The more they resist Him, the more furiously in His love the Son of God presses Himself upon them: but always for what He is, never in false colours to humour their predilections. At last, irritated to frenzy by His importunate pretensions, they decide to destroy Him, and He, changing the tactics of love, ceases His assault and suffers them to do their worst. When they see how meek He can be without surrender of principle, they will have their last chance of recognizing God for what He is. At least Saul of Tarsus will take it. From his eyes the scales will fall.

" Your sin remaineth." So ends the ninth chapter of St. John's Gospel. From that point to the end it is exclusively a treatise on divine love. But already, in the very heart of the treatise on sin, to show what sin is, God's love of sinners has inevitably exhibited itself. Between the miracles worked by Jesus on the Sabbath day to provoke the Pharisees, St. John had interpolated the story of the woman taken in adultery. This passage is missing from many early texts, and some have suggested that it is unlike St. John's writings and like the style of the other Gospels, from which they would like to conclude that it has been lifted. But it could not be more in place or in character, and without it the doctrine of sin would be greatly obscured. It is the Johannine counterpart to the parable of the Pharisee and the Publican. Each is a masterpiece, the parable as a vignette, the other as a tableau enlarging and clarifying the finer points implicit in the smaller picture. It brings out very vividly our Lord's attitude both to the Scribes and Pharisees and to any sinner who is not as the Scribes and Pharisees.

These last are trapped into a tacit admission that they are sinners, and into an exhibition of their habitual behaviour whenever their conscience faces them with the fact: they immediately slink away from the accuser, to stalk about a moment later as self-complacent as ever. Simultaneously, they are forced to a fleeting acknowledgment that Christ knows the secret labyrinth of their souls as well as they know it themselves, and better: for He calmly faces the truth about them, whereas they have to torture themselves into maintaining a lie. It is further brought home to them that their refusal to face the truth about themselves is bound up with their refusal to face the truth about Him. They are revealed to themselves, at one and the same time, as self-blinded, and as closing their eyes immediately even to that. The subtlety of the simplicity with which Jesus exposes them to themselves could be pursued indefinitely. But the most delicately exquisite touch of all is that Jesus, in keeping with His constant protestation, refrains from judging either them or the sinful woman. His words to her when He is alone with her are amongst the most beautiful and most moving that ever fell from His kind lips: " Has no one condemned you? " " No one, Lord." " Neither will I condemn you; go, and sin no more." He has told her as plainly as He has ever told the Pharisees that she is a sinner. She knows it, and knows compunction. So He has told her the truth in tones not of anger but of love. Strange that anyone should question this being in the style of St. John.

The division into chapters that has been imposed on the books of the Bible coincide, sometimes very well, sometimes very imperfectly, with pauses in the sense. The division between the ninth and tenth chapters of St. John's Gospel is a case apart. There is no break here in our Lord's discourse, and no change in His audience (x. 21). But the change of tone and of subject matter is abrupt. In a twinkling we have passed from darkness to light; from all that sin is to all that love is.

The shepherd knows his sheep, each by its name. He leads, and they follow because they know his voice. " I am the good shepherd." He is come that His sheep may have life, abundance of it. A good shepherd lays down his life for his sheep. He knows them and they know him, just as the Father knows the Son. The Father loves the Son because He lays down His life for His sheep. He lays down His life of His own accord, to take it up again. " No one can take it from me. I alone have power to lay it down and take it up again. This is what my father has commanded me to do."

This starts a dispute among His hearers, some defending and some attacking Him. Time passes and the scene changes, but the argument goes on uninterrupted. Some come insisting that He say openly who He is. He will not be drawn. Whatever He says they will not believe,

whatever He does gains Him no credit with them, because they are not
His sheep. They may rob Him of His life, but not of His sheep. That
He will permit, not this. His Father gave Him both, bidding Him
sacrifice His life but not His sheep. No one can rob Him of anything
against His will, for no one can rob His Father, and He and His Father
are one. They pick up stones again, but this time He faces it out
and they are powerless. They begin to hatch plots for seizing Him.

He retires beyond the Jordan, followed by many, and many believe
in Him. Word comes from the sisters Martha and Mary[1] that their
brother Lazarus is sick. " Now Jesus loved Martha and Mary and their
brother Lazarus." He stays where He is until He knows that Lazarus
is dead, and then shapes to go, inviting His disciples to go with Him.
They protest. He is walking to His death, and would lead them to
theirs. He assures them He is going with His eyes open. Thomas,
who could never bear losing sight of Him or being out of touch with
Him, calls on his fellows: " Come, let us too go and die with him."

When Martha hears that Jesus is approaching Bethany she goes
to meet Him outside the gate. " O Lord," she says, " if you had been
here my brother would not have died; but I know that God will grant
whatever you ask." This opens up a conversation calmly sustained
on both sides until Christ has elicited from Martha a confession of
faith unsurpassed even by Peter's. She returns to the house and in a
whisper says to her sister—of whose devotion to Jesus, so different
from her own, she had formerly complained—" The Master is here
and is asking for you." As far as we have heard He has not mentioned
Mary's name. It would seem that Martha now better understands the
nature of the special bond between her sister and Jesus, and approves.
Mary rushes out, followed by the many visitors who have come to
condole with her. They think she is going to weep at her brother's
tomb. She is a woman of notoriously strong emotions. She greets
Him in exactly the same words as Martha: " O Lord, if you had been
here my brother would not have died," but can say no more. She is
sobbing at the feet of Jesus, as we always find her. Her grief infects
everybody, especially Jesus. He is very profoundly disturbed, groaning
from the depths of His soul. His speech is choked, and His few
sentences are short and sharp. " Where have you laid him? " He is

---

[1] Traditionally, in the liturgy and in the devotion of the faithful, Mary the
sister of Martha has always been identified with "the woman who was a sinner"
(Luke vii. 37) and "Mary Magdalene out of whom he had cast seven devils"
(Luke viii. 2). Certain difficulties, chiefly topographical, are solved by assuming
three distinct Maries. This scruple is ignored here. The difficulties are not
insuperable. And the character described under the three titles is so identical,
and so unique in history, that one cannot conceive its having existed in triplicate
in the small circle of our Lord's devoted followers, especially as all the others
were such strongly contrasted types.

weeping now. The visitors suppose His tears are for Lazarus, but recognize that love is their cause. At the tomb, groaning anew, He finds voice enough to say: " Take away the stone." Martha, practical as ever and seeing Him beside Himself, intervenes protectively: " Lord, he has been dead four days; he is stinking now." Jesus almost scolds her. " Have I not told you that if you believe me you will see the glory of God? " It is His longest speech since Mary's grief upset Him. But now He looks up and at greater length speaks to His Father: " Father, I thank you for having heard me. I knew you always do, but I said that for the sake of these standing near, so that they may believe that you have sent me." Then, shouting loudly: "Lazarus, come out!" Bound so that he can move neither hand nor foot nor see where he is going, Lazarus obeys. "Loose him, and let him go," says Jesus.

The point of the story, as of all the Gospel, is to show that Christ is divine. But it shows just as powerfully that He is human. The Word was made flesh—genuine human flesh, alive with feeling. The Word is who He was; the flesh is what He was, though not all He was. What happens humanly in His flesh comes out of His Person and reacts on His Person. When His Body is shaken with human emotion His Being is in the emotion though it cannot at its divine roots be moved by anything but itself. Just as Christ says He cannot die or rise again but of Himself. When two people move Him to different emotions they are different to Him at the depth of His Being, though at the depth of His Being He is the same to both. Which means that God loves all alike but with a difference; the difference being that they are different to Him. When our love of one another approaches this perfection, we call it sympathy. So in Christ it is revealed to us that God is a sympathetic Lover.

" Now Jesus loved Martha and her sister Mary and Lazarus." He was not merely a friend of the family: he was the sympathetic lover of each. He loved Martha as though there were only Martha, and Mary as though there were only Mary. Alone with each, He was of one mood and tense with each. With Martha He was calm, conversational, practical, going straight to the point methodically by way of the head; as quick to check her as she was to fuss busily about many trivial duties. With Mary He could languish in love, heave with it, go straight to the heart of love by way of the heart. It was by the gradual way of clear question and answer that He led Martha to the act of love He most desires from those He loves: her act of faith in His divine nature and mission—the " one thing necessary " (because none can be saved without it) that He had long before elicited from Mary in one spontaneous burst of love. " Go in peace, thy faith hath saved thee " (Luke vii. 50).

Jesus loved Lazarus also. St. John does not correct the impression
of the observant visitors, that His tears were more for Lazarus dead
than for Mary sobbing. They may as well have been for poor Lazarus'
having to come back to this vale of tears and die a second time. What
harder thing than dying can befall any man? What happier thing than
being happily dead? Jesus died once for Lazarus; Lazarus died twice
for Jesus; but surely Lazarus was there after Pentecost to be given
the Body of Jesus to eat. So Jesus got the better of it. How like a
man He loved His friend! The love between man and man is different
from the love between men and women. No man will be outdone in
love by a man; but unless as well as man He is the God to whom all
things are possible, no man can help being outdone in love by a woman.

By this story of the two sisters and their brother, John reconciles
for us the love and the violence of the most cruelly hard thing that
Jesus ever said: " Unless a man hate father and mother and sister and
brother and wife and children for my name's sake, he cannot be my
disciple." " Who is my mother? " Jesus loved Martha, and Mary,
and Lazarus: not all, but each. The Good Shepherd lays down His life
for His sheep; not for the flock, but for each sheep in the flock. If one
should stray, the flock is forgotten. The first thing for which Jesus
showed His love was a marriage. But he showed a greater and more
tender love for the issue of marriage, and warned us all that unless we
become as little children we cannot enter the kingdom where all are
one with Him and His Father in the Holy Spirit who is Love. That
is easy, for every one of us, married or unmarried, is somebody's
child. We all are, or have been, young. We are not all old, nor will
all be old. But we are to be children hating father and mother and all
our family. That is the cruel condition. The Jews were one family,
all children of Abraham. Were they to hate Abraham? As they used
it they made the name of Abraham odious to John the Baptist and to
Christ. Neither spoke anything but good of Abraham, it was " Father
Abraham " they railed at. Jesus was sent, as John before Him, to break
down tribalism in religion: to teach us to value ourselves for what we
are in ourselves, not for what our father was or for what our family is.
That is how Jesus values us and loves us. He did not love Martha
because she was Mary's sister, or Mary because she was Martha's,
or Lazarus because he was their brother. When He blessed the family
with the first of all His miracles at Cana He established it, not as the
end of all things, but as the primitive bodily means to the end. Its
immediate end is children, the more the merrier if the bread and
wine is there; its ultimate end is the everlasting life of each child.
An end is to be loved for its own sake; a means only for the sake of
the end, for its own sake not at all. For the sake of the end we must

be as ready to sacrifice it as to use it; both of which imply contempt
of it. Insofar as there is good in a thing ordained to be a means it is
apt matter for sacrifice to something better as a pledge of our love for
the better thing. Is there anything better than my father for which I
show my love by sacrificing him to it? It all depends on whether he is
only my father, or my father and friend as well. I give proof of a love
than which none can be greater as between men, when I sacrifice my
life for my friend. My father then, as my friend, is dearer to me than
my life. But as my father merely, is he not simply a means provided
by nature to the end which is my life? It is the burning question of
mother and child—which shall die for which. When Christ said
" Who is my mother? " did He mean that she ought to die for Him?
If that was ever a controversy between them, there could never have
been an end to it. It is the one quarrel that can never end in agreement
between friends. Yet Christ sacrificed His Mother, and she sacrificed
her Son. He consented to her homelessness and dereliction, and she,
with His Father, consented in His death. For whose sake? The Father's
and ours. So they both loved us more than they loved one another?
That does not follow. All they sacrificed for us was life, comfort,
home, wealth, mutual society and the rest: all temporal goods. And
this sacrifice they made, not for our temporal welfare, or social welfare,
or freedom from war, or from death, or for anything common, but for
that in us, our person, which makes each of us, in God's sight, an
utterly distinct creature from any other that He has made. Hence
the intimate personal nature of our love for these two. They have
loved us as God loved us: each one apart, as though there were no other.
The Son loved us as though He had no Mother; but not the Mother
as though she had no Son, for her Son was her God.

After the story of Lazarus and his sisters the Gospel of St. John
calls for no further commentary here. There is no violence in it any
more, except the violence of men, which did not proceed, like Christ's,
from love. Of Christ the rest of the Gospel relates only meek, patient,
self-annihilating love. To the last breath of His Body and the last drop
of His Blood, He gave us that gift, than which, as Man, He could not
give greater. Then having bankrupted Himself as Man, He went
as Son to His Father to ask, sure of success, that together they should
give us all they have to give one another: the Eternal Gift of God
to God—God.

ANATHEMA-MARANATHA: LOVE AND WRATH IN ST. PAUL

Victor White, O.P.

In the whole history of Christendom, there can be few who confront us more remorselessly with the problem of love and wrath in Christianity than does St. Paul. The influence of his presentation of the subject on subsequent Christian thought and practice has been incalculable. But, equally, there can be no denying that much of it hardly makes congenial reading for the modern reader, even for such as are not prepared (as many have been) to diagnose and dismiss the Apostle as a paranoid, an epileptoid, or at best an unintegrated fanatic. It is no longer fashionable to present " Paulinism " as an early adulteration of the pure milk of the Gospel, but neither can it be said that St. Paul can always be read without offence. He himself was convinced that the very Gospel of Love will be found offensive—" unto the Jews a stumbling block, and unto the Gentiles foolishness " (1 Cor. i. 23).[1] Christ Himself in the written Gospels comes " not to send peace but a sword " (Matt. x. 34), and He in fact arouses conflict, division, hatred, malice and enmity such as are hardly to be found in the history of any other religious or moral teacher. But even this may not prepare us for the difficulties which confront us in the life and writing of St. Paul, still less for the sad story of intolerance, aggressiveness, *odium theologicum*, anathema, persecution, proselytism, fear, spitefulness, cruelty and bigotry with which the history of Christendom—alongside much that is wholly admirable—offends everything in us that we nowadays tend to regard as most authentically Christian. All this—the ever-ready theme of the satirist—will be neither explained nor justified by St. Paul. But he may be found to concentrate the problem for us, and, even though he may not provide us with blueprints for its practical solution in the twentieth century, he will at least offer us principles without which the problem is scarcely intelligible, let alone soluble.

We must beware of too readily reading into St. Paul our own or our contemporaries' meanings of " love ". But it should not be necessary

---

[1] In the scriptural quotations in this essay we sometimes make use of the Douay and Knox translations of the Vulgate; but, even at the expense of consistency, we have sometimes employed or made direct translations from the Greek original when it appeared desirable.

for us to consult Greek philologists or biblical scholars in order to find clues to his own understanding of *agape*—the word he most often uses, and which our translations render as " love " or " charity ". In the famous, resounding phrases of 1 Corinthians xiii, he is himself at some considerable pains to indicate what he understands by the word.

Agape is, in the first place, St. Paul tells us, something quite indispensable. But before attempting to tell us what it is, he finds it well to tell us what it is not: to differentiate it from all those high gifts, virtues and values which are mistaken for it, but which, without it, are worthless:

> " If I speak with the tongues of men and of angels, and have not *agape*, I am as clanging brass or a tinkling cymbal. And if I should have prophetic insight, and fathom all mysteries and secret lore; and if I should have such absolute faith that I could move mountains, and have not *agape*, I am nothing at all. And if I should give away all that I possess, and if I give my own body to be burned, and have not *agape*, I make nothing of it."

Agape, then, is not sublime " spiritual " talk or understanding. It is not even charity in any usual sense of the word—not even the most generous and selfless charity. Nor is it heroic courage even unto death.

What, then, is it? It is, in the first place, something very simple and homely; human and humane: *Agape* is something that is

> " patient and kind; *agape* is not jealous or boastful, it is not arrogant or rude. *Agape* does not insist on having one's own way, it is not irritable or resentful. It is never glad when others go wrong; it is gladdened by what is true".

In Romans xii. 9 ff., also, St. Paul stresses this humanity, this simplicity of *agape*:

> " Let *agape* be without sham . . . Love one another like brothers, outdo one another in showing respect . . . Rejoice with those who rejoice, be sorry with those who are sad. Live in harmony of mind, falling in with the opinions of common folk, instead of following conceited opinions."

But in verse 7 of 1 Corinthians xiii we become aware of a transition. *Agape* is indeed human, matter-of-fact, practical; but it is no ordinary, average human love that " bears all things, believes all things, endures all things ". And presently we know that *agape*, like Jesus Christ Himself, is not only absolutely human, but also absolutely divine; something transcendental and changeless with the unchangeableness of God:

" *Agape* never ends. As for prophetic knowledge, it will pass away; as for tongues, they will cease; as for spiritual insight [*gnosis*], it will be superseded."

Though all else is subject to change and decay and destruction, *agape* abides; and its possession is the condition of our human maturity as well as of our participation in the eternity of God:

" When I was a child, I spoke like a child, I thought like a child, I reasoned like a child; but when I became a man I gave up childish ways."

It is, St. Paul has just said, characteristic of *agape* that it is all-believing, all-hoping, all-trusting. Faith and hope are for him the indispensable conditions for the attainment of this *agape*; and these three are somehow one. Not certain knowledge but faith, not secure present possession but hope, must be the response to true *agape* in this world.[1] For I do not, St. Paul has just said, *know* the Beloved: I am known *by* Him. " For now we see in a mirror dimly, but then face to face. Now I know only in part, but I shall understand fully, even as I am now fully understood."

These words take us to the very heart of St. Paul's experience and teaching on the love of God. " The Love of God " is notoriously an ambiguous phrase: it can mean either God's love for us or our love for God. But St. Paul himself soon settles the ambiguity for us. In his Epistles, and in his sermons in Acts, we find little about our love for God, no autobiographical account of his own love for God, no instructions on methods or techniques for loving God—not even many exhortations to us to love God. What is important for him is not our love for God; what is all-important is God's love for man. The few passages which might seem to be exceptions prove the rule. For St. Paul we are lovers of God only in so far as we are passive and receptive to God's loving knowledge of, and loving action towards, His chosen. So in 1 Corinthians viii. 3: " If anyone loves God, he is known by him "; Galatians iv. 9: " Now you have come to know God, or rather to be known by God "; Philippians iii. 12: " I am not already perfect, but I follow after [perfection] to make it my own, because Christ Jesus has made me his own." Though St. Paul speaks, in Romans viii. 28, of " those who love God ", he goes on at once to explain that these are

[1] In his fine pages on " The Purifying of Love " Gustave Thibon graphically describes how the illusion of knowing and possessing the other must be purged by faith and hope, which respect the otherness and mystery of the partner, if human love is to be real and lasting. See *What God Has Joined Together*, Hollis and Carter, 1952, 114 ff.

" those who are called according to God's purpose ". True, he closes
I Corinthians with the extraordinary curse (to which we must return):
" If any one has no love for the Lord, let him be anathema "; but this
is because the Lord Jesus is the " son of God's love " without which
we are reprobate and accursed. But the initiative is always God's
love for us; and what matters supremely is not whether we love God
but whether God loves us. St. Paul does not say in so many words,
as does St. John, " in this *agape* consists: not as though we had loved
God, but because he has first loved us " (I John iv. 10), nor that
"God is greater than our heart, and knoweth all things" (I John iii. 20).
But faith and hope in God's love for us is for St. Paul, no less than
for St. John, the centre of his preaching. Beside this the talk of our
love for God, which occupies so much of later devotional literature,
must appear somewhat of an egocentric impertinence. Our response
in faith, hope and love to God's love is indeed indispensable, and a
token that we are beloved of God. But the primary fact to which it is
a response is the overwhelming fact of God's love for us. We might
express it, in later categories, by saying that *agape* is, in the first instance,
not a matter of morals, still less of technique in " spirituality ", but
rather of dogma, of response to revealed fact.

For what, in St. Paul's belief, is this divine *agape*? We cannot
evade the fact that his is a stern, a grimly realistic doctrine. His God
is a God of love, but also a God of wrath. He bids us

> " See then the goodness and the severity of God: towards them
> indeed that are fallen, the severity; but towards thee, the goodness
> of God if thou abide in goodness " (Rom. xi. 22).

And it is only against this background of wrath and severity that he
will expound to us the love and the goodness; apart from it his doctrine
of the divine *agape* makes no sense.

This doctrine often shows itself in attitudes and statements which
may shock everything in us which is liberal, tolerant—or just sentimental—and may sometimes incline us to suspect him of something
like hypocrisy. We recall again that astonishing mixture of valediction
and malediction at the end of I Corinthians—a postscript written, he
tells us, with his own hand:

> " If anyone has no love for the Lord, let him be anathema.
> Maranatha [May the Lord come]! The grace of the Lord Jesus
> be with you. My love be with you all in Christ Jesus."

St. James remarks, " Out of the same mouth proceed blessing and
cursing; my brethren, these things ought not so to be " (Jas. iii. 10).
But with St. Paul blessing and cursing seem to come often in the same

breath; and the love and wrath of God, and the love and wrath of Paul, seem often so entangled with one another as to startle, if not to scandalize, the modern reader. We remember the fierce crescendo of anger in Galatians—the passionate threats, denunciations and pleadings—" O fools of Galatians, who has bewitched you? . . . My little children, of whom I am in labour again." It mounts in querulousness and fury until the fifth chapter, in which it might seem that passion has blinded Paul to all logical consistency. (In verse 3 the Galatians are told that if they submit to circumcision they will be bound by the whole Old Testament Law; in verse 6 that neither circumcision nor uncircumcision is of any importance at all.) In verse 12 we have, " I wish those who unsettle you would castrate themselves." We wonder what has happened to all the fine talk about *agape* in 1 Corinthians xiii —the *agape* which is not arrogant or rude, not irritable or resentful. And yet, in this same chapter of Galatians, St. Paul is presently telling us, " The whole law is fulfilled in one word, ' Thou shalt love thy neighbour as thyself'. But if you bite and devour one another, take heed that you are not consumed by one another." And then, that " the works of the *flesh* are enmity, strife, jealousy, anger ", while " the fruit of the *Spirit* is love, joy, peace, patience, kindness . . . gentleness, self-control".

What are we to make of this blend of love and violence, of blessing and cursing, in St. Paul? Are we to say just that even St. Paul failed sometimes to practise what he preached?—that he was naturally a passionate and irascible man? Certainly he was that, and we cannot leave the fact out of account. We know he was a man of intense loves and intense hates. We first meet him as a young ruffian, taking part in the brutal stoning of Stephen (Acts vii. 58–60). Then we find him making " havoc of the church, entering in from house to house; he dragged off men and women and committed them to prison " (Acts viii. 3); then, " breathing out threats and slaughter against the disciples " (Acts ix. 1).

In Philippians iii. 5–6 he tells us why that had been. He was " of the people of Israel, of the tribe of Benjamin, a Hebrew born of Hebrews; as to the Law, a Pharisee; as to zeal, a persecutor of the church; as to righteousness, in accordance with the Law, blameless ". His great hate then had been the by-product of a great love—love of morality, love of the Law, love of his people and of God's choice of them: and this love, at least, would never leave him, for always there would be something in him that wished to be anathema even from Christ for his kinsmen according to the flesh (Rom. ix. 3). There had been love, too, for good works, personal righteousness, punctilious observance, and for the Pharisee party which, against powerful opposition, upheld these things. His great love had been, then, for those very things which most aroused the anger and the irony of Jesus Christ (e.g. in Matt. xxiii).

On the road to Damascus he was literally thrown from his high horse. His was a conversion, not only in the religious sense, but also in the psychological sense of a sudden and complete reversal of personality, a turning upside down of all his previous values. His ego now becomes identified with what had hitherto been his shadow. What had been his great hate—Christ and His followers—now becomes his great love. What had been his great love—the moral righteousness of good, law-abiding deeds as the all-in-all of salvation, exact observance, racial exclusivism—now become his great hate, as almost every page of Romans and Galatians bears witness.

But the fundamental complementarity of love and hate remained. Each fed the other, and each was intensified by the other. This may offend our idealism and our romanticism, and may strike us as neither humanistic nor humane; but we must recognize that it is still very commonly human.

A Hebrew, steeped in the Old Testament, could hardly view things otherwise. The realistic *agape* of the Hebrews had always differed in this respect from the idealized *eros* of later Greek theory. As Kittel's New Testament *Theologisches Wörterbuch* puts it:

" The essential characteristic of love in Israel is actually its tendency towards exclusiveness. The Greek Eros is fundamentally universal, undiscriminating, undisciplined, broadminded. The love which is commended in the Old Testament is the jealous love which chooses one object among thousands and holds it fast with all the strength of its passion and its will, brooking no relaxation of the bond of loyalty. It is just this jealousy which reveals the divine strength of such love. It is no accident by which, in the Song of Songs (viii. 6) love strong as death is inseparably connected, in the poetic parallelism, with jealousy hard as hell. Jacob has two wives, but his love is given to only one of them (Gen. xxix); he has twelve sons, but loves one of them more than all the others (Gen. xxxvii. 3). God has set many peoples in the world, but gives his love to the elect nation. With this he makes a covenant which he loyally keeps and jealously guards—as if it were a bond of marriage (Hosea i ff.). To break the law is a breach of faith, to worship strange gods is adultery, calling forth the passionate jealousy of Yahwe . . ."[1]

[1] Translated in *Manuals from Kittel*, vol. i, "Love" (Quell and Stauffer), Adam and Charles Black, 1949, pp. 32, 33.

Divine love is thus very human in its exclusiveness, in its association with anger and jealousy. And human love is to be in its image and likeness. The *Wörterbuch* continues:

" The principle of loving one's neighbour is [in the Old Testament] marked by the same motif of exclusiveness. It is a love that makes distinctions, choosing, preferring, rejecting—not a cosmopolitan love, embracing millions. The Israelite begins his social activity at home, loving Israel first as God does . . . The scope of social responsibility is thus always defined in terms of a particular organization and a concrete situation. The cosmopolitan Greek loves all the world; the patriotic Israelite his neighbour . . ."

The conversion of Saul of Tarsus into Paul the Apostle of the nations did not, and could not, eradicate this fundamental apprehension of love as selective and concrete, and as the complementary opposite of wrath. For St. Paul, as for St. John, the manifestation of the greater light only intensifies the darkness; and, by contrast, the darkness sets in relief the brightness of the light. Becoming a Christian, accepting Christ as the embodiment and manifestation of God's love, did not mean the rejection of the God of Israel with all the characteristics of His loyal and jealous love, and the substitution of a God of universal amiability. On the contrary, the love of God shown in Christ manifests by contrast the unlovableness and incompetence of man without that love, and, reciprocally, human hatefulness and sin manifest not only the extent of man's desperate need, but also the intensity and immensity of the response in God's love. That surely is why we find (quantitatively, at least) as much about God's wrath in St. Paul as about His love—perhaps very much more. St. Paul will not allow us any sentimental illusions about God's love, nor about our own lovableness, nor about our own harmony with the Creator, with His creation, or with ourselves. We are by birth, as members of the human race, children of wrath (Ephes. ii. 3); and this wrath sets the stage for the drama of divine love, and is indeed itself a vehicle of that love.

Such is the burden of St. Paul's most methodical account of the ways of divine love—his Epistle to the Romans. It opens with a long, detailed and tart description of the demoralization of the Gentiles, " working that which is filthy and receiving in themselves the recompense due to their error " (i. 27). The Jews condemn the Gentiles, but do the things which they condemn, and having the written Law have less excuse (ii. 1 and *passim*). Jews and Gentiles are all under sin (iii. 9); all have sinned and need the glory of God (iii. 23). There is no salvation in morality, let alone in a morality which nobody possesses;

and though Israel has the Law, it has never been able to keep it, and the Law has served rather as a reproach: " by the law is knowledge of sin " (iii. 20). Abraham, David and the rest were not saved by morality but by unswerving faith in God's forgiveness and love (iv *passim*). This is written " also for us ".

" Therefore, since we are justified by faith,[1] we have peace with God through Jesus Christ our Lord. Through him we have obtained access to this grace whereby we stand, and glory in the hope of sharing the glory of God . . . And hope does not disappoint us, because God's love has been poured into our hearts through the holy Spirit which has been given to us. For while we were yet helpless, at the right time Christ died for the ungodly. . . . But God shows his love towards us in that, while we were still sinners, Christ died for us. Since, therefore, we are now justified by his blood, much more shall we be saved through him from the wrath of God . . . The law entered in that sin might abound. And where sin abounded, grace did the more abound" (Rom. v. 1, 2, 5, 6, 8, 9, 20).

Here we have the quintessence of St. Paul's apprehension of God's *agape*. We might paraphrase it by saying that God and man have become at loggerheads—the human race is an accursed race, as verses 12–19 of this same chapter explain, and as the behaviour of Jew and Gentile make manifest. It is manifested also in the inward conflict of our spirituality and carnality (chapter vii) and in our outer disharmony with our natural environment (viii. 20–23). Man, without faith and hope in God's love, tends to hate God; and God hates what man has become. But God loves Christ, and Christ loves God; Christ in God loves us, and we in Christ love God. The sure pragmatic test of the presence of this love is (for St. Paul as also for St. John) the presence of Christ's Spirit poured upon His chosen. So

" What Paul means by the love of God is clear. It is ᵗhe directing of God's sovereign will towards this world and its salvation. Love in action is the goal towards which God has been striving since the very beginning. Ever since Abraham's days God has envisaged a people free from the domination of the law. He has created this people through the sending of the Son and finally of the Spirit. . . . The aim of God's loving action is the new man. But this is not achieved

---

[1] This has, of course, nothing to do with the Lutheran slogan of salvation by faith *alone*; nor is it an exhaustive statement of the function and interrelation of faith and deeds. As the word implies, it is of the essence of heresy to pick and choose; Luther (however he be interpreted) crystallized into a " nothing but " dogma this " moment " in St. Paul's inner " dialectical " struggle.

without loving action on the part of man himself. . . . God's sovereign call is a call to freedom. God's new man is a free man . . ." [1]

We should note that this divine *agape* is (to use a later phraseology) strictly *trinitarian* and *incarnational*.

It is *trinitarian*. For, in St. Paul's mind we are not beloved of God—indeed God is not loving but wrathful—apart from " *the* Beloved " (Eph. i. 6), the Son of His love (Col. i. 13). " The love of . . . God is in Christ Jesus our Lord " (Rom. viii. 39) and reaches us through " conformity to the Son ", who is thus the first-born among many brethren (Rom. xvi. 29). And this can only be insofar as we partake of His Spirit: " anyone who does not have the Spirit of Christ does not belong to him " (Rom. viii. 9), while " through Christ we have access in one Spirit to the Father " (Eph. ii. 18), and it is in this Spirit that we are the beloved children of God and can address Him as " Abba, Father " (Rom. viii. 14, 15).

Then, it is *incarnational*—human, fleshly, of the earth earthy. We have already seen how St. Paul insists on its homeliness, its ordinariness: its patience, kindness, sympathy in joy and sorrow. For all its unchangeableness and divinity, it is neither something purely transcendental and other-worldly, nor a romantic, idealized love, nor yet only a cold, unemotional benevolence. Such had not been the love of Jesus in the Gospels, and such could not be the love of His passionate disciple Paul.

Yet it may well seem to us that Paul's love is not only human, but all too human in its turbulence and the wrath which accompanies it. Must it not seem to our minds, enlightened by modern psychology, that he all too easily identifies his own loves and hates with the love and wrath of God? And that with dubious propriety and dubious piety he projects his own pattern of love-aggression into the divine sphere?

Such questions as these are bound to occur to the modern reader so inevitably and spontaneously that he may forget how heavily loaded they are. The theocentric standpoint of St. Paul and the anthropocentric standpoint of most modern psychology are not easy to reconcile. We can hardly even guess how St. Paul himself would meet our misgivings. The tacit assumption behind them that wrath, anger, even aggressiveness, were somehow " bad " or " infantile " in themselves would be unintelligible to him; still more so our view that righteous indignation is the most reprehensible form of indignation, and necessarily a symptom of hypocrisy, immaturity or a lack of self-awareness. He would doubtless agree with St. James that " the wrath of man does not achieve the righteousness of God "

[1] *Manuals from Kittel*, vol. i, " Love ", pp. 55, 56.

(Jas. i. 20); but we may note that the Epistle of St. James is also an exceedingly wrathful Epistle. It is precisely the wrath of *man*, egocentric wrath, which St. James and St. Paul alike condemn. St. Paul, we may suppose, would regard it as a compliment rather than a reproach that he identifies his loves and hates with the love and wrath of God. He would say (we may guess) that the fact that his love and indignation reflect and image the love and wrath of God was their one and only justification. He will not merely admit, but boldly proclaim, the identity of his own evaluations with those of God Almighty. " We have the mind of Christ" (1 Cor. ii. 16); "We have received the Spirit who is of God, that we may know the things that are given us by God . . . the spiritual man judges all things " (ibid., 12, 15); " he who is joined to the Lord is one Spirit with him " (1 Cor. vi. 17). Even when he offers his own counsel, on matters concerning which he has " no commandment of the Lord ", he does so " as one who by the Lord's mercy is trustworthy " (1 Cor. vii. 25), and he adds " I think that I also have the Spirit of God " (ibid., 40). The things that anger him so much in writing to the Galatians and the Corinthians are the things which, he is convinced, invite the anger of God, and which imply a rejection of God's love as shown in Christ—the ceremonial and regulations which would imply an insufficiency in His atoning work of loving forgiveness, and which would lead to an infringement of that freedom of the children of God whereby Christ has made us free (Gal. iv. 31: *al.* v. 1). And if sometimes there enters a note of more personal petulance—the complaint that his disciples are not faithful to himself, or are ungrateful for all he has done and suffered for them, or have disloyally followed other teachers—we must not forget that he is a " chosen instrument " of God to carry Christ's name to all peoples and to the children of Israel (Acts ix. 15), and therefore that to spurn him is to spurn Christ and God Himself (cf. Luke x. 16).

These considerations will not recommend St. Paul to the modern " good pagan ". On the contrary, they will confirm his worst suspicions. But though he may consider unfounded and extravagant St. Paul's claim to identification of his mind, and of his love and wrath, with the mind and the love and wrath of God, he cannot easily contend that it is pathological or even (given Paul's premisses) irrational. The identification is fully conscious and freely accepted. It is something quite different from that compulsive identification with the superego—that God-almightiness, as Alfred Adler called it—which we rightly recognize as psychopathological. Moreover (though this is perhaps only another way of saying the same thing), the identification is not subjective but purely objective. St. Paul does not identify *himself* with God, consciously or unconsciously; on the contrary, he is only God's creature and minister. What he does claim, at least implicitly, is that the *objects* of his love and wrath are also the objects of divine love and wrath. This is not an irrational aim for anyone who believes he is made in the image and likeness of God, or indeed who believes in a God at all. Nor is it true that Paul, in any accepted clinical sense, projects his own emotional pattern upon God: his God is no subject of changing moods or arbitrary oscillations between love and hate. On the contrary, the changeless fidelity and constancy of God's love is St. Paul's central conviction, and forms the basis and motive of the faith and trust which that love demands; and it is that love, and its very constancy, which explains and justifies the wrath. God, for him, is all love, and constant love; but that selfsame insistent love, which is experienced as love by those who accept it in faith and trust, must be experienced as wrath by those who reject or ignore it. Of such sort had love always been as Paul had experienced it, whether as a Pharisee or as a Christian. He would have understood Ian Suttie's *Origins of Love and Hate*, which sees wrath, fear and aggression as always the by-product of frustrated love, as (by implication) does St. Thomas Aquinas. He would perhaps have understood less well those Freudians, whom Suttie criticises, who present love and aggression, Eros and Thanatos, as two ultimate and mutually irreducible constituents of human nature. He would have understood the contention of St. John of the Cross that it is the same " Living Flame of Love" which purges and hurts and stifles, and which warms, soothes and comforts. St. Paul sees it to be his calling to proclaim the divine love which casts out fear; but does not hesitate to proclaim the fearful divine wrath which summons us to accept that love. It is not perhaps entirely amiss to ask ourselves if our scandal at the wrath of St. Paul, and at his doctrine of divine wrath, is not itself a projection of a split in our own personality, of our own inability to correlate these opposites, to accept and acknowledge the wrathful aspect either of our own personalities, or of our mental and emotional picture of an idealized God.

Neither Hebrews nor Christians, if they are honest,[1] have ever been able to by-pass or repress the severity or aggressive factor which is

---

[1] Cf. Kierkegaard: " Quite simply: I want honesty . . . I am not a Christian severity as opposed to a Christian leniency . . . But one thing I will not do, not for anything in the world. I will not by suppression, or by performing tricks, try to produce the impression that the ordinary Christianity in the land and the Christianity of the New Testament are alike " (*Attack upon Christendom*, p. 37). " To put an end to coquetry I have had to apply severity—and have applied it precisely in order to give impetus to the resort to leniency. If I had only understood its frightful severity, I would have kept silent. I think I dare say of myself that I undoubtedly have at my disposal a profounder pathos in preaching the leniency of Christianity than anyone in our land " (*Journals*, X2 A 525, p. 378; quoted, *Attack*, p. 94).

inseparable from love in its temporal, human situation. No one of the Apostles—any more than was St. Paul—was exclusively placid, lenient, tranquil, amiable. All of them, we may say, had had to work through the aggressive passionate counterpart to love if the fullness of love was to be attained. St. John is the Beloved Disciple, a foremost witness to the love of God in Christ: " God so loved the world . . .", " A new commandment I give you . . .", " My little children, love one another . . ." Yet he was a Boanerges, a son of thunder, calling fire and slaughter on those who rejected his Beloved—and what vials of wrath are poured forth in his Apocalypse! The Epistles of St. Peter or St. Jude are far from being all sweetness and gentleness, and what an angry Epistle is that of St. James! Yet there is hardly more wrath in these than in Christ's own denunciations of the Pharisees in Matthew xxiii. For ideal, tranquil love, the New Testament compares unfavourably with Plato's *Symposium*—but perhaps it is far more realistic and descriptive of what love really is.

We might nevertheless like to think that St. Paul found his way to what we should consider a more tranquil, more integrated, less tempestuous love. And indeed, when we come to read his later Epistles we seem to find ourselves in somewhat calmer waters. The doctrine of divine love and wrath remains the same, but the positive affirmations of love now push the wrath—both God's and Paul's—relatively into the background. The Epistles to the Ephesians, the Philippians and the Colossians must all be read as almost lyrical praises of the ways of divine love, followed in each case by exhortations to the brotherly love and loving behaviour which divine love requires of us. The opening words of Ephesians set their tone:

" Blessed be the God and Father of our Lord Jesus Christ, who has blessed us in Christ . . . even as he chose us in him before the establishment of the world, that we should be holy and blameless in his sight. In love he destined us to be his children through Jesus Christ, by the set purpose of his will, to the praise of his glorious grace which he freely bestowed on us in the Beloved . . ." (i. 3–6).

And St. Paul prays:

" that Christ may dwell in your hearts through faith, that you, being rooted and grounded in love, may be able to comprehend, like all holy people, what is the breadth and length and height and depth, and to know that love of Christ which surpasses knowledge, that you may be filled with all the fulness of God who, by the power at work within us, is able to do far more abundantly than we ask or suppose " (Eph. iii. 17ff.).

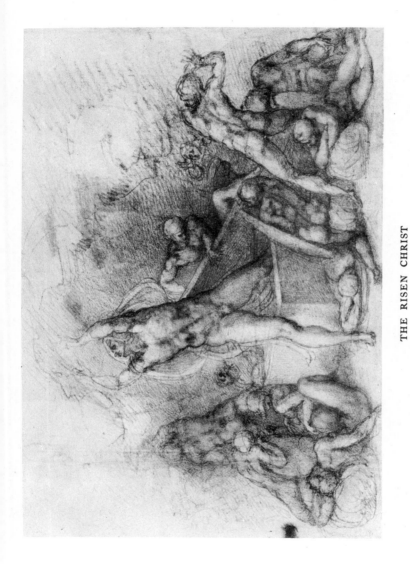

THE RISEN CHRIST

Michelangelo: Windsor Castle, Royal Library: by gracious permission of H.M. the Queen

This growth in realization of the inner power of divine love seems now almost to have consumed the former anger; but it is not that the occasions for it have been done away, or that Paul is now closing his eyes to unpleasantness or calling evil good. Still, in Ephesians as in Romans, " the gentiles live in futility of their minds; they are darkened in their understandings, alienated from the life of God because of the ignorance that is in them . . . become callous and given up to licentiousness " (iv. 17–19): but in Ephesians the matter is disposed of in a verse or two, without the long, censorious detail of Romans. In Philippians there are still those " who preach Christ from envy and rivalry . . . who proclaim Christ out of partisanship, not sincerely, thinking to afflict me in my imprisonment." But now the writer seems to have overcome the resentment of Galatians and Corinthians, and to have reconciled himself with the fact. " What does it matter? " he now asks, " provided only, whether in pretence or in sincerity, Christ is proclaimed " (Phil. i. 15–17). In Colossians we read again, as we did in Galatians, of those who would impose on believers regulations " about food and drink, or a festival or a new moon or a sabbath ", or who would propagate their pet devotions, " insisting on self-abasement and worship of angels, basing themselves on visions, puffed up without reason " (Col. ii. 16ff.). But now there is much less of the sound and fury of Galatians, even against these infringements of Christian liberty. These things are only obsolete " shadows of things to come ", but now come: they " have an appearance of wisdom in promoting rigour of devotion and humility and severity ", and can do no good. But there seems no longer the same assurance that these concessions to frailty, and to the human " fear of freedom ", can do much harm; though the Colossians must put them in their place. For, " if with Christ you died to the elemental spirits of the universe, why do you still submit to regulations—Do not handle, Do not taste, Do not touch? "

But although we may perhaps trace a certain development, a certain mellowing, in St. Paul's presentation of love, he never did, and never could, see it as something which in this world could be cosy and undemanding. It was something ever burning, breaking, making new; something which must always arouse resistance from human egotism. The love of God shown in Christ demanded utter surrender to Jesus and to the Spirit of Jesus, in complete faith and hope, until it could be said, " I live, now not I, but Christ lives in me " (Gal. ii. 20). God's love for us might evoke our love for God in contemplative rapture and ecstasy, but not in this lay its principal and most exacting demand. Paul had experienced these things—" caught up to the third heaven . . . and heard things that cannot be told, which men may not utter "

(2 Cor. xii. 2)—but they were nothing to boast about. If boast he must, it is of his labours, his floggings, imprisonments, stonings, dishonour, shipwrecks, sleeplessness, hunger, journeys, dangers, on behalf of his fellow human beings. For what the love of God demands of him is the transmission of that love to his fellow-men. God's love, as he sees it, is something ever outflowing from its divine centre; never that of the *solus soli*, the sterile, closed circuit of lover and beloved. " Thou shalt love the Lord thy God . . . thou shalt love thy neighbour as thyself " are not, for him, so much two commandments; the second is the fulfilment of the first, and the meaning of brotherly love is the extension and radiation to others of divine love. For,

> " the purpose of divine love is not that we should return to God, not that we should attain freedom for our own sakes; it is that he who is called should put himself in love and freedom at the service of his neighbour: ' Through love be servants one to another; for the whole law is fulfilled in one word—thou shalt love thy neighbour as thyself ' (Gal. v. 13f.). Paul takes up Jesus' demand for love of neighbours, and establishes it in the same sense as the Lord. But his main interest is in brotherly love: ' Let us work that which is good toward all men, and especially toward them that are of the household of the faith ' (Gal. vi. 10) . . . ' Beloved ' and ' Brother ' become interchangeable terms (1 Thess. ii. 8; Phil. xvi)."[1]

So St. Paul's teaching on divine love is not only trinitarian and incarnational, it is also ecclesiological, and therefore eschatological:

> " The decisive importance of brotherly love is seen in relation to the unique moment in cosmic history (καιρός, Gal. vi. 10; Rom. xiii. 11) which makes it imperative. During the whole of this age of decision between the Cross and the ' End ', brotherly love is the only relevant behaviour—the only principle that is sure of the future. Its sign is the sign of the Cross. It is willingness to serve and sacrifice, to forgive and make allowances, to share and sympathise, to lift up the fallen and restore the erring (Gal. v. 25ff.; Rom. xii. 9f.; 1 Cor. xiii. 4ff.) in a community which owes its whole existence to the mercy of God and the sacrificial death of his Christ (Phil. ii. 1ff.; 1 Cor. viii. 11; Col. iii. 14ff.). The apostle's own highest ambition is to help forward the salvation of the Church by the imitation of Christ. He is willing to fill up that which was lacking of the afflictions of Christ (Col. i. 24). At the same time the humblest act of human love finds its place in the service of the great loving activity of God—

---

[1] *Manuals from Kittel*, vol. i, " Love ", pp. 57, 58.

in harmony with Paul's fundamental idea of the relation between divine and human operations. It is in love that the working of God and man achieves unity. Love builds up (1 Cor. viii. 1)—it builds the work of the future. Love's sign is the sign of the end . . . Love is the power of the coming age already breaking into the world. For Paul, as for Jesus, love is the only life-force that has a future in this age of death."[1]

In the foregoing pages we have attempted to present Love and Wrath in St. Paul as objectively as possible. A few more personal reflections may be permitted by way of conclusion.

We are not called upon to *like* St. Paul's presentation of the Love and Wrath of God, and on St. Paul's own principles our unredeemed, self-centred, comfort-loving, *laissez-faire* egotism cannot be expected to like it. It is not, however, alien to universal tradition as revealed by comparative religion. A " God without Thunder " has never been the God of any realistic religion; and it may be safely asserted that any religion which ignores or represses the hostile manifestations of Divinity is already in decay and out of touch with the realities of the human situation, whether in relation to nature, to society, or to the realm of grace and salvation. Every living religion has always made it its special concern to direct human awareness first and foremost to the more disagreeable and hostile aspects of Divinity. It is a commonplace that, in many of the more " primitive " cults, while perfunctory acknowledgment is made of a supreme and all-beneficent God, conscious attention in myth and ritual is directed much more to divine or diabolic power which is more hostile to common human aspiration and endeavour. A similar pattern, demanding the facing of the " dark side " of Divinity, may be found in all the " higher " religions and mythologies and spiritual paths. In India, we are told, he who has chosen the divine saviour Rama (the " joy-giver ") as his master must first pay homage to Shiva the Destroyer for three or six months. In Greece, the terrifying Medusa's head on Pallas Athene's shield must first be faced and overcome before the benign aspects of the goddess will be revealed. In Tibet, confrontation with the " wrathful deities " is the condition of attaining the " peaceful deities " and the " clear light of the Void ". Examples could be multiplied indefinitely. In Israel, Job must be shaken out of his pious contentment through the afflictions sent through Satan as the emissary of God's love, and by the overwhelming vision of divine might. Christ comes, not only for the rise, but also for the fall of many in Israel (Luke ii. 34); He brings not peace but a sword (Matt. x. 34); his coming enhances

[1] *Manuals from Kittel*, vol. i, " Love ", pp. 58, 59.

the heinousness of sin (John xv. 22); His sending of the holy Spirit imparts the sense of sin (John xvi. 8). In its essentials, St. Paul's teaching on the love and wrath of God is homogeneous with the Gospels, and they are essentials which we neglect at our peril. They have never been forgotten, and cannot be forgotten, by the Church.

St. Paul's tremendous confidence in his mission, his single-minded devotion, his indignation at everything that conflicts with his convictions, may sometimes more appal than edify or stimulate us. The irascibility of his letters was evidently a joke even to their first recipients; and his naïve, " I warn you that, when we visit you, our actions will not belie the impression which our letters make when we are at a distance " could hardly have assuaged their mirth (see 2 Cor. x. 10, 11). But we are not required to regard him as a notable specimen of psychological maturity or as a model of tact—even of tact in the best sense of " touch " with the other fellow's point of view. He sees himself as seeking, but not having attained, the full measure of the stature of Christ; and as only one of many very different organs of the Body of Christ. We cannot invoke him to justify any sort of sectarian bitterness, bigotry or intolerance whose hidden motive is very different from that faith and trust in God's love which animated him.

THE GOD OF WRATH AND THE *MYSTERIUM TREMENDUM*

Michael Mason

" To Cariathiarim hill . . . they went up, great and small, to fetch the ark home . . . putting it on a newly made wagon, with Oza and Oza's brother for drivers. They had reached the threshing floor of Chidon, when one of the oxen, frisking as it went, tilted the ark a little to one side, whereupon Oza put out his hand to steady it. This rashness of his in touching the ark provoked the Lord's anger; there, in the divine presence, the Lord smote him and he fell dead."

1 Paral. xiv. 6-11.

" When certain human passions are predicated of the Godhead metaphorically, this is done because of a likeness in the effect . . . hence a thing that is in us a sign of some passion is signified metaphorically in God under the name of that passion."

Summa Theologica, 1, q. xix, a. 11.

" And behold one of the ancients said to me; Weep not; behold the lion of the tribe of Juda . . . And I saw . . . a lamb standing, as it were slain."

Apoc. v. 5-6

The Christian life consists in learning how to love. Perfect love casts out fear; so that the nearer we get to being truly Christian, the nearer we get to being without fear. So that learning how to love obviously implies learning how to be unafraid. Yet the Christian life does also mean learning how to fear, in another sense of that word. And since one love implies a twofold relationship to fear, it's very important to become clear as to which sort of fear is which. For if one works hard to foster the sort of fear which is incompatible with love, and to get rid of the kind which is part of it, then learning how to love is made a good deal harder than it need be.

Broadly speaking, we have to get rid of fear on the psychological plane and learn how to fear properly on the metaphysical plane.

Take psychological fear first. Psychological fear is, at root, caused by sin—though it by no means follows from this that a man crushed by psychological fear of God is a wicked man. In order to see how psychological fear of God arises, and why it is incompatible with love of God, we must look at sin from the psychological viewpoint. What are the psychological mechanisms of sin and of its effects?

To give an answer to that question we have to go, for a moment, below psychology into theology; for psychology does not set out to answer such questions as " What is sin? " any more than biology sets out to answer questions like " What is a repression? " Moral theology tells us that sin is a rejection of God; just that. It's worth while pausing to let the fact sink in, for many people find it very hard to think of sin in any terms other than those of the police-court. But if sin is to make any sense to us as an idea—as we shall see, sin does not *in itself* make sense at all—the picture we must associate it with is not ultimately that of the policeman and the dock but that of the jilted lover; sin is a refusal of love and a refusal to love. It is transgression of law, certainly; but it is that only in the second place; basically, it is refusal of love and must be firmly grasped as such before the transgression-of-law aspect can make any sense to us.

Outside the mental order, love necessarily means a person loving, so that the refusal of love is, in practice, the refusal of a lover. In this case the lover is God. And here we must make a digression if our thinking is to stay married to reality. For it cannot be denied that, as far as England at any rate is concerned, the effect of the spiritual history of the last few centuries has been to drain most of the *mana* out of the phrase " the love of God ". One thinks of it as painted on peeling notice-boards outside disused chapels; it tends to bring with it a train of associations with everything that is unpleasant—disagreeable duties done in a smother of suppressed resentment, and all the hundred and one gloomy experiences which are summed up in the *cri du coeur* " O God make the bad people good and the good people pleasant." If one sees sin as a refusal of love conceived in such uninviting terms as these then one is not, in honesty, going to see it as any very great tragedy. And under the circumstances that is scarcely surprising.

It is therefore worthwhile to use as a stepping-off point for one's thinking about divine love the experience of human love—the sort of thing that happens, for example, when you have been waiting for a few minutes at the appointed rendezvous and the figure you have been waiting for appears round the corner. That particular dress and no other; that particular way of walking and no other; those particular eyes, those particular lips, that unique leap of the heart in yourself. Hardly a dour sort of experience, and hardly a wishy-washy one of the kind which one doesn't mind going without. But the love of God differs from that not in being something other than that but in being that stepped up *ad infinitum*—to borrow the language of mathematics, " raised to the power of infinity ". Like love of a human person, love of a divine person is " the movement and rush of the heart which follows fondness and culminates in union ", to quote St. Francis de Sales. It is not a dreary altruism smelling faintly of disinfectant; it is every bit as much a passionate pull of desire toward a given concrete being as is the love of the bridal bed. And such a desire to possess the beloved implies all the paradoxes summed up in the saying that he who will save his life must lose it—conquest of the one loved is possible only through surrender to the one loved, possession of the beloved is possible only through self-giving to the beloved and so on into the bottomless mystery of the " death of love ".

Human love is certainly something which even the most un-religious will, in most cases, readily concede to be in every sense charged with life and joy and power—much cynicism on this score is in itself an inside-out tribute to the high opinion naturally held of love, for the experiences of the promiscuous are of lust rather than love, and their disillusionment a record of the difference between what was needed and what was received as a result of this disastrous confusion. But when we use human love as a jumping-off point for thinking about divine love we have to remember that contact with God does not mean becoming airborne so much as going so deep into matter that we get past its very roots to an order of being more concrete than matter itself. Our very materiality and sexuality are not things opposed to our spirituality; God being the prototype of all that is, which is at all only insofar as it is like Him, our materiality and sexuality—which are essential elements in human love—are stamped with God's image just like everything else. The transcending of materiality and sexuality which we find in God does not mean that, in divine love, the concreteness and immediacy which change the very heartbeat in human lovers are replaced by something thinned-out and ghostly, like the life that goes on in the mind. If human love is fine scarlet, divine love is not a washed-out and genteel " ethereal " pink, but the colour of flame. And again, we have to remember that when we say that everything in human love is present in divine love in its concentrated essence—i.e. that the only " aspects of human love " which aren't there are precisely those things which make the difference between love and lust—it is important to remember how far contemporary muddled thinking has succeeded in confusing passion with greed and mere animalism— perhaps in revenge against the " angelism " which is the devil's stock trap for the man who wants purity. Greed and animalism are no more part of love at its physical level than they are part of it at its spiritual level; they are the cancer of love. The defence of purity obliges no-one to the lie that lust is not an intense experience. But love is an experience of greater intensity in the same order; it is chastity which puts the fine edge of delectation on legitimate sexual pleasure, and this not by reason of a sort of super-lasciviousness hidden in the very heart of purity, but because lasciviousness is a caricature of purity's sensitivity of palate.[1]

It is therefore no mere figure of speech to say that just as everything which makes for human love, as opposed to lust, makes for greater intensity of experience in those very regions which are lust's concern, so also everything which makes divine love what it is surpasses at their own game the most intense experiences of human love. Since spirit is being more concrete than matter itself, love of the supreme Spirit, who alone of Himself is, is supreme among experiences in density of being; more concrete, more intense a fulfilment of man, body and soul, than was ever dreamed of by the most frenzied pervert who ever racked human nature in the attempt to extort from it a satisfaction of the completeness desired. The very pain which lies at the heart of the joy of human love—since the " other ", the beloved, always remains outside oneself in a sort of ultimate chastity—and is the dynamic of desire, is a symbol of the infinite degree by which God's love is intenser yet, both to Him the Giver and us the receivers. For the insatiability of the desire of finite beings to possess the beloved, and to give themselves to the beloved, is the measure of their limited capacity as lovers; but there is no limit to God's capacity as Lover.

When by means of some such meditation as this we have replaced some—at any rate—of the proper mental stuffing of the phrase " the love of God ", it begins to be easier to see why refusal of this love is not an academic affair, the breaking of an arbitrary set of rules, the keeping of which will be rewarded by a very rarified sort of pie in a very far-off sky. Sin is not a question of getting ourselves in wrong with a particularly crusty celestial magistrate; it is a question of locking ourselves out of our bridal chamber. For just as the forces of human desire are resolved only in union with the human beloved, so the forces of divine desire are only resolved in our eternal union—glorified body and redeemed soul—with God in the beatific vision. From the Song of Songs onward through all the writings of the mystics, the truth of the matter is not that marriage is a rather *risqué* symbol for the union of man with his God, but that the ultimate union of Creator with creature—creature possessing Creator, creature surrendered to Creator —is the archetype of marriage.

That union is what we are made for. And this fact—that sin is frustration, a frustration far more profound than the " sexual frus-

---

[1] Cf. *Summa Theologica*, I, q. xcviii, a. 2, ad. 3: "In the state of innocence . . . sensible delight [would] have been the greater in proportion to the greater purity of nature and the greater sensibility of the body. "

tration" of vulgarized materialistic psychology—brings us up from the depths of theology to the less profound level of psychology. By sin, we starve ourselves of something which we really desire at a level deeper than even that of instinct. It is the psychological mechanism of that process of self-frustration, and of its effects, that we must grasp if we are to understand the nature of psychological fear of God and see why it is, unlike metaphysical fear, incompatible with love of Him.

The key lies in the fact that what we are made for is what is natural to us, in the fundamental sense of that word. Union with God is what is natural to us, in the sense that it is what we are made for. True, we can't achieve it by our own natural powers. But the supernatural grace which we need in order to achieve it is no denial of nature or riding roughshod over it. It is a fulfilling and perfecting of nature. We are made for union with God for ever in the beatific vision as surely as a razor is made for shaving; and the first thing to grasp about the psychological mechanism of sin is that it is an infinitely greater violence to nature than using a razor to cut linoleum.

That seems, on the face of it, a flat contradiction of experience. Most of us find sin no trouble at all, and often very pleasant indeed. Living in luxury on the money you swindled out of the shareholders is pleasant; solitary vice is the line of least resistance; hating is easy, bullying feeds you fat, glutting spite and lust and *Schadenfreude* and greed for power can make you feel fine; fornication goes admirably with a summer night and anger is as intoxicating as the smell of blood. Far from being any violence done to ourselves, evil seems to consist in " doing what comes nat'rally ".

Indeed evil does " come naturally "—to human nature as we know it, damaged by original sin. But this state is not its natural state. Exactly insofar as it is eaten into by original sin human nature is denatured, robbed of its " humannatureness ". When we come across evil in the physical order—disease—we say, significantly, that the sufferer is " not quite himself ". The phrase can be applied to evil in the spiritual order with even greater significance. A man suffering from the self-induced sickness of sin is spiritually " not quite himself "; and inasmuch as he is not quite himself spiritually, so far sin will be " natural " to him: inasmuch as he is his true self—good and not evil—evil will be a violence done to himself. We are spiritually atrophied to the degree to which we are evil; and that which is atrophied is no longer sensitive; which is why most of us are largely unaware of the unnaturalness of sin, and in consequence of the horror of it. The saints, being largely free from this atrophy, react to sin as we would to a red-hot iron; their tremendous compassion is rooted in a horror at sin greater than any we would feel at the sight of the most ghastly disease. That is why their own estimates of their own sins often seem unrealistic to us and strike the sceptic as either morbid or exhibitionistic. When we say " horror of sin " we so often mean " dread of sin's punishment " : but the saints mean " horror of sin "—which is why they say it.

We can see, then, why the contradiction between our knowledge of sin as violence done to nature, and our experience of sin as the easiest thing imaginable, is a contradiction in appearance only, the removal of which is effected by distinguishing the different senses of the word " natural ". This elucidation clears the way to a further and subtler puzzle: how do we manage to do it? The fact that we manage it very easily does not make the action of sin any less extraordinary *in itself*. For sin demands knowledge and consent; the fact that we have powerful instruments available for breaking the control of reason and will does not alter the fact that, if the conditions of sin are to be fulfilled, the violation of will and reason must be known and chosen. Sin implies responsibility; and responsibility here implies a deliberate frustration of our deepest needs. And that must always remain *in itself* an extraordinary thing, however easily understandable it may be made in any actual instance by all or any of the circumstances which modify our responsibility for acts of their own nature evil. I say, *in itself;* the words sum up the unavoidable method of an enquiry such as this. In order to grasp firmly the effects of sin existential—the individual sins that we commit—we have to squeeze out of it sin essential, " pure sin ", with all that impairs its sinfulness strained away. We have to strain away " material " sin—act evil in itself for which, none the less, we are not fully responsible through lack of knowledge or lack of freedom in choice. We have to strain away venial sin—act which is only triflingly evil, although we are fully responsible for it. That leaves us with mortal sin—act gravely evil in itself, for which moreover we are fully responsible, since we are fully aware of its serious wrongness, and freely choose to do it. In mortal sin are visible, clearly magnified, all the elements which are present to some degree, however small, in the most trifling of venial sins. In mortal sin the self-destructive nature of sin becomes quite clear, and the question posed above repeats itself with sharper insistency: How do we manage it? However overpowering the temptation, there must nevertheless, for mortal sin, be an instant in which we freely and knowingly do the act of self-destruction it urges; and in that instant lies the secret of sin's destructiveness.

What we do is to induce in ourselves what we must call, in inverted commas, " madness "; a kind of momentary madness in which we " see " things as they are not. In that state the self-destructive activity of sin becomes possible to us. We shall see in a moment how this sinister conjuring trick is performed; *why* we should want to perform it is a question which, when followed right down to its root, even theology cannot answer. There is no reason, ultimately, why a man should choose self-destruction as such; you do not begin to understand sin until you have grasped that, basically, sin does not make sense. If a real reason could be given why a man should sin, then sin would not be itself; for it is, precisely, irrational; the false " mystery " which cannot be fathomed because there is nothing there to fathom, put up by the ape of God to try and bluff us away from the real mystery, which can never be fathomed because there is no seabed. How then, is the state of " madness " induced? Psychologically speaking, the process may be described as one of self-hallucination. If we are to choose any particular thing, we must see it as good; for our wills, which are what we do our choosing with, can get no purchase on any evil seen as such. And if we are to " see " any evil thing as good, we must in some sense choose to do so; for of itself our intellect can't get any purchase on anything but what is actually there; and what is actually there is only actually there insofar as it is good, for evil is privation of being. Thus in the act of sin intellect and will, which are intrinsically incapable of being deceived, are each clashed with the other in order to produce an apparent deception by both. And if it be objected that this is an impossible situation, the answer is " Precisely ". If any account could be given of sin which made sin really intelligible, it would not have been sin that one was talking about. You have to abuse language to talk about sin, just as you have to abuse being in order to sin. The impossible is attempted when you crash the gears of a car; but you can crash them for all that, and go on crashing them.

Thus the sinner hauls himself out of reality by his own bootlaces, so to speak. And the nonsensical pattern of the vicious circle follows all the way through the analysis of sin. We know that, because God loves us, what He wills for us is our good—not in the sense of the dire childhood phrase " It's for your own good " when the " good " was some peculiarly unpleasant thing resentfully submitted to through fear of punishment—but in the adult sense of the term, as the one loved is the good of the lover. When we sin, we do something which is not what God wills for us. And as we have seen, the will must be provided with a good as its object if we are to be able to operate it at all. So, we have to induce in ourselves the hallucination that what God does not will for us is our good. And this involves an implication which is crucial from the psychological viewpoint. For to choose is, in the strict sense of the word, to make a distinction between good and evil. If what we do not will to another is his good, then what we do will to him is his evil; there is no third alternative. At rock bottom the only possible relationship of one rational being to another is one of either love or hostility. " Indifference " is the label we use to cover the fact that both of these can be potential as well as actual—put six strangers on a raft in mid-Atlantic and see what happens as provisions run lower. So, to not-will to another what is his good, is to will him his evil. And if—as the sinner has to persuade himself—God not-wills our good, then God wills our evil. He is a hostile " God ". To sin, we have to hallucinate a hostile " God " to cover the real loving God from us; and it is in the unreal world sustained in being by the unreal " God " that we choose the unreal good. And here again we encounter the pattern of the vicious circle, the impossible situation. The process of hallucinating the unreal " God " can only follow from a desire to do what is not God's will—as we have seen. But insofar as you desire to do what is not God's will you do not love Him; and insofar as you do not love Him, you must, ultimately, be hostile to him: " He that is not with me is against me ". So that the act of hallucinating a hostile " God" presupposes hostility to God in the first place; and that hostility to God presupposes a hostile " God " since, as we have seen, we cannot reject with our wills something which we see as good . . .

Thus the hostile " God " is the cause of hostility to God; and hostility to God is the cause of the hostile " God ". This is the vicious circle of sin—a vertigo that has to be kept effective by a continued effort against nature and reason. In order to sin you have to do at the metaphysical level what you do at the logical level when you assume your conclusion to prove your premises—choose nonsense.

So much for the psychological mechanism of sin. It explains nothing because there is nothing explainable. The psychological mechanism of its effects follows the same pattern of the vicious circle. And if the picture seems to be too hopeless, it should be remembered that a psychological account of sin must of necessity leave out the redeeming feature of the situation—the divine grace which harrows through the walls of hell; for once we have sinned we are indeed, *psychologically* speaking, " y-bounden in a bond "—impotent to put right the harm we have done ourselves; though we do retain the power to defy our own self-induced hallucinations and call upon the outside power which can break through into our private worlds of unreality. And it is precisely in this matter of calling for help that an understanding of the psychological effect of sin can help us greatly in co-operating with God; which is why it is worth making an analysis that does not deal with the rôle of grace.

The act of self-hallucination which is at once cause and effect of the hostile " God " is, like other acts, habit-forming. There is of course no reason why a man who has sinned should not, by the grace of God, repent so completely as to make a complete about-turn from the nothingness he chose back to the God he rejected by choosing it; thus completely banishing to its proper nonentity the hostile-God mirage which he called up to mask the real God so that the act of turning away should be possible. But experience, both of ourselves and others, shows that this complete co-operation with the grace of God is, in an enormous number of cases, not achieved. Although the guilt of our sin is forgiven—that is, although things are put right on the spiritual level—the psychological effects of it remain, to a greater or lesser extent; so that things are not completely right at the psychological level, and some traces at least of the hostile-God mirage hover in front of the face of the true God to whom we return.

The deeper the roots of the habit of sin—psychologically, not, necessarily, spiritually—the greater the proportion of the hallucination which tends to remain and the harder it is to distinguish from the reality on which it is superimposed. We are again involved in the vicious circle. In order to sin, one has made an appearance do duty for reality; when one comes to repent, one finds that to a greater or lesser extent one *seems* to be asking it not of the reality but of the appearance. One believes in the loving God and not in the hostile " God "; but because of the wisps of hallucination which still linger before His face, the belief in the loving God is to some extent ineffective—" notional "—and the belief in the hostile " God " effective—" real ". We have so much experience ourselves of reacting to offences against ourselves with fear, anger and vindictiveness, and so little experience of reacting to them with understanding and forgiveness, that the hostile reaction does in any case always tend to be far more real to us than the loving one. Most people have had, not once but many times, the experience of asking forgiveness of a " God " who says something like this:

" Ah. So you're back. Thought as much. Got the wind up, eh? Well you may have, too. I shall have to forgive you of course, much as I should like to pitch you into hell. I can tell you that I find this forgiving business every bit as much of a strain as you do, if not more. You think it costs you a lot of effort to be charitable—you should just see the effort it costs me. When you carry on like you've been doing recently I sit up here with the veins standing out on my temples like cords—at this very moment I am only managing to hold myself back from giving you hell by a supreme effort of self-control which I won't guarantee to keep up *ad infinitum*. The last straw breaks the camel's back, you know, as you've so often said yourself. So from now on, watch out. You can't say I haven't made perfectly clear what is required of you—and don't go snivelling and making excuses and saying it's very hard—nonsense. You just aren't trying. I can tell you, you won't get much help from me unless you make a lot more effort than this—you don't think I am going to go on helping people who keep on letting me down, do you? And of course you won't be *able* to make the effort without my help—which you won't get unless you deserve it—so what with one thing and another you had better be on your toes from now on, hadn't you? You can take it from me that I shan't put myself in the wrong by being unjust to you. But it will be very easy for me to hurl you into hell with perfect justice, and from now on, in order to recompense myself for the present frustration of my fury against you, I shall be watching you like a hawk for the first chance to do it. So thank God—that's me—for getting away with it this time, and heaven help you if you come up here again on the same charge. And in case you don't know, this is me being very very fond of you."

Put like that, explicitly, it is obviously fantastic; no one would claim that that was the God of Christianity as Christianity teaches Him to be. Yet very many people have a picture of that type hovering at the back of their minds when there is question of asking God's forgiveness, even for quite small sins. " At the back of the mind "—that is the point. The hostile " God " has to be implicit. A hostile " God " is a contradiction in terms; ultimately, you cannot go on conceiving him. But an implicit hostile " God" manages to preserve at once his contradictions and his place in the mind by keeping those contradictions out of the way of direct awareness—that is why the process of self-hallucination is in the great majority of cases conducted implicitly; the act of sin necessarily involves, among other things, a refusal to follow one's own thought to its logical conclusion. This helps to account, incidentally, for the difference noted earlier between sin existential—sin as we encounter it in the concrete instance—and sin essential—sin as we encounter it in the laboratory conditions of intellectual analysis. Much of what becomes clear-cut in such an analysis is always, in the concrete instance, confused, anguished and obscure; but it does not follow from this that the analysis is in any way inhuman or unrealistic. A housewife buying her groceries does not formulate in a chain of conscious syllogisms the reasoning which leads her to refuse small hard green apples; yet this does not mean that she is not using the mental processes which are analysed for us in the textbooks of logic. And if one is to handle sin existential, in oneself or in others, with the compassion and delicacy of touch which charity demands, this can only be in virtue of a firm grasp of sin essential. A deeply human casuistry demands the sharpest black-and-white distinction between good and evil, counterbalanced by an equally sharp awareness of the power and complexity of the forces against which man has to struggle in his attempts to live according to that distinction.

As we have seen, the habit-forming properties of sin's act of self-hallucination tend to leave us, at the psychological level at least, confronted with a confusing mixture of real God and hallucination God. In consequence of this our reactions to God become confused and self-contradictory. For insofar as we are honest with ourselves we hate the hostile " God ", the monstrous caricature which I have just depicted. And we are right to do so; it is the only sense in which the word " hate " can have a Christian meaning—that of *horror vacui*, the healthy recoil from what is not, from the false abyss of the nonsensical. Our hostile " God " is a diabolical caricature and we are quite right to reject him. But because this caricature " God " is, as far as we are concerned, more or less mixed up with the real God, our healthy rebellion against the diabolical domination of unreality often seems to us to be a rebellion against the real God. And since we are totally dependent on the real God for everything—our very existence, let alone the necessary help against the unpredictable turns of life—we dare not admit to ourselves—save in rare Job-like moments of terrifying honesty—the hatred and resentment which we harbour within us. So we nervously reassure ourselves that we love God at the very moment when there is, in the depths of our being, an apparent intense hatred of Him; and thus our very idea of love becomes poisoned. For when we hallucinate the hostile " God " we are already projecting onto God—that is, disowning—a hostility which is actually in ourselves; as we have seen. The more hatred and hostility we have in our own depths, the more there is to be attributed to the hostile " God "; and the more there is to project thus onto God, the more hostile a " God " He can become; and the more of a hostile " God " He can become, the more the hatred and hostility He can arouse in us for yet further disowning and projection. Again, the pattern is that of the vicious circle, the diabolical aping of the charmed circle of love.

If this were all there was to be said about the mechanism of sin and of its effects the resultant picture would be a very mixed blessing to most sufferers from psychological fear of God. For if the hostile " God " is the by-product of our sins, then surely the more hostile the " God " that terrifies us, the more desperately sinful we must have been?

One answer to this is that even if our worst fears are true on this score—and we should be slow to presume that they are, however terrifying our feelings—it does not alter the fact that the monster " God " is not true; the whole point of the analysis is not to convince ourselves that we are not evil, but to convince ourselves that God is good, in the tenderest and most human sense of that word, so that in the light of this love we may be able to face the evil that is in us, whether it be more or less than we fear. Yet this does not cover a fact of which every confessor has experience—that many people who go in terror of God and struggle hopelessly to fulfil the remorseless demands of the most pitiless celestial slave-driver, are in point of fact not worse than far happier men; on the contrary, they are often people who do try hard to live a good life. Frequently they are the victims of failures in charity which, at an age when they were, psychologically speaking, quite defenceless, branded them with needless terrors which many years of adult life have not succeeded in obliterating. These people suffer at the hands of the angry " God " all right; yet how can their fear-distorted caricature of reality be due to sin?

The answer carries us from the consideration of psychological fear to that of metaphysical fear. Even though the life of a fear-ridden man be near to blameless, it still remains true that fear and its reverse side of hatred are the consequence of sin: but in such a case, original sin as opposed to actual sin; original sin actualized not so much in the man who fears as in those who stamped upon him, either directly or indirectly, either intentionally or (as is far more often the case) unintentionally, their own fear and their own hatred. The statement that the sins of the fathers shall be visited on the children is not one of gloating vindictiveness, but the statement of a tragic fact; its ultimate context is that of Christ's tears over Jerusalem.

We have considered in some detail the individual act of sin. It is organically related, as part is to whole, to the archetypal sin which is the original sin of Adam; actual sin is original sin actualized. Adam's archetypal sin, thus manifested in our actual sins at the level of the individual, is manifested at the level of sacred history in the story of man from the Fall to the Incarnation. The story of Adam, the story of pre-incarnation man, the story of each individual man—these are neither just parallels as an allegory is a parallel; nor one and the same thing; they are an organic unity. The relation between the three is not unlike that between the redeeming self-sacrifice of the Son, the historic event of Calvary, and the celebration of Mass. Our self-exile from the paradise of our baptismal innocence into the unreal world of sin is the perpetuation through time of the archetypal self-exile of Adam from the Garden of Paradise. For Adam may be said to have a threefold reality; as the archetypal man, as a given historical individual, and as humanity.

Now, as we have seen, a given fear-ridden individual may well be in the eyes of God a comparatively innocent man, though his own suffering lies largely in the very fact that he cannot believe it; his fear, and the hostility which is its other side, may be an off-print of the fear and hostility of others. But they in their turn may well be also all but blameless in the eyes of God, having suffered similarly at the hands of others; and so back and back till we come to the only man to commit a sin outside the framework of original sin—that is, with an undamaged human nature. The man is Adam and the sin his original sin of disobedience. In that sin alone—as far as human beings are concerned—sin existential and sin essential are one. All the factors which can enter to modify responsibility in actual sin—the weakening effects of original sin itself, the influence of others, ignorance, confusion, fear, strain, sickness mental and physical, environment and a thousand other things—did not, and could not, enter to modify Adam's responsibility for his archetypal sin. The act of self-hallucination which we have isolated as the essence of actual sin was, in Adam's case, performed in " laboratory conditions "; in it knowledge was full and consent free to a degree which the more vulnerable intellect and will of fallen human nature can never equal. It was pure self-hallucination, pure hostility to God; all our sins are closer or remoter approximations to it. And as such it is the source, under the devil, of all human fear and hostility, whatever also may be our personal responsibilities.

We have seen that as far as man's own psychological condition is concerned, the after-effects of sin lie in the fact that he has to make his way back to God through the hostile image which he called up in order to be able to turn away. So much for the individual level; the Old Testament—" the pedagogue to Christ "—shows us the same thing happening on the historical level. The warped mentality of post-Fall pre-Incarnation man provides the crooked conceptual lines with which God has to write straight. Sin had put between God and man (to vary the metaphor) a false abyss of unreality—the devil's ape of the real abyss that divides Creator from creature. If God was not to violate the human freewill which had put it there—and He would have done so if He had closed the gap by forcing us to be good—the only alternative was to leap it, as an electric charge leaps from positive to negative pole. The bigger the gap between the points, the bigger the charge needed to leap it; and so it was here. If God was to arrive among men while respecting the conditions men had set up, He had to arrive with all the shock of that tremendous impetus behind Him, as a lightning stroke of naked *mysterium tremendum*: similarly, in the fullness of time, He had to submit to the helplessness of childhood if He was to arrive among us as incarnate *mysterium fascinans*. " No man can look upon God and live ": that holds from the moment Adam hid among the trees to the moment when human eyes first looked upon the newborn Christ; all the elaborate ritual of the Old Law is a sort of safety drill to insulate men against the unbearable power of the Divinity that must, for a time, come like a thunderclap. The nearer men come to God, the smaller the false abyss and the smaller the momentum needed to carry across it: hence the gradual emergence of the God who will have mercy and not sacrifice in and through the God who speaks in thunder from Sinai, and strikes dead, like a high voltage current, the man that merely touches His dwelling-place. The Lamb is revealed in the Lion, but the Lion remains in the Lamb; only those who are strong can dare to be gentle, and the supreme tenderness of God is possible only because He has absolute power over us—there is, ultimately, no avoiding the absoluteness of God's rule, which violates our pride beyond the last reaches of humiliation. There is, at bottom, only one thing which God reveals to man—God. He only becomes Someone who is many distinct things—just *and* merciful *and* loving *and* powerful and so on—when He passes through the composing-and-dividing filter of the human mind. This mode-ification of the Being who is beyond all modes of being " modifies " God without falsifying Him—providing we realize that human knowledge of God (apart, it may be, from the special case of certain mystical experiences) does " modify " Him, and that knowledge of God without modification belongs to God alone. Quite apart from sin, the very nature of our created intelligence makes it inevitable that we should see as distinct the justice and the mercy which that very seeing shows us to be one; but the additional fact of sin means that we bang ourselves and the world against the irresistible love of God and, in view of the psychological distortions we have considered, interpret the experience as God's banging us. The Old Testament tells an archetypal story manifested at the individual level in every period that lies between a sin committed and forgiveness received: if we are to understand its violence, and the relation of its " God of Wrath " to the *mysterium tremendum*, we must turn our minds toward the function of purgatory. The blaze of the heavenly glory, which is ecstasy to those freed from the cancer of sin, would be agony to those not so purified if—*per impossibile*—they were able to be present therein. Indeed, the love of God is, precisely, what torments the damned; damnation is, by definition, so acting that you turn God's love into a torment, as a suspicious husband turns the love shown toward him by a faithful wife. In purgatory the love of God is experienced as pain, because it is destroying what stands between God and us. The Old Testament period, either of mankind as a whole or of any individual life, is a purgatorial period during which a " totalitarian " love ruthlessly burns away, by degrees, the inadequacies through which it has to come to us. The cauterizing process is ruthless, not only in what it has to do to us, but in the way in which it bends evil itself to its own purposes: it is through the slaying, threatening, revenging God of the Old Testament, as through the monstrous caricatures of our own guilt and fear, that the God of total love makes His way, and must make His way if He is not to do us the real violence of overriding our freewill. In God Himself God is His love, God is His justice, God is His mercy: so that His love is His justice and His justice His mercy. The *mysterium tremendum* and the *mysterium fascinans* are one and the same; the Old Law mentality faithfully transmits Him so, but the man with the Old Law mentality speaks truer than he realizes, and it is only in the light of the New Law, which fulfils the Old without destroying it, that we can at last understand how the apparent violence of the *mysterium tremendum* is not our hostile violence of weakness, but the insatiable possessiveness of omnipotent love. Just as God's creatorhood dwarfs our creatureliness beyond the ultimate degree of humiliation, so His absolute power over us, which can in the last analysis be neither withstood nor frustrated, is a mastery of which defeat by violence is a pale caricature. The terror of Sinai is the ecstatic panic of the beloved overwhelmed by the Lover; the cry " It is a fearful thing to fall into the hand of the living God " is that of the lover lost in the embrace of the Beloved. The Holy Ghost, love personified, was manifest at Pentecost in the beauty and terror of fire.

It is a standing temptation, to confuse the undefeatableness of total love with the vicious vindictiveness of man's projected malice—to confuse negative psychological fear with positive metaphysical fear. Metaphysical fear is part of love, the astringency which prevents it from becoming sickly-sweet. We are quite right to get a feeling in the pit of the stomach when we look over the edge of God's hand, which alone sustains us in being, into the abyss of nothingness above which it sustains us; otherwise how can we ever sense the tenderness with which that hand encloses us? We are right to go dry in the mouth at the approach of the divine Lover/Beloved since, just as the sharpness of the delight of the union of human lovers is born out of the pain of their separateness, so the ecstasy of union between creature and Creator is born from the agony of full experience of the nothingness in virtue of which we are created, not self-existent, beings. Without the panic-striking awareness of our own helplessness, the God of the moral theology manuals must remain a mere merciless drawer-up of rules: for the illusion of our own self-sufficiency will at once compel us to

attempt the impossible, and to picture God as in justice keeping
merciless tally of our failures. Metaphysical fear is the root of the
wisdom of love; with it, Lion and Lamb become one. " It is because
He is just that He is ' compassionate, and merciful, long-suffering and
plenteous in mercy. For He knoweth our frame, He remembereth
that we are dust. As a father hath compassion on his children, so hath
the Lord compassion on them that fear Him'."

LOVE AND VIOLENCE IN THE APOCALYPSE

George Lamb

THE Apocalypse of St. John the Apostle, it is probably true to say, is not very much read these days—if indeed it ever was; and when you do come to read it, you find it fairly easy to understand why. The difficulty concerns communication. The Apocalypse is made up of a vision, or rather two visions; but of what? Of eternity? Of the temporal future? Of both? At one time it was widely believed to describe the end of the world, which was to occur after a thousand years of Christianity. St. John himself says that it concerns " the things which must shortly come to pass ". But how long is " shortly "? Already we are near the end of the second millennium; and the earth is being transformed so rapidly that no great effort of the imagination is needed to foresee that the apocalyptic mentality of nearly a thousand years ago could easily be revived as the twentieth century nears its end. Even today, the signs are not lacking: only a truly heroic faith can conquer the general unease, the secret disease, the malaise of our civilisation.

Nevertheless, a thousand years is a long time; two thousand years is twice as long; and though we may feel that St. John's " shortly " " speaks to our condition ", we know from our history that this is an illusion—temporally speaking—a mere accident of words. If we were to say, even, that St. John shared a sense of impending misfortune common to all who believe and long for the coming of the kingdom, we should be on dangerous ground; for the inference might be that the Apostle, like those who lived nearly a thousand years after him, like those sectarian Christians of today who can give you chapter and verse for the date of the end of the world, was historically and prophetically in error. And dare one say that? Indeed a merely superficial reading of his Revelation is sufficient to make one thing startlingly clear, and that is that the inspired author is not in the first place concerned with time and temporal events in themselves. He is caught up in ecstasy; he witnesses things never before or since revealed to man; and if he sees in St. Paul's dark glass and not face to face, it is nevertheless in as highly polished a glass as has ever been granted a man in which to see the reflection of divine truth.

In that highly polished glass St. John saw strange sights. " Strange " is a weak word to describe all those creatures and catastrophes: the beasts covered with eyes, the dragon that swishes its tail and a third of the stars of the firmament disappear, the darkening of the sun and moon, the blood, the hail . . . The list could be extended indefinitely, to infinity almost; very nearly, to eternity. Nevertheless there is something strange about it all: there is this major difficulty of communication —to know exactly (or even vaguely) what is being communicated. A great deal has been written recently about the need for universal myths, for a generally accepted pattern that can be used as a medium for the expression of symbolic truth. But the difficulty in St. John is of a different order. When poets and philosophers lament the lack of a valid system of communication, they mean that they find it difficult to convey to others what they themselves have discovered: they find themselves obliged to hunt for metaphors, symbols, myths, that will somehow " make contact ". It is a difficulty of expression. There was no such difficulty for St. John. For St. John simply wrote down what he saw, as he was told to do. It was not a man-made truth or a man-made vision that he attempted to convey, but something God-given, a Revelation. That is to say, it was not a matter of imagination, but of inspiration, and as such it had power, it was dogmatic: " If any man shall add to these things, God shall add unto him the plagues written in this book. And if any man shall take away . . ." Not even Blake could write like that: it is either madness, or the word of God.

Therefore, when we come to read the Apocalypse, we have to accept it in much the same way as we accept any of the Christian mysteries. We cannot, strictly speaking, interpret it; all we can do is to attempt to comprehend, to some extent or other, its relationships—relationships, because the book as a whole gives the impression of a network of communication between spiritual realities with their own consistency, their own harmony, their own unity. But this system is not ours. We cannot say *this* means *this*, and go on to deduce something further: we should probably be wrong if we did. The Apocalypse is as " objective " as any piece of writing could be: it is its own pure diamond, and we have to look at it and attempt to see it for what it is.

Since, however, it is a vision of spiritual reality, and since we are spiritual as well as material beings, there is another method of at least partly comprehending it, and that is the method of analogy. It would be a mistake to consider the various wonderful and fearful creatures who appear in the Apocalypse as being, in the ordinary meaning of the word, allegorical. An allegory attempts to convey abstract truth by means of personified counters. It is a device, a mental construct. St. John saw, not personifications of abstract truth, but the movement of a living spiritual reality: hence its strangeness. But spiritual truth is reflected, so to speak, even though in an obscure form, in our world of matter, in the world of materialized forms, in history. Analogically, we are justified in transposing his vision on to our own level—or, rather (but this is more difficult), in seeing our own diurnal reality in the light of his vision. Whichever method we attempt to adopt, we have justification for it in the great truth that grace perfects nature, that the created world reveals some of the attributes of its Creator, that the world of history can teach lessons which are not utterly value-less, not entirely misleading, as pointers to eternity. The problem of what exactly is being prophesied in the Apocalypse has not been satisfactorily solved; this does not mean that we shall be mistaken if we attempt to see in it some relevance to our human history.

Furthermore, the Apocalypse is one of the books of the Canon, and as such exists for one purpose only: to bind the soul to God. How can it help to do this? There is one obvious though quite subsidiary way, and that is by means of those direct instructions which occur principally in the course of the first few chapters addressed to the seven Churches: words of encouragement, words of warning; exhorta-tions to patience, penance, steadfastness in works, faith, charity. " But because thou art lukewarm, and neither cold not hot ", the Laodiceans are admonished, " I will begin to vomit thee out of my mouth. Because thou sayest: I am rich and made wealthy, and have need of nothing; and knowest not that thou art wretched and miser-able and poor and blind and naked." " Such as I love," they are told a little later, " I rebuke and chastise. Be zealous therefore, and do penance."

But the primary purpose of the Apocalypse is the imparting of a vision, which is conveyed, and is meant to be received, with a sense of urgency: " The Revelation of Jesus Christ . . . to make known to his servants the things which must shortly come to pass "—such are its opening words. After the messages to the seven Churches, before the vision proper, " a door " is " opened in heaven ", and a voice says to St. John, " I will shew thee the things which must be done hereafter ". And at the very end occurs a phrase which has recurred before: " Surely I come quickly "; to which St. John replies: "Amen. Come, Lord Jesus."

In between, we have had visions of the most appalling catastrophes. It is true that the final vision is of " the holy city, the new Jerusalem coming down out of heaven from God, prepared as a bride adorned for her husband "; and that earlier there are moments of peace, of jubilation, " the voice of harpers harping on their harps ", adoration of God: "Amen. Benediction, and glory, and wisdom, and thanks-giving, honour and power, and strength to our God for ever and ever." But these are no more than momentary interludes between scenes of spiritual, material, world and universal disaster. The book with seven seals is opened: at the opening of the first seal a figure on a white horse appears and goes forth conquering. This crowned Rider is Christ; but He is immediately followed, at the opening of the second, third and fourth seals, by other riders, and these are War, Famine, and Death. The opening of the fifth seal reveals " under the altar " " the souls of them that were slain for the word of God "; with the opening of the sixth comes a great earthquake; the seventh brings the seven Trumpeters, with their hail, fire, blood, darkness, and—with the fifth blast—the opening of the bottomless pit; " and the smoke of the pit arose, as the smoke of a great furnace "—and out come locusts, like scorpions: "And in those days men shall seek death and shall not find it ". The sixth angel blows his trumpet and four angels are loosed, " to kill the third part of men ". There is an army of horse-men, " twenty thousand times ten thousand "; the heads of the horses are as the heads of lions; those that sit on them have breast-plates " of fire and of hyacinth and of brimstone "; the horses' tails " are like to serpents, and have heads; and with them they hurt ". Before the seventh trumpet is blown, there has been another war, bodies left lying in streets, an earthquake, in which " the tenth part of the city fell "—seven thousand men are slain, and the rest are " cast into a fear ". " The second woe is past ", we read; and are prepared to utter a sigh of relief. But we find we have been premature, for the sentence has not ended. "And behold," it goes on, " the third woe will come quickly."

And of course it does. The seventh trumpet is blown. A woman clothed with the sun appears, then a great red dragon, who fights against the woman, then Michael and his angels, who fight against the dragon. Beasts appear, one coming up out of the sea, another out of the earth. The vineyard of the earth is reaped, and cast into the great press of the wrath of God; " and blood came out of the press, up to the horses' bridles for a thousand and six hundred furlongs ". There follow the seven last plagues, which issue from " the seven vials of the wrath of God "—we can guess their characteristics: earthquakes, blood, hail, falling stars, darkening of the sun and the moon . . . And finally comes the greatest disaster of all: " Babylon the great is fallen, is fallen "—Babylon, the great harlot, the woman seated (like Rome) on seven hills. Then Satan is bound and cast into the bottomless pit for a thousand years. Finally, the holy city descends from heaven; there is a new heaven and a new earth, a river of life flows through the city, and beside the river the tree of life: " and the leaves of the tree were for the healing of the nations ".

This whole vision lasts, in simple numerical terms, for thirty-four pages. The disasters occur, almost without intermission, for thirty of those pages; in terms of chapters, seventeen out of the nineteen are concerned with violence. In any consideration of the Apocalypse as a vision concerned essentially with Love and Violence, this is the proportion to keep in mind.

Ultimately love triumphs: the dragon, the beasts, all sinners, are defeated. Their torment goes on for ever, but they are impotent against love, against the Lamb, against the patience and faith of the saints. But this is " ultimately ", and we in our daily lives are rarely concerned with ultimates, except in the veiled form in which they reach us through the endless conflict of relatives—conditioned goods, greater or lesser evils. Down into this conditioned world of conflict, violence, disaster, the martyrdom of saints, comes ultimately the holy city, Jerusalem. Meanwhile we must reconcile ourselves to violence. There is very little encouragement to be drawn from the Revelation of St. John by those who hanker after peace on earth and think that in some way this is a necessary result of the Incarnation and Redemption and the establishment of the Catholic Church. We are subject, historically, to the reign of violence: Satan was to be bound for a thousand years, and then loosed for " a little time ", to " seduce the nations ". How long, we asked, was " shortly "? And how long is " a little time "? From the Apocalypse the answer seems clear: the " little time " will last till the end of time —time which is itself little, a mere drop in the ocean, compared with eternity.

It is not surprising that outside the Catholic faith the Apocalypse became the particular field of interest of a minute minority of end-of-the-worlders during the nineteenth century. For except by an act of drastic foreshortening it can hardly be looked upon as an optimistic picture of world history. Non-Catholic Christianity at least was considerably affected by the spirit of that age, with the result that the end-of-the-worlders were spiritual and often social outcasts; but by casting them out and ignoring them the age was ignoring an essential element in Christianity, an element which we in the twentieth century find it less easy to ignore: the awful temporal interregnum of violence and degradation. Civilization advances, and by advancing declines. A sex, a class, a race, a nation works for its emancipation, and in emancipating itself seems to tend to destroy its own essential nature. Were the suffragettes wise to make martyrs of themselves, to create conditions whereby young girls have the right and privilege to suffer equal boredom with their menfolk at factory benches or anywhere else rather than in the home? Has Western civilization worked wonders in Africa, India, China, from the point of view of the indigenous? Are the workers greatly benefited by exchanging the tyranny of a private owner for the

mass-tyranny of a trade union? We have succeeded in changing the
pattern of society, superficially; but the essential design remains—
turn the tapestry over and it looks just as it did a hundred years ago,
a thousand . . . just the same as it did when St. John wrote his
Apocalypse. The dragon Satan is still with us; and even his great
beasts, coming up out of the sea to the west or from the land to the east.
The souls of the saints are still hidden under the altar: only rarely does
one come noticeably within our sight—a Thomas More, a Bernadette,
a Thérèse of Lisieux. St. John's vision was a Revelation concerned
with spiritual realities—the victory of the good, the defeat of the wicked
—but it could be taken as a description, accurate even in its minute
particulars, of the past history of Europe, of present-day events, of—
we may safely say—the history of the future. We are promised every
kind of murderous violence; universal convulsions; suffering for the
godly—" Such as I love I rebuke and chastise "—suffering for the
ungodly—" Babylon the great is fallen, is fallen ", when all those
who live " in delicacies ", who imagine, like the Laodiceans, " I am
rich, and made wealthy, and have need of nothing ", discover to their
everlasting discomfiture that they are " wretched and miserable and
poor and blind and naked". Nothing could be more shocking to the
apostles of progress—if any still remain to be shocked—than this
vision of St. John's; nothing to be more quickly discarded, forgotten,
damned as pessimistic, in a forward-looking age.

But we no longer live in a forward-looking age. Our age, on the contrary, is one of universal homesickness, and those who are homesick look
backwards rather than forwards. We find sham Gothic more attractive
than our fathers did; we hold exhibitions of curios at which we
laugh, perhaps, but sympathetically. The great Victorians—how we
envy them! If we think of them as eminent, there is now no longer any
sting in that word. We envy them their solidity, their breadth, their
vastness, their great beards—so comfortable and warm as well as
prophetic. Compared with them we are not only pygmies, but there is,
as it were, no flesh on our bones. We are lean and scraggy, and worried
to death. And to us St. John speaks more directly: we may not be quite
so ready to admire his literary skill, his brilliant imagery, his poetic
quality, for we realise with a dreadful sinking feeling that he is not
indulging in any flights of fancy, any romantic hyperbole: he is not
describing from a safe distance—as, say, Macaulay could, or Gibbon—
terrible events in the remote past or an even remoter future. No;
he is talking about Now—his now and our now; the everlasting Now
of human history, with cities always rich and riotous, living " in
delicacies " like Rome and Babylon, Paris and New York; or falling,
falling, like Berlin, Vienna, London. " Unreal city ": to the poetic eye

the city we see may be unreal, to us immersed in its daily activity it is only too real—tremendous, wonderful, frightening as Babylon, whether in its temporary heyday or its permanent collapse: the city that seems all-powerful—elegant, the centre of civilization, Dr. Johnson's London—the monstrous city, the *megalopolis* that attracts and perverts and ruins the sensitive and ambitious: Paris that terrified Rilke, Paris that raised the prices of Impressionist paintings when it discovered their colossal money-value, Paris of hectic students and feverish tourists, mobs, whistles, endlessly collapsing Governments; Paris of the factory-worker priests, hidden like saints under the altar—for though they may not be saints, they have borne the victuals and medicaments of sanctity into the heart of the abomination of desolation, into—say—a car factory, experiencing as Simone Weil experienced the cold steel of affliction, the need to become as a dumb brute, to be crushed under the heel of necessity; learning in the bone—and not, like an intellectual, with the head only—the actual weight of gravity, and hence the need for the counterweight of grace. An apple fell at Isaac Newton's feet, and from that simple occurrence first he, then we, have learned a good deal. But it takes more than a walk in an orchard to bring home to our heads the spiritual gravity of the world: we need to walk for years with the outcast, the displaced persons, or with those millions who are only not displaced because they exist at the bottom of society as its broad foundations, everlastingly complaining but everlastingly there. Such do not need to read St. John to know that the city is cruel, that the great harlot lives in delicacies which they provide and for which they get small thanks. They know as bitterly as Karl Marx knew that society as actually existent rests upon a basis of profound human injustice. Sometimes they know, as he did not know, that the humans who have created the system will be unable to transform it; that if there is to be any justice in the city, it will have to come from some other source than the hearts of men; that it is unlikely to come; that if it comes at all, it will be at the end of time. " And I John saw the holy city descending " —but that was not as part of the temporal order: it signified the end of the temporal order.

"And God shall wipe away all tears from their eyes"; the Apocalypse ends on a note of immense, because infinite, compassion; but it is an End—the end of the world. Meanwhile the best thing of all, the only ultimately valid thing—circumstances, the world, cities and the fallen angels being what they are—the only genuinely good thing for us as we are in the temporal order, immersed in history, choosing the greater good or the greater evil, is—martyrdom: the crucifixion of good by evil and its rebirth into everlasting life. The martyrdom may be spectacular or it may be hidden, private; but things being what they are, martyrdom it must be: inflicted either by the great city, who herself will come crumbling down in torment and shame, or voluntarily, by those who can learn " the patience of the saints ". Martyrdom it must be, the way of the Cross, the way that must be trodden daily, hour by hour, minute by minute, to the end of the world. " Le Christ sera en agonie jusqu'à la fin du monde ": that is our motto, our watchword.

What support is there for poor human nature upon these quicksands of violence, in this air infested and infected with plagues, falling stars, frightening thunder, shrilly blasting trumpets? What consolation is there for outraged human nature, doomed to a terrestrial sojourn so black and uncompromising? There is the consolation the saints have known, the only consolation that exists: which is not to be found in things of the senses, nor in constructions of the mind, nor in our human friendships, nor in our work: the consolation of our faith, " the folly of the Cross "—" to the Jews a stumbling block, to the Gentiles foolishness ". In St. John's vision all temporalities are whittled away: reading him is a thorough spiritual stripping. Do we seek for consolations in temporal recorded history? It is the region of terror, trial, disaster. There is the vision of the End: the Holy City. But we have to realise that it is the End; it is not for us here and now.

The word *Hope* does not occur in the Apocalypse. Faith is mentioned, and charity, and patience, and works; but not hope. Perhaps this is because it is a vision of the End, when hope will be swallowed up in knowledge. Nevertheless it is a striking omission. And certainly the Apocalypse as a whole does not give any grounds for hope—except that which is aroused by the supernatural vision of the End: the ultimate establishment of the holy city, that city in which there is " no temple ". " For the Lord God Almighty is the temple thereof, and the Lamb." Now the only kind of hope that this vision can arouse is what one must call an utterly supernatural hope, from which all temporal elements—i.e. illusions—have been eliminated. The only hope we are entitled to keep—are indeed obliged to keep—is the hope that we shall ultimately be inhabitants of that holy city—which means that we shall be saints—which means that we shall be worthy of some kind of martyrdom. We may hope that the world, the flesh and the devil may not prevail against us; this means that we shall lay ourselves open to attacks from, to battles with, these three antagonists. We must be prepared for the utmost violence to be exerted against us, hoping that ultimately, in and through us, Love will prevail. This Love is a terrible thing: it does not enable us to escape the violence; it is, at most, a light shining through the violence; even more frequently it is not a light but a darkness, the " dark night " of the soul. Just as in the Apocalypse the sun and moon are darkened, and the sea is turned into blood, so our earthly hopes have to be extinguished—fall like the stars swished away by the tail of the dragon.

So, in fact, they do fall and die, during the course of our earthly life. From the moment we know that we shall never be engine-drivers after all, disappointment sets in. We long for love, and we find ourselves married, and discover that things are not what they seem. The worldly-wise tell us to learn moderation, not to expect too much (that would be " selfish "). Marriage, for instance, is " a matter of give and take ": the worldly-wise ask us to cut down our expectation of happiness and be satisfied with a kind of business arrangement, counting ourselves lucky if at the end of the year our spiritual account book shows the debit and credit columns balanced without overmuch trickery or heart- and candle-burning. But the worldly-wise have never found anyone to believe them. They do not even believe themselves. So frequently we find them betraying their disappointment—and what is disappoint-ment but disappointed hope? The vision of our ultimate End, our final Home, our eternal Resting-place, is not intended to deaden hope but to supernaturalize it. It asks us to spiritualize our hope; not to defer it (though in a sense its object is distant) but to develop it here and now, directed towards its ultimate object: Him who alone can satisfy the soul.

Perhaps St. John does not tell us to hope because he knows that we can do no other. Instead, he shows us what we are intended for, where our hope should lie. " I am Alpha and Omega, the first and the last, the beginning and the end. Blessed are they that wash their robes in the blood of the Lamb, that they may have a right to the tree of life, and may enter in by the gate into the city." We must wash our robes in the blood of the Lamb. And blood is red. In the heavenly city our robes will be white; but not here below, not on earth. On earth, if we wish to wear the white robes of sanctity we must be prepared to wash them in red—in the red blood of martyrdom, in the kingdom of violence. The pure white, the pure Love, are for later.

One final point. The Apocalypse is a vision of violence—of the most extreme, the most unrelieved violence to be found in the whole of the Bible. It is perhaps worth remembering that the Apostle who saw this, and who wrote down what he saw, was the Apostle of Love, the dis-ciple whom Jesus loved; not the rash Peter, not that blacksmith of the Lord, Paul, but the gentle John. He who loved most, to whom after our Lord's death it was given to look after the Blessed Virgin Mary, the reserved, domestic John—so one thinks of him, as a retiring figure, a kind of Newman, etherealized, a creature of light and phil-osophy, a lover, possibly, of music—he it is who sees these most appalling visions. We may imagine that he remained unchanged to the end, fortified by the Holy Spirit, his love intensified, his nature as mild outwardly, as forgiving (until seventy times seven), devoted to our Lord and His blessed Mother. His behaviour was not violent: it was the behaviour of a mortified saint, all sweetness and light. It was his visions that were bitter and dark.

We must not confuse the spiritual eye with the eye of flesh and blood. We must not confuse a vision of violence with the behaviour of violence. These things are opposites: they go by contraries. The thug does not have violent visions. He has no visions at all. With his inner eye he sees nothing. Blindly, destructively, he spreads violence all around him. Hitler had no spiritual vision: he saw, not Michael and his angels, but himself as world-conquering *homo sapiens*. It is those who stay at home who see the most: into a small room, behind closed doors, comes the sound of a mighty rushing wind, and tongues of fire descend upon those " gathered together with one accord in prayer ". It would be a great mistake to confuse these two utterly separate things, to take an analogy for an identity. Political strife, domestic strife, psychological strife, mirror the spiritual war in heaven, Michael and his angels fighting on behalf of the woman clothed with the sun against the devil and his angels. As citizens of one world and potential citizens of another, we have to fight on at least two fronts at once. But not all the fronts are of equal importance. The earthly city, great Babylon, that city in which we are compelled to earn our bread, must fall—it is a temporal city; and only the City of God, the Holy City, will remain. If we have to choose, we know where our first allegiance lies.